THE

MADMAN

and the

ASSASSIN

---

the strange life of

BOSTON CORBETT,

the man who killed

JOHN WILKES BOOTH

S C O T T   M A R T E L L E

CHICAGO
REVIEW
PRESS

Published by Chicago Review Press Incorporated
814 North Franklin Street
Chicago, IL 60610
ISBN 978-1-61373-018-8

Library of Congress Cataloging-in-Publication Data
Is available from the Library of Congress.

Interior design: PerfecType, Nashville, TN

Printed in the United States of America
5 4 3 2 1

For the Lovely Margaret

CONTENTS

PROLOGUE

April 26, 1865

If they could have been seen from above on the moonless Virginia night, the two groups of men on horseback would have made for an odd sight. A squadron of more than two dozen mounted Union cavalrymen and one prisoner slowly guided their horses over a sand roadway, struggling at times against the unstable terrain. Three other men on horseback rode a few hundred yards ahead, scanning a fence line to their right. Two of the men were detectives. The third, Willie Jett, a former member of the Confederate Ninth Virginia Cavalry, was another prisoner of the detectives, one they hoped was leading them to a couple of fugitives.

Jett was searching for a break in the roadside fence, the rails obscured by bushes thickening with spring growth. They talked quietly, the detectives trying to keep their impatience, and their suspicion that Jett was lying to them, in check. But Jett insisted the gap was somewhere along this stretch of road. He had been here just two days ago, had turned off the road and through a gate and on up to Richard Garrett's farm beyond. But the murky night swallowed landmarks. He couldn't get his bearings, couldn't say for sure exactly where the gap was. Maybe, Jett suggested, it was just ahead. A few hundred more yards at the most.[1]

One of the detectives, Everton Conger, a former Union army officer mustered out because of war wounds, spurred his horse forward, staying close to the south side of the road until, as Jett had promised, he found ruts in the grassy earth leading to a latched gate. There were two gates, Jett said after he and the other detective, Luther Byron Baker, caught up with Conger—one gate here at the road and another farther along the lane leading to the farm. After the soldiers passed through the second gate, Jett said, they would need to turn left to get into the farmyard, which was surrounded by locust trees.

Baker decided to find the second gate himself. He sent Conger back to warn the cavalrymen into silence. The squadron had been assigned to help Baker and Conger with their manhunt. If Jett was telling the truth and the Garrett farm was where they would find the two fugitives they were looking for, then Baker wanted the element of surprise. He assumed that the fugitives had guns. One of them was the actor John Wilkes Booth, who had killed Abraham Lincoln just twelve days before. Any man facing the gallows for assassinating a president would surely try to shoot his way to freedom, even if he was hobbled by a broken leg.

As the soldiers reached the cut, one was assigned to stay at the road with Jett and the other prisoner, a local fisherman named William Rollins, to keep them from shouting a warning. The rest of the soldiers gathered at the second gate, where two sergeants passed along whispered orders from Baker and their commander, Lieutenant Edward P. Doherty. The troops' energy had been fading after two long days of riding with barely a break, and no sleep beyond stolen catnaps. Just a few minutes more, Baker told them, and they would have their man. They had come too far, and worked too hard, to miss their chance now. They would need to move quickly to cut off any opportunity for escape. Speed and surprise—in addition to their overwhelming numbers—were on their side.

Baker quietly unlatched the gate, pushed it open, and remounted his horse. The members of the Sixteenth New York Cavalry moved up the lane, turned left at the entry to the homestead, and at Doherty's shouted command "Open file to the right and left—gallop!" thundered into the farmyard.

The ground-shaking din set off howls from dogs sleeping under the porch and roused the Garretts inside the two-and-a-half-story pine-board farmhouse. Nearby, two Garrett sons, both recently returned from the

Confederate army, jolted awake from where they had bedded down in a corncrib next to the tobacco barn. The soldiers dismounted in a clatter, then rushed to surround the buildings, directed by Conger and Doherty as Baker raced up the front porch steps and began pounding on the door.

As Jett had promised, Booth and the other fugitive, David Herold, were at the farm. They had spun a lie to the Garretts about being two Rebel brothers trying to make their way home at the end of the war. The family had let the two men sleep in the house the first night but then became increasingly suspicious; they ordered them to the tobacco barn at bedtime on this night. The two Garrett brothers, fearing the strangers would steal the family's horses during the dead of night, had quietly locked them in and bedded down themselves in the adjacent corncrib so they could react quickly should the two strangers try to break out.

As the horses thundered into the yard, Booth knew instantly who, or at least what, the noise meant: Union cavalrymen, and they had come for him. Booth quietly awakened Herold and told him Union soldiers had arrived and surrounded the barn. Herold, rattled, wanted to quit. "You had better give up," Herold whispered in the darkness. "I will suffer death first," Booth whispered back. "Don't make any noise. Maybe they will go off, thinking we are not here." But Herold had trouble remaining still; he moved about, rustling the hay, as soldiers stood alert in the farmyard, a half-dozen of them behind the barn to ensure that no one ran off into the woods or fields. Booth and Herold could hear the noise in the yard, the hollering from the porch as the soldiers tried to get the Garretts to come to the door. There was no easy escape for a man with a broken leg and no horse at hand. If Booth was worried, Herold didn't pick up on it. But then, Herold's own nerves were fraying.[2]

Doherty and Conger had joined Baker on the porch. They continued banging on the door and hollering at the Garretts to come out. It took several minutes for Richard Garrett, the patriarch of the small farming family, to make his way downstairs, where, unarmed, partially dressed, and disheveled, he opened the door.

"Where are the men who stopped at the house?" Conger demanded. They had left, the old man said warily. Where did they go? "To the woods."

"What?" Baker mocked. "A lame man gone into the woods?" Garrett offered to lead them to the hiding spot if they'd let him put on his clothes. He could get dressed, the detectives said, but he wasn't going back into the house to do it. A relative handed clothes through the open door and the old man slowly put them on, testing the detectives' patience.

"Well, sir," Conger asked with forced politeness as Garrett finished, "whereabouts in the woods have they gone?" Garrett launched into a meandering explanation but Conger cut him off with a terse "I just want to know where these men went." Garrett resumed his explanation; Conger turned to one of the soldiers. "Bring a lariat here and I will put that man up to the top of those locust trees." As the soldier trotted off, another cavalryman approached from the shadows propelling John Garrett, one of the sons.

"Don't hurt the old man," the son said. "He is scared. I will tell you where the men are." Baker grabbed the younger Garrett by the shirt, dragging him back down to the yard as he pointed his revolver at Garrett's head. The tobacco barn, the son said. "Show me," Doherty said.

Conger ordered all two dozen soldiers to ring the sixty-square-foot barn as he, Baker, Doherty, and the Garretts, joined now by the second Garrett son, moved closer to the still-locked barn entrance. Conger told John Garrett to enter the barn, collect the weapons from Booth and Herold, and bring the two men outside. "They know you," Baker said, "and you can go in."

Baker shouted into the barn that he was sending in Garrett, "and you must come out and deliver yourselves up." The young man nervously unlocked the door and stepped inside, but reappeared moments later, visibly shaken. "This man says, 'Damn you, you have betrayed me,' and threatened to shoot me. [He] reached into the hay and came up with a revolver."

Conger and Baker discussed their options and decided to try to flush the two men out with fire. A sergeant came forward and offered to go in alone and take the captives. The cavalry might have the numbers, he argued, but the men in the barn had the advantage. They could see the soldiers outside the gaps between the wall planks, but the soldiers could not see the men inside. There would be less bloodshed, the sergeant said, if Doherty would let him enter and take the men alone. Doherty rejected the offer and sent the sergeant back to his position in the cordon around the barn. Baker ordered the Garrett brothers to start piling brush against the back wall and hollered at Booth and Herold to come out in five minutes or they'd burn them out.

None of the Union men had identified themselves to Booth, and he started shouting out demands to know who they were and what they wanted. Baker danced around the question, answering that they knew who he was, and that they wanted him, and that he should come out. Booth asked for time to consider the demand. The pursuers preferred to take Booth alive, so they agreed, and for about ten minutes all that was heard in the yard were the soft shuffles of the soldiers and their tethered horses, and the chirps and chirrs of the Virginia night.

Two conversations eventually arose—one inside the barn between Booth and Herold, the other between Booth and the men outside. Booth at times taunted, saying he couldn't give up his guns because he needed them to shoot the soldiers. At other times he seemed to be trying to set the stage for his own death, asking Conger to line up his soldiers a hundred feet from the barn so he could come out and fight for his freedom. The Union men held firm until Booth finally shouted, after accusing Herold of betraying and abandoning him, that "there's a man in here wants to come out." Baker said they would let him, but he had to toss out his weapons first, a demand that launched another debate, with Booth finally persuading Baker that the only weapons in the barn were his, that Herold was unarmed, and that Booth would not give up his guns.

Cutting the number of men in the barn in half was worth letting Booth keep his guns, so Baker, standing outside the door with Doherty, agreed to let Herold come out. When the young man reached the door, Baker grabbed him by the arms and yanked him into the night, binding his wrists. Conger, who had already moved to the back of the barn, lit a fistful of hay and jammed it into the piled dry brush, which ignited with a fury. Conger peered through a gap in the boards that made up the barn wall; the flames and smoke were quickly spreading, the yellow flickering glow lighting up both the yard and the inside of the barn. Booth dropped his crutch and spun around, looking at the walls as though trying to find an escape route with the firelight's help. He carried a rifle and hobbled toward the back of the barn, trying to figure a way to put out the fire, then shuffled along the side of the barn, stopping briefly to peer out through cracks before making his way back to the doorway, still ajar from Herold's exit. As the flames spread and smoke billowed, Booth raised his rifle, the barrel pointed toward the opening in the doorway, with Baker, Doherty, and a handful of solders beyond.[3]

At the side of the barn, the sergeant who had offered to take Booth and Herold alone kept a steady gaze on the injured actor through a hand-wide gap between two planks. The sergeant was a slender man, about five feet, four inches tall, with longish dark hair parted in the middle and slicked back behind his ears. He wore a scraggly beard and had soft brown eyes. He had served with the Union army off and on since the start of the war, and steadily since late 1863. He'd earned a reputation for religious zealotry that at one point landed him in the stockade for calling out a superior officer who swore while dressing down his troops. But that deep faith had also helped him survive four months in the notorious Andersonville prison.

Only the sergeant himself knew exactly what was running through his mind at that moment. Flames were crawling up inside the back wall of the barn, illuminating Lincoln's killer. Doherty and Baker were standing on the far side of the partly open barn door. Soldiers were spaced about ten yards from each other around the barn to ensure Booth couldn't flee. In the flickering light of the growing flames, the sergeant saw Booth raise his rifle toward the open door and the soldiers and detectives beyond. He believed the killer was about to kill again. So the right-handed sergeant steadied his gun on his opposite forearm, took careful aim through the gap at Booth's shoulder, and fired.

The soldier would later credit—or blame—Providence for the decision to shoot, and for the path the bullet took. It only had a few yards to travel, but it yawed a bit from its intended mark and hit Booth at the left base of the skull, shattered the fourth and fifth cervical vertebrae—and severing the spinal cord within—then tore on out the other side. Booth collapsed, paralyzed and mortally wounded. Within seconds Doherty, Conger, and some of the soldiers pulled him from the blazing building and moved him into the yard, and then, as the fire roared and grew, placed the assassin on the Garretts' porch, where he clung to life for about three hours.

The sergeant who fired the fatal shot was named Boston Corbett. And with that guiding hand of Providence, his troubled life became the stuff of legend, infatuation, and invention. And, eventually, institutionalization, for Sergeant Boston Corbett was mad as a hatter.

1

LOSS AND REDEMPTION

The 630-ton *Zenobia*, sailing from New York under the command of Captain Nathaniel Putnam, arrived in Liverpool in late July 1840 laden with passengers and cargo, including five hundred barrels of turpentine, more than seven hundred bales of cotton, some peach brandy, and other goods bound for British importers. By August 14, the empty ship was tied up at the Galt, Barff and Company dock to be loaded for the return trip. The records don't reveal exactly what day the ship moved out of the harbor and into the Irish Sea to start the westward journey, but the *Zenobia* arrived back in New York around October 2, which suggests the ship left England by early September.[1]

Europeans had first inhabited New York some two hundred years earlier, so it was a mature shipping port the *Zenobia* reached on that early autumn day. Most of the transatlantic ships glided up the East River to dock, and the seascape presented an impressive sight with "the many sails, which were tending toward it, the expanding river and opening harbor, and at last the broad way, with its tall ships setting in from the sea," one traveler wrote several years later. "And the Great Metropolis itself stretching into the distance, with its domes and spires, its towers, its cupolas and 'steepled chimneys' rising through a canopy of smoke in the gray dawn of a cloudless September morning."[2]

In addition to its unspecified trading cargo and crew, the *Zenobia* carried 8 presumably well-to-do cabin passengers and 206 steerage passengers—men, women, and children in search of a different future from what they faced in the places whence they came. England and Ireland, mostly, but the passengers also included a few American-born travelers returning home. There were laborers and mechanics, butchers and farmers, whole families, broken families, and single adults destined for New York and points beyond: Pennsylvania and Connecticut and farther inland to Illinois. Some of the passengers would be taking seats on the burgeoning network of railroads connecting cities across the Northeast. A few were heading in a different direction, on to the Deep South—Charleston and New Orleans, primarily, where the economies were built on the backs of slaves but where the white immigrants hoped they might find paid work as mechanics, butchers, or laborers. A handful of the passengers planned to go even farther, using New York as a way stop en route to Canada or the West Indies.[3]

Some were looking to reunite families. Sarah Levi and her four children, ages five to thirteen, were joining her husband in New York. For some, the voyage would bring tragedy. James McFarland, a mechanic, and his wife, Betty, were traveling from Scotland to Pennsylvania with their two children. The youngest, Mary Jane, just one year old, died at sea on September 20. The next day, six-month-old British-born John Rowe, Ohio-bound with his twenty-three-year-old mother, Anne, and his two-year-old sister, Elizabeth, also died.

Bartholomew Corbett was among the passengers who planned to go no farther than New York, where he hoped to earn his living as a taxidermist and naturalist. At age fifty-nine, Corbett was among the oldest of the *Zenobia* passengers, and it must have been a challenging trip for him and his children, thirteen-year-old Emma, ten-year-old John, and eight-year-old Thomas, the future "Boston" Corbett. Bartholomew's wife and the children's mother, Elizabeth, was not with them. Had she died? The records are unclear. The records also don't reveal passengers' motives, but her death could have been the catalyst that sent Bartholomew, his children, and their nine pieces of luggage off to the United States for a fresh start.

The Corbetts settled at 276 Mott Street, a few blocks north of the infamous Five Points slum. New York was already the nation's largest city, covering the lower third of Manhattan Island. Since the 1825 opening of the Erie Canal, it was also becoming the nation's dominant port and a doorway to the world. Of course, a door offers passage both ways, and the Corbetts were part of a flood of immigrants that would only increase over the next two decades, adding to the wealth and chaos of the city. That influx remade Manhattan, forcing construction of new homes northward on the island even as the poorest of the poor, both American-born and the freshly arrived, overflowed Five Points' dilapidated buildings and mud streets. The congestion, poverty, and relentless vice fed cycles of disease and pestilence that swept far beyond the neighborhood's ill-defined borders.[4]

Still, Manhattan was the place to be, despite its drawbacks. A financial panic in 1837 brought down several large banks on Wall Street, then as now the nexus of American financial power and influence, and the city's economy had yet to fully recover. Even with the fiscal uncertainty, municipal leaders were beginning to lay the foundations for the modern city, establishing in 1842 a $12 million aqueduct from the Croton Reservoir at Forty-Second Street and Fifth Avenue. The lower tip of the island, the footprint of the original city, was quickly shifting from residential to commercial as the city expanded northward, driven by the rapidly growing population and the amassing of wealth.

For the next two decades, as the debate over slavery tore the nation North from South, New York would be an anomaly as a source of a surprising level of support for the secessionists—particularly among those who recognized that the city's fortunes were built in part as the major exporting hub between slave-harvested cotton from the South and markets in England and the rest of Europe.[5]

Despite New York's status as the nation's most vibrant city, and the boom-and-bust cycles of the business and financing classes, poverty was endemic. Ships disgorged Europe's poor by the hundreds. Manhattan's population increased by 60 percent during the 1840s, fueled in part by the potato famine–driven exodus from Ireland. The slow recovery from the 1837 financial panic and the rapid addition of immigrant laborers meant high unemployment and low wages. Horace Greeley, the journalist and social chronicler, noted that two out of three New Yorkers took in less than one dollar a week in wages. He estimated there were fifty thousand city residents who were one week away from being out of money for food and rent. In the Fourteenth Ward (bordered north and south by Houston and Canal, and east and west by Broadway and Bowery), only 125 of the 3,700 residents in 1850 owned their homes. And the Fourteenth Ward was not the city's poorest district.[6]

Bartholomew Corbett was among the renters. He also joined Manhattan's internal northern migration; by 1849 he had moved his family to 395 Fourth Avenue. It's unclear how Bartholomew made his living as a naturalist, an emerging occupation at a time when amateur science was on the cusp of an intellectual division. "Empiricism was being replaced by theory, amateurs by professionals," according to historian Thomas Bender. "The ideology of professionalism in science was beginning to insist upon the purity and moral aura of scientific inquiry in an effort to separate science from the common life and commercial values" of New York City.[7] The role of the naturalist was among those undergoing a metamorphosis. In England, the Royal Geographic Society had been founded in 1830, supporting a wide range of explorations around the globe. The next year, Charles Darwin embarked on his five-year world voyage aboard the HMS *Beagle*, gathering the samples and observations that would eventually form the core evidence for his theories on natural selection. In 1836, Louis Agassiz theorized that large swaths of the earth had once been covered in ice. In Washington, DC, a $500,000 bequest by British scientist James Smithson led, in 1846, to the Smithsonian Institution.

It's unclear what if any formal background Bartholomew Corbett had in studying the natural world. His name shows up in none of the growing literature of the era, which suggests that his role was limited as the professionalism of the science progressed. Most likely, he prepared dead animals for displays—hunters' game and other collectibles—while satiating his curiosity by reading deeply in the natural sciences. By his final years of life he had amassed a significant personal library that he kept in what, to an outside eye, were piles of junk—he was a nineteenth-century hoarder. It doesn't seem as though Bartholomew found much success in his trade or satisfaction in America; sometime in the 1850s, when he was in his seventies, Bartholomew returned to England.[8] By then, Thomas, the baby of the family, was out in the world on his own.

Few records remain of Thomas Corbett's childhood and entry into adulthood. As a teenager, he gravitated to the hatmaker's trade, a vibrant business centered around Nassau Street, just north of Wall Street. Corbett trained as a finisher of silk hats, a skilled trade undergoing seismic changes just as he was entering the workforce—changes that affected other industries as well.

The hat-making trade began with small craftsmen, often farmers filling in hours during the winter who would make only one or two hats a day as they slowly pressed animal hair into felt, then shaped it into a stiff block to create the frame for each hat. Some then sold the blocks to hat finishers; others finished off the hats themselves with a coating of beaver pelt or other material. For most craftsmen, markets were limited by proximity: places they could reach by horseback or, occasionally, stagecoach or boat. The hats, or hat frames for those supplying craft shops in town, were bulky, further limiting the amount of product the makers could carry to market.

Revolutions in production techniques and machines as well as transportation changed not only hat making but American industry at large. Canals, railroads, and turnpikes shortened the time it took to get products to markets and increased the amount of goods a manufacturer could ship. With better access to markets, small producers could sell more products, which led to expansion of the more successful businesses and the clustering of production in areas with the easiest access to labor, supplies, and cash markets (as opposed to more localized bartering economies).

For the hat-making trade, that meant the emergence of craft centers, which divided loosely along style lines. In 1835 silk hats became fashionable, and production centered in New York City and Philadelphia. Hatmakers specializing in the more traditional beaver and other fur hats, and in wool and felt hats, gravitated to different cities. "Soft" hat manufacturers clustered in Orange and Newark, New Jersey; for wool hats, Boston and Danbury, Connecticut, were the key centers. (Danbury, in fact, had been a hat-making city since the Revolutionary War era.) Richmond, Virginia, Troy in upstate New York, and Cleveland had smaller localized hat industries as well, but the geography of the industry was primarily in New England, New York City and nearby New Jersey, and Philadelphia. And thus that would be the geography of Corbett's young adult life.[9]

The labor itself was fragmenting, too. In the early 1800s inventors and tinkerers concocted new machines that could make the basic hat block in minutes, compared with the hours it took by hand. So hatmakers began specializing. Some became machine operators; others focused on the distinguishing latter stages of production. Local unions, or guilds, controlled who was accepted as an apprentice and who was allowed to work in shops. They also struggled to set floor wages, with some success—it was one of the earliest American trades to unionize. Some of the factories were large, with scores of workers, but most of the shops were tight spaces with only a handful of crafters, all men except for the women who affixed ribbons, belts, and other decorative touches before the hats were shipped off. It was a hard-drinking workforce as well: guild initiations inevitably involved a night of drunkenness, an offshoot of the work conditions. It was generally believed that drinking on the job helped "increase . . . vigor and activity." After the workday, the hatmakers simply moved the party to a nearby alehouse.[10]

It was into that close-knit, hard-drinking world of skilled tradesmen that Corbett entered as an apprentice silk hat finisher. And while it was a skilled trade, it was also a dangerous one, primarily because of the mercury-based compounds used to form the felt. The mercury stiffened fur while it was still on the hide, making it easier to remove and, with the application of liquids and heat, press into the basic felt forms around which the hats—including silk hats—were made. The rest of the processes involved more heat and water, which gave off a mercury-infused mist.

Hatmakers of the time who inhaled and ingested the mercury often became irritable, with slurred speech and unsteady balance. Those more heavily exposed were prone to fits of paranoia. The link between these symptoms and exposure to mercury would not be established for another three decades, but by the 1930s a phrase had arisen in England to describe such behavior: "mad as a hatter."[11]

Exactly how much exposure the young Corbett had to mercury as a silk hat finisher is unknowable. Later in life he would exhibit some of the traits associated with mercury poisoning, including bouts of paranoia. But for now it was a chance for a young man to make his way in the world.

Sometime in the early 1850s, Thomas Corbett met a woman named Susan Rebecca (her last name does not appear in the records), who was thirteen years his senior. They married and moved into rooms on East Ninth Street just east of Tompkins Square Park. The particulars of their relationship are elusive, although census records, city directories, and later reports by friends offer some clues. It's also unclear how much of a role religion played in their life together. Decades later, a friend wrote that Corbett had told him about "what a good Christian wife and what a pleasant home he had," but there are no other references to Corbett being a particularly God-fearing man at the time.[12]

Corbett continued to work as a silk hat finisher, and the couple migrated from one hat-making city to another, including a stint beginning around October 1854 in Troy, New York. Corbett, who had been in the United States since he was eight years old, decided to make his transition from British citizen to American, and on June 9, 1855, Thomas H. Corbett took the oath in a Troy courthouse.[13] At the time, he and Susan were living in the home of a couple named George and Sarah Robinson, along with the Robinsons' two young children and Sarah's mother. The Corbetts didn't stay in Troy very long, though, eventually making their way south to Richmond, Virginia.

By some accounts, Corbett had a hard time finding and keeping work there, in large part because of his vociferous opposition to slavery in a time and place where divisions on that issue were stark and unforgiving. Richmond would have an even darker legacy for Corbett: his wife took ill, and as they were returning to New York City by ship, Susan died at sea on August 18, 1856. The body continued on to New York, where the death was recorded and Susan was buried.

Susan's death devastated Corbett, and in the common telling of the story passed along initially by friends, Corbett began drinking heavily and constantly. At the depths of a binge he encountered some evangelical temperance Christians and, as one version of the story goes, was detained by them until he sobered up, undergoing a religious epiphany in the process.[14]

Corbett's conversion was singular, but not his alone. It occurred as the nation was seized by the third in a series of religious paroxysms marked by surges of interest and new membership in evangelical Protestant churches and the creation of new sects and communities.

The First Great Awakening came before the American Revolution and lasted roughly from 1730 to 1750, giving rise to the Shakers and other Christian sects. The Second Great Awakening occurred from 1790 through 1840, during which preachers of all stripes encountered God and Jesus in various miraculous circumstances and claimed fresh and exclusive insights or pending Armageddon. The movement reenergized mainstream religions while propelling new churches that rose and fell with the visions, personalities, and persistence of those claiming direct connections to God. Upstate New York picked up the nickname "the burned over district" for the numbers of evangelists who emerged there. Methodism thrived with its emphasis on religious rebirth and conversion of sinners at open revivals. William Miller in the Adirondacks preached that Saturday was the true Sabbath and that the second coming of Christ was imminent, likely by 1843. His prediction was wrong, but his preaching gave rise to Adventism, and eventually the Seventh-Day Adventists. In Palmyra, near Rochester, the angel Moroni revealed himself and the golden Book of Mormon to Joseph Smith.[15]

The Second Great Awakening also coincided with the Industrial Revolution, which upended the American economy and society. Farmers—or at least their offspring—began giving up the land for city life and factory work, particularly in the Northeast and in burgeoning cities such as Chicago and Detroit. By the 1850s, those changes had merged with the increasingly acrimonious debate over slavery.

Against that backdrop of existential tension and dehumanizing industrialization, missionary Jeremiah Calvin Lanphier began holding a weekly lunchtime prayer meeting for Manhattan businessmen at the North Dutch Church at the corner of William and Fulton Streets, just a few blocks from Wall Street. The first meeting started inauspiciously on September 23, 1857, as Lanphier sat alone for thirty minutes before a half-dozen men stopped in out of curiosity. The next weekly session drew twenty men; the third session drew up to forty, and so it grew as the pace of the sessions increased from weekly to daily and became known simply as the Fulton Street prayer meeting.

The noontime meetings grew into a religious phenomenon that rapidly spread across the nation, and expanded far beyond local businessmen's prayer lunches. Open-air revival meetings drew sinners like moths to a flame, and converts swelled congregations. James Gordon Bennett spotlighted the trend in February 1858 in his *New York Herald* newspaper, which had the largest circulation among New York's popular press. Horace Greeley quickly picked up the coverage in his competing *Tribune* newspaper, and the Great Revival became a national media event. Yet Bennett and Greeley were late to the story; the nation's religious weeklies, most of which were based in New York, had been chronicling the rise for months. And as with the Second Great Awakening, Methodist churches benefited greatly.[16]

By the summer of 1858, Corbett—already converted—had followed his trade to Boston, where he fell in with members of the Methodist Episcopal Church and found a religious home and a calling. He became a proselytizer and street preacher, exhorting fellow sinners to heed the word of God and avoid the temptations of drink and sin.

But Corbett was still human. After Susan's death, and after his conversion, Corbett sought to remain chaste but struggled against sexual urges. A "Bible Christian," Corbett pored over chapters 18–19 of the Gospel of Matthew, in which Jesus advises his followers that unless they approached their faith with the openness and acceptance of a child, they couldn't gain entry to heaven. And if their actions offend the faithful, "woe to that man by whom the offence cometh! Wherefore if thy hand or thy foot offend thee, cut them off, and cast them from thee: it is better for thee to enter into life halt or maimed, rather than having two hands or two feet to be cast into everlasting fire. And if thine eye offend thee, pluck it out, and cast it from thee: it is better for thee to enter into life with one eye, rather than having two eyes to be cast into hell fire."

What made Corbett stumble weren't his hands or his feet or his eyes, but his libido, and "he prayed for strength to overcome" his desires. Matthew 19 offered, he believed, the answer. "Eunuchs, which have made themselves eunuchs for the kingdom of heaven's sake" would fall under God's good graces. "Finally," a friend recorded years later, "he said that the Lord directed him, in a vision or in some way, to castrate himself."[17]

On July 16, 1858, Corbett took a pair of scissors, sliced open the bottom of his scrotum, pulled the testicles downward, and then cut them free. The procedure must have been incredibly painful, but Corbett handled it with remarkable stoicism. Records from Massachusetts General Hospital note that he afterward "went to a prayer meeting, walked about some and ate a hearty dinner. But the wound was heavily clotted, and blood and fluids backed up in the scrotum which swelled enormously, and was black." Corbett returned to his rooms and someone sent for Dr. Richard Manning Hodges, who cleaned out the wound and drained the fluid, tied off the epididymis and the vas deferens, dressed the incision, and sent Corbett to Massachusetts General.[18] There, Corbett had more medical issues to face. With his scrotum and penis still painfully swollen, he began having intestinal trouble, which the doctors treated with an enema the day after the self-castration. Corbett was, in a word, a mess. But he healed quickly. The records indicate that by July 18 he was feeling better and suffering less pain. On July 19 some of the sutures were removed. On August 15, Corbett was pronounced healed and released from the hospital. "[After] his recovery he was very much gratified with the result as his passion was not trouble any more," the friend wrote. "He said that his object was that he might preach the gospel without being tormented by his passions."

Two weeks after Corbett left the hospital, he formalized his affiliation with the Methodist Episcopal Church. The Reverend Richard Pope, who would remain a friend for decades to come, baptized Corbett on August 29 in a ceremony at Boston's Back Bay. Corbett, thinking he was following a tradition of apostles changing their names, abandoned Thomas for Boston as his first name, reflecting the city in which his conversion, and his rebirth, took place.

Corbett began to pattern himself after Jesus Christ. He grew his jet-black hair out long and parted it in the middle, comporting with artistic depictions of Christ. He was a fiery if unimposing man of God, with a compact body, a short neck, a low, wide forehead, and dark eyes to match his hair. Friends described him as having a "mild" look to his face, with a beard and mustache that came in thin when he let them grow. To some, a clean-shaven Corbett looked "like a woman."[19] He was friendly and open, helpful to those he saw in need, but also quick to condemn those he thought were out of step with God. He tended to tuck in his chin and affected a strange, and to some annoying, manner of speech during church or prayer services in which he would add an "er" to the ends of words, as in "Lord-er, hear-er our prayer."[20] He was fast during sermons with a loud "Amen!" and, more often, "Glory to God!" belted out in a high, driving voice, a phrase that earned him the nickname of "Glory to God man."

Corbett worked in Boston for a time, then moved back to New York City, where he became a hat finisher for James H. Brown beginning in 1859. But his main engagement was as a minister to lost souls. He joined in sermons with an evangelist named Orville Gardner who, like Corbett, had come to find faith after leading a dissolute life.[21] Gardner, though, had a much more freighted past than Corbett.

A native of Maine, Gardner was a physically powerful, heavyset man who rose in the hard-edged world of bare-knuckle prizefighting. In 1847, Gardner won $800 by outlasting Allen McFee in a fight that went thirty-three rounds and took one hour and nineteen minutes to complete.[22] A habitué of Five Points, Gardner brawled whether there was a scheduled match and prize money on the table or just as part of a night out on the town. Nicknamed "Awful Gardner," he was jailed numerous times for bar fights and other legal transgressions. In February 1851, he accosted a woman on the street near the Fulton Ferry on the East River, knocked her down, and began fighting with her husband. A crowd formed and other men joined in to help the assaulted couple, overwhelming Gardner and chasing him to a nearby hotel. As the small mob grappled to keep him from finding safety inside the door, Gardner pulled out a gun and fired two shots, wounding one man in the face. Gardner was arrested, but it's unclear whether any penalty was ever exacted.

Two years later, Gardner was arrested again after biting off a chunk of a fellow fighter's left ear during an unsanctioned brawl. In 1855 he was sentenced to six months in jail after punching and breaking the jaw of a touring businessman from Utica when the visitor refused to go to a bar Gardner insisted he patronize. The next year, Gardner and four friends crossed the Hudson River to Jersey City for a night on the town and drew the attention of police "after committing several disorderly acts, and breaking a city lamp by maliciously throwing a brick through it. He got into a difficulty with Charles Ross, one of his companions, and was then arrested and locked up in the City Prison."[23]

Then Gardner found Jesus. The brawler was visiting his brother, who had already been swept up in the religious fervor of the 1857–58 Great Revival movement, and Gardner decided, out of politeness, to join his brother's family as they attended a series of meetings at their church. "The Lord's spirit was powerfully displayed, and went from heart to heart all through the church," Gardner said later. "It worked upon me three or four nights. The pastor of the church came to me and asked me if I would not like to get religion and serve God." Gardner demurred, but with an uneasy feeling. He decided to "leave that part of the country; it was getting too warm for me."

But Gardner kept feeling drawn to the prayer sessions and after a few more days found himself at the front of the church confessing his sins. He felt nothing, and began to sense that the Lord had forsaken him until, while riding to White Plains with a friend, he started singing a hymn. "The first thing I knew, God spoke peace to my soul. It came like a shot, when I was not anticipating it, and the first thing I said was, 'Glory! God blessed.'" At least, that's how Gardner described it a few months later in an account that was widely reprinted in newspapers by editors still grappling with the idea that such a recidivist could actually turn his life around.[24]

Giving up the fight game, Gardner and his brother opened a short-lived shoe-making business before Gardner turned to evangelizing full time, preaching to an initially skeptical world about his conversion and redemption and his newfound sobriety. But Gardner stayed the course, eventually opening a coffee shop for fellow fallen men on Bowery and running it for several years with donations from well-heeled New Yorkers. He made prison visits, particularly to Sing Sing, and spoke at regional "camp meetings," the same circuit that Corbett traveled.

Corbett did more than preach, though. In many ways, he lived the Gospel as he believed it. Corbett routinely gathered up drunken sinners from the New York streets and took them to his rooms, which for a time were at 91 Attorney Street, south of Houston about ten blocks from the East River. Once a sinner was in his clutches, Corbett would sober him up and feed him, restoring the sinner's health as best he could while trying to bring the man to God. On a practical level, Corbett also tried to help his charges find work. "He continually expended all his own money for such purposes," Brown, his hat-making boss, wrote years later, "and frequently borrowed from his friends." Given that his friends were fellow devoted Christians, they loaned in faith, and he repaid within days of incurring the debt.[25]

"When he worked for me, he lived a very singular life," Brown wrote. "He kept bachelor's hall in one room. He would find some poor devil and take him in, feed and cloth [sic] him, and when he got him in good condition he would tell him to go so he could make room for another one. And go through the same process until [Corbett] would not have decent clothes for himself, and no amount of talk would change his ways. And all the answer I could get from him was that he was 'doing the Lord's work.' I don't think there was ever another person born just like him. But he was a good man, for all of his faults were of the head, and not of the heart."

Corbett's brother John, who suffered from ill health, had married "in a wealthy family and lived on the Fifth Avenue." He regularly visited Boston "and sent quite a number of letters for him in my care that contained money," Brown wrote. "He told me that he would like to give him more but he knew that he would give it all away. So he would only give him a little at a time, but as often as he wanted it, he would give it to him."

Corbett also developed a reputation for recalcitrant righteousness. If he felt an employer was not acting in a Christian way, he would walk out. Similarly, cursing by a fellow hatter would send Corbett to his knees for a prayer of repentance and forgiveness. He quit one shop because he thought the owner was reconstituting used hats and selling them as new.

At the same time, Corbett seemed to begin a pattern that he would follow in later years, working at one place long enough to earn enough money to support his preaching, then going to spread the Word of God and heal the sinners. And he was a regular at the Fulton Street prayer meeting, where "he generally had his seat under the clock. He would sit quietly until the requests for prayers were read, and if any one struck him with peculiar force, as was generally the case, he would spring up the instant the reading was finished, and pour out his heart to God in prayer."[26]

A follower needs a leader, and Corbett had not only God and Jesus Christ but also Phoebe Palmer, a traveling preacher and theologian of mystical Methodism. She lived in Manhattan with her husband, Walter C. Palmer, a homeopathic physician who occasionally joined his wife in her evangelistic efforts.

Phoebe Palmer was born in Manhattan in 1807, one of sixteen siblings (ten would survive into adulthood) raised by the fairly well-to-do Henry and Dorothea Worrall. Her father, a Yorkshire man, had as a teenager fallen under the influence of John Wesley, who laid out his belief in a "perfecting grace," a moment of personal epiphany in which his "heart was strangely warmed" at the knowledge that God works through the hearts of his followers. It gave Wesley the power, he believed, to resist temptation and to build a ministry to help others find their connections with God. That formed the foundation of Methodism. As a young girl, Phoebe read deeply and regularly of Wesley's works as well as those of another Methodist theologian, John Fletcher. And her father led the family in daily religious readings.[27]

Palmer came of age during the Second Great Awakening. With her family she attended camp meetings and other gatherings in which sinners would move to the "mourner's bench" at the front of the gathering, renounce their sins, and, often in a paroxysm of the spirit, turn their lives over to God. Yet Palmer was bothered by a perceived difference between herself and fellow believers who, like Wesley with his "warm heart," described feelings of repentance and acceptance by God. They were often overcome at that moment of personal epiphany by a flood of tears and convulsive emotions. Palmer felt none of that; as a lifelong believer, she had no conversion to make, even though Wesley and others taught that there would be a second awaking of the acceptance of Jesus. Palmer eventually determined that rather than warming her heart, God spoke to her through Scripture, and that she had entered a state of sanctification without, for lack of a better phrase, the theatrics.

All of which laid the groundwork for a broad theology that fed the Methodist revival movement and pushed the church toward a mysticism that left traditionalists wary and spurred debates over the nature and expression of Christian faith. On a personal level, Palmer's faith had unusual repercussions and interpretations. She and her husband had six children. Three died young. Their first child, Alexander, died at nine months. Their second, Samuel, died after seven weeks. Palmer suffered a mother's grief but also "saw the deaths as divine chastening for having loved her children too much. Rather than embittering her toward God, the deaths of her first two children caused Palmer to rethink her priorities in life and to consecrate herself more fully to God." That interpretation grew from Wesley's teachings that women should remain single, since marriage and motherhood put others between them and God. Then Palmer's daughter died in a tragic crib fire, and Palmer was stricken with repeated illnesses (most likely a kidney ailment). She perceived them all as punishments from a jealous God. Her prayers and meditation led her to an unusual conclusion: her husband and children were standing between her and God. So she marginalized them in her life, and in her emotions, to devote herself to God.[28]

In 1835, Palmer and her sister, Sarah Lankford, whose families shared a large home at 54 Rivington Street at Stuyvesant Square, began weekly prayer sessions for women. Held on Tuesdays in Dr. Palmer's office in a back room of the house, they were informal gatherings that usually included the sharing of personal testimony of God's role in some of the women's lives, a sermon, and readings of religious texts. The prayer meetings became immensely popular and soon were moved to a large second-floor parlor. When Lankford and her family moved out of the city following a new job for her husband, Palmer took over the meetings alone, and slowly began allowing men to attend as well. In 1839, she made history as the first Methodist-sanctioned woman to be appointed permanent leader of a "mixed"—male and female—religious meeting. Soon as many as three hundred people were cramming into the house for the Tuesday sessions.

Palmer was now in demand as a lecturer, and she honored countless invitations to speak at tent meetings and camp revivals. She wrote eighteen books (*The Way of Holiness* became something of a religious hit) and a steady stream of articles for religious magazines and newspapers, and she eventually edited the *Guide to Holiness* periodical. Her works helped spawn the Pilgrim Holiness Church, the Church of the Nazarene, and the Salvation Army.

It's unknown when Corbett first crossed paths with Palmer, but they became friends in faith. Corbett also became a regular at Palmer's Tuesday prayer sessions. Under her influence, Corbett "imbibed some peculiar beliefs, which he was honestly trying to carry into practice . . . [that] it is possible to live for days, weeks, months, and years in succession, without committing any sin in thought, word, or deed."[29]

That belief—that he could lead a Christian life one moment, one act, at a time—would frame the rest of Boston Corbett's life.

2

Boston Corbett
Goes to War

As Boston Corbett was finding peace with God, his country was falling apart.

The Southern secession movement began like a dominoes trick. South Carolina was the first to fall, on December 20, 1860, some six weeks after Abraham Lincoln won the presidency yet more than two months before he would assume office. Then over three successive days in January, legislatures in Mississippi, Florida, and Alabama voted to join the exodus. Georgia and Louisiana followed by the end of the month, and Texas jumped aboard in February, shortly before the seven rebellious states met in Montgomery, Alabama, to create the constitution for their Confederate States of America.

The secessionists had demands. They wanted outgoing US President James Buchanan, who believed slavery was a states' rights issue and not the federal government's business, to cede federal forts to the new confederacy. Buchanan refused, though he also failed to defend the forts. The Southern states seized all but four and blockaded the most significant of the remainder, Fort Sumter in South Carolina's Charleston Harbor.

So by the time Lincoln was sworn in on March 4 as the sixteenth president of the United States, the nation was already disunited, with six states along the Gulf of Mexico, and Georgia and South Carolina on the Atlantic coast, forming a solid Southern tier of slaveholding states in rebellion. (Four more states—Virginia, Arkansas, North Carolina, and Tennessee—would soon join them.) Lincoln's election, which slavery supporters felt would mean the end of the peculiar institution that fed their economy and defined their society, had been the final bit of pressure that cracked the union.

Inauguration Day started ominously, with brisk winds and a leaden sky—Confederate gray, in fact. Rumors of Southern plots ran rampant, and many expected someone would try to kill Lincoln before he could take office. It wasn't just idle chitchat. The seat of the federal government had the misfortune of being surrounded by two slaveholding states, Virginia and Maryland. Lincoln had traveled by train from his Springfield, Illinois, home along a circuitous northern route to reduce risk. (As it was, someone tried unsuccessfully to block the rail line with debris.) He made it to the capital safely, though exhausted, after sneaking unannounced past rebellious Baltimore. Lincoln kept a low profile at his suite in the Willard Hotel, the seat of power for unofficial Washington and the lodging place for everyone from job applicants to contractors to incoming members of Congress.

Lincoln restricted his visits to only a handful of guests—no easy task given the size and nature of the Willard. "It is a quadrangular mass of rooms, six stories high, and some hundred yards square," British journalist W. H. Russell wrote after a visit the next year.

> It probably contains at this moment more scheming, plotting, planning heads, more aching and joyful hearts, than any building of the same size ever held in the world. . . . Up and down the long passages doors were opening and shutting for men with papers bulging out of their pockets, who hurried as if for their life in and out. . . . There were crowds in the hall through which one could scarce make his way— the writing-room was crowded, and the rustle of pens rose to a little breeze—the smoking-room, the bar, the barber's, the reception-room,

the ladies' drawing-room—all were crowded. At present not less than 2,500 people dine in the public room every day.[1]

Lincoln might have wanted to stay out of sight, but on Inauguration Day there was no hiding.

By the time Lincoln emerged onto the East Portico of the Capitol shortly after noon, the morning's hard weather had turned, as though winter had passed into spring within just a few hours, leaving the air warm and the sky clear and blue. But the fear of assassination remained. As a precaution, Lincoln's open-top brett carriage was surrounded on the trip to the Capitol by a human shield of soldiers on horseback. During the ceremony, Horace Greeley, the New York newspaper editor, sat immediately behind Lincoln. As the new president read his first inaugural address, Greeley was "expecting to hear its delivery arrested by the crack of a rifle aimed at his heart."[2]

There was ample space for an assassin to hide himself. Some twenty-five thousand people had gathered outside the Capitol, many more than could hear the unamplified oath and speech. They watched an odd scene unfold as Lincoln, dressed all in black, ran out of hands. He had his speech, his gold-headed ebony cane, his eyeglass case, and his hat, which he sought to lay down somewhere. But there was no side table. Stephen A. Douglas, whom Lincoln had beaten in the November election, was on the platform as a ranking member of the US Senate, and he reached out and took the hat as though he were Lincoln's valet, a moment of unintended poignancy. Nearby, ready to administer the oath, sat Chief Justice Roger Taney, author of the Supreme Court's 1857 Dred Scott decision that denied blacks, whether free or slave, basic rights of citizenship and extended slavery into the territories. The controversy over that decision had fed the tensions that were now cracking apart the union, and the presence of all three men represented the heart of the American crisis.[3]

Lincoln placed his handwritten speech on a desktop and laid his walking stick across the top of the sheets as a paperweight. In his high, thin voice, he told the nation that he had no intention of challenging the Southern states' declared right to maintain the slavery system, or to move militarily against the forts that the Southerners had seized. But he did intend to enforce federal laws. States couldn't unilaterally back out of the union. Much like a contract, he argued, one party might violate the agreement and pay the consequences, but both parties have to agree to end it, and the rest of the states had not given the rebellious slaveholders permission to leave. These were the *United* States of America, and the oath he was taking on the steps of the still-incomplete Capitol building required that he defend the federal authority across all thirty-four members of the Union—whether they still considered themselves to be members or not.

"In doing this there needs to be no bloodshed or violence; and there shall be none, unless it be forced upon the national authority," Lincoln said. "The power confided in me, will be used to hold, occupy, and possess the property, and places belonging to the government, and to collect the duties and imposts; but beyond what may be necessary for these objects, there will be no invasion—no using of force against or among the people anywhere."

Five weeks later, Confederate cannons bombarded Fort Sumter, and Lincoln's dream of a peaceful resolution to the disintegrating union disappeared. The war was on. The president hastily convened his cabinet, and within days he sent out a call for volunteers from the Northern states to defend the republic. He wanted seventy-five thousand men, each pledged to serve ninety days. The request was sent by letter and telegram to state capitals and was reprinted in newspapers across the remaining union. Some states, such as Tennessee, rejected the call-up. Within days, Virginia voted to secede, bringing the rebellion to the capital's southern edge. Three more states—Arkansas, North Carolina, and Tennessee—quickly followed suit.

But the rest held firm. Even Maryland, despite its sympathies, stayed with the Union, though many of its citizens' hearts went with the secessionists, making the state a dangerous place for Union troops to traverse. And mountain-dwellers in western Virginia soon staged their own secession, beginning the process of splitting off from the Virginia commonwealth and the Confederacy, eventually forming West Virginia. But north of the Mason-Dixon Line, which defined the Maryland-Pennsylvania border, militias—some already formed, some hastily patched together—offered their services to the president and the Union.

Most of the New York newspapers were filled with details about which militias were accepting volunteers where, and what new militias were being formed. New York State's quota under the call-up was seventeen regiments of 1,780 men each, for a total of more than 30,000 men. A sense of urgency propelled the drive, especially after Virginia seceded, leaving Washington and the new president exposed to mortal risk. Telegrams zipped around the North, many of them to and from Washington, warning of an anticipated Rebel march on the ill-defended Union capital, and spreading reports of destroyed bridges and rail lines that increased the physical isolation of Lincoln and the seat of the US government. "Such, in variety, were the multitudinous messages of alarm and counsel which kept the electric wires in constant action. They were throbbings of the great heart of the people—spontaneous, irrepressible," Lockwood L. Doty, chief of the bureau of the military records of New York, wrote in an official report on the New York militias.[4] Losing the Capitol in the opening days of the rebellion would be catastrophic; losing Lincoln would be even worse. In Manhattan, business and industrial leaders met in a hurried conference and pledged $20,000 to move local soldiers and their equipment to Washington via trains and ships.[5]

Among the militia organizers was Elmer Ellsworth, a lover of military discipline and organization who was based in Washington. He immediately perceived the peril Washington faced, and he had a clear idea of how to quickly raise a well-trained regiment of tough, courageous men. Three days after the Rebel shelling of Fort Sumter, Ellsworth was in Manhattan, dropping in on Greeley and other newspaper editors and making the rounds of the city's vibrant but fractious volunteer firefighting companies. The fire departments comprised a culture of predominately Irish hypermasculinity: hard-drinking, hard-fighting men who were heavily drilled in working as teams to fight fires—traits also key to a successful military unit. Ellsworth saw the fire companies as the foundation for an effective fighting force to defend Washington, and he quickly persuaded most of them to come together as the First New York Fire Zouaves.[6]

Further support came from the city's existing militias, including the Twelfth Regiment, a National Guard outfit under the command of Colonel

Daniel Butterfield, who by day was in charge of the New York telegraph office of American Express, a company cofounded by his father.[7] In the run-up to the war, the regiment held regular training sessions for its members, about 425 men, and hosted a series of evening lectures on the latest in military strategies, usually delivered by guest speakers. Before the inauguration, leaders of the militia had offered the regiment's services as plainclothes escorts for the president-elect on the train ride to Washington, though the offer wasn't accepted.[8] With Lincoln's call for volunteers, the Twelfth sent out a notice that it would enroll new members at its Eighth Avenue "drill room" between Forty-First and Forty-Second Streets, and shortly afterward opened recruiting offices at 552 Grand Street and at 594 Broadway, where steady streams of men showed up to fill out their papers.

The ever-excitable Boston Corbett, still living and working as a hatter in New York, was caught up in the exuberant rush to war. He was living on East Ninth Street, between Avenues A and B, but worked on Eighth Avenue on the west side of the island for his hat-making friend James Brown. Corbett had had his issues with other employers, most of them stemming from his eccentric expressions of faith. But in Brown he found something of a patron. Brown himself was deeply religious, which was likely the glue that bound them. Older than Corbett, Brown seemed to take a paternal interest in his employee. Outside of the business, Brown was a member of the Twelfth Regiment, so when the call went out that the Twelfth was mustering for action, Brown found himself in a bind. His health was not good, and his business would not run well without him. So he approached the antislavery Corbett and asked him—probably for a fee; the records don't say—to serve as his substitute.[9]

Corbett was twenty-eight years old when he signed up on April 19, 1861, for a three-month stint. In addition to the existing members of the Twelfth Regiment—and substitutes such as Corbett—there was a flood of recruits. So many, in fact, that the Twelfth Regiment had to turn away several hundred would-be fighters, leaving them to join later-forming regiments, a decision made on the most pragmatic of grounds: there weren't enough guns to arm them all.[10]

The members of the Twelfth might have been volunteering in New York, but they wouldn't be formally mustered in until they reached Washington,

DC. The different militias and other military units scrambled to get ready, and some—including the Twelfth—left before they were fully provisioned. The departures were to begin with a rally at Union Square on April 21, two days after Corbett enlisted and was assigned to I Company. For the occasion, the city sprouted a coat of bunting, with red, white, and blue flapping from windows of five- and six-story office buildings as well as street-level bars and restaurants. There was a touch of mob mentality to the cause. The *New York Herald*, whose editor was slow to line up behind the war effort, was besieged by Union loyalists, and the building was at risk of being overrun by a flag-waving mob until the editor published a pro-Union editorial and flags and bunting began appearing in *Herald* office windows too.

But at Union Square, there were no backsliders. Some ten thousand people crowded into the open space in the middle of the explosively growing city. Different regiments made their way through the throngs. The Twelfth Regiment was ordered to report "in full fatigue, with overcoats and knapsacks" to the Fourteenth Street edge of the park, and allowed to carry only one extra change of underclothes. Their single trunks were to have been dropped off at the 594 Broadway office the night before for loading on the *Baltic*, the steamship that would take them to Annapolis.

Corbett showed up that day dressed in a gray uniform close to the unit's colors, which would soon change, given that the unit was fighting for the blue-clad North. Corbett cut an odd figure, short and stocky with "a round pleasant face and abundance of long black hair parted in the middle so that he resembled a woman," according to Edward Kirk, recently promoted from private to corporal and "assigned to drill and care for a squad of new men."[11]

The regiment comprised ten companies, each delineated by a letter, with more than 100 per company for a total of 1,192 troops. This was more than double the size of the militia from just a few days before but fewer than the 1,780 sought in the call-up. They'd had no time to drill and nearly half had no uniforms. But they were ready to fight. The units were ordered to gather at different armories around the city by 7 AM, then march to arrive at the rendezvous point on Fourteenth Street by 9 AM. Individual soldiers led their own small parades of friends and relatives to the armories for cheerful and tearful farewells. As the companies came together a patriotic party broke out at Washington Square Park, including a stage from which speakers, unheard over the din, offered prayers and best wishes and tried to rally the hearts of men who didn't really need rallying. Yet.

The thickening crowd slowed the military convergence, delaying for hours the scheduled parade departures from Union Square to the ships. Finally, in the early afternoon, the regiments began leaving. Corbett and the other volunteers of the Twelfth fell into the best-disciplined parade formation they could manage. Following the uniformed Butterfield atop a prancing black horse, they marched down Broadway, then cut a block west to Mercer and then south to Canal Street and finally westward to the piers at the North River (the name then for that stretch of the Hudson). Broadway, normally empty on a Sunday, looked like a holiday celebration, according to a reporter for the *Herald*:

> Every window, door, housetop, awning, was crowded. The street itself was thronged as though the populace were wedged together in one solid living mass. This extended as far as the eye could reach in both directions, except in the small central space kept clear by the police. Bright eyes, more numerous than the stars, flashed towards the military from every point to which they turned, and in one instance a laurel wreath was thrown among the soldiers. The cheers rang through the atmosphere in thrilling contrast to the usual quiet of Sunday morning. The hats and handkerchiefs waved everywhere over the sea of humanity in such profusion that they resembled the migration of an immense flock of pigeons across one of our great western lakes. The Stars and Stripes waved everywhere, and one banner displayed the words, "Fort Sumter and its Band of 70 Heroes. No Surrender to traitors."

With that many people, and that many soldiers to move, confusion was inevitable. Butterfield and his men reached the *Baltic* to find another regiment already aboard. After some hurried discussions, a different ship was found for the misdirected regiment, whose soldiers were cleared out of the *Baltic* to let the Twelfth board.

Hearing that the regiments would reach the piers at 11 AM, hundreds of people showed up at the river's edge to send off the troops, only to have to wait most of the day before the men finally marched into view. A few arrived hoping to enlist on the spot. "One came with a rusty musket, a cartridge box at his belt, and his pockets full of ginger snaps," the *New York Sun* reported. "Another had nothing but a six barreled revolver. . . . Scores came with the most outré equipment, and some tolerably well accoutered, and all alike were sent away to some of the recruiting offices to enroll their names."

By late afternoon, the troops were finally squared away, and around five o'clock deckhands loosened the ropes and the *Baltic* pushed away from the pier and out into the river, then began steaming south through the harbor to the Atlantic Ocean beyond.

For those accustomed to the sea, it was an uneventful voyage. For the land-lubber soldiers, the steady roll of the Atlantic left many of them ill, and the pitching ship doomed efforts to get a jump on training with open-deck drills. "Although a fine day, the *Baltic* rolled heavily, and every time the soldiers moved or changed position of their pieces, they lost their balance," reported a *New York Herald* journalist traveling with the Twelfth Regiment. "The Colonel supported himself against one of the masts, and the Adjutant presented the appearance of a person dancing." The rest of the troops, he reported, looked as though they had been drinking and "spectators were convulsed with laughter" as they watched the ragtag band of soldiers try to retain some semblance of military bearing and dignity.[12] More serious issues arose, too. One soldier fell overboard, another wounded himself with his own sidearm, and a third was sliced open by a bayonet when the rolling seas tossed a colleague off balance. All three apparently survived, but a fourth soldier was reported dead from sunstroke by the time the Twelfth finally moved from ship to shore at Annapolis on April 26.[13]

"It was at this time that we began to see the peculiarities about this comrade" Boston Corbett, Corporal Kirk wrote years later. The Twelfth Regiment soldiers had been ordered to fill their haversacks with as much crackers and cheese as each soldier could manage, which would be their sustenance during the march from Annapolis to Washington. Kirk went one step better and ordered his soldiers to eat as much as they could before they started out, hoping to give them enough fuel to move quickly over the long distance. "Corbett said he would eat no more until on the shore of the enemy," Kirk recalled. "Almost daily something would occur which would mark him as different from others." Still, Corbett had many positive qualities. "He was a very religious man, faithful at his post of duty, a good speaker, and a skillful and helpful nurse to those who were ill or in distress, and [he] knew no fear."[14]

The regiment initially was assigned to guard a series of bridges leading south from Baltimore to Washington, a bulwark against sabotage by Rebels and their supporters in Maryland.[15] The precarious position of the capital became clear when secessionists in Baltimore severed the telegraph connections between Washington and the North, and railroad lines were torn up, isolating Lincoln in his hastily emptying city. And Rebel forces were on the move in Virginia, reinforcing seized federal positions at places like Norfolk and Harpers Ferry. But the first casualties of the war occurred in Baltimore as the Sixth Massachusetts Regiment tried to march from one train station to another to get to Washington. A mob formed, streets were blockaded, and violence broke out, forcing the regiment to fight its way through. Twelve civilians and four soldiers were killed, a harbinger of what would become four blood-soaked years.[16]

As the Twelfth Regiment worked its way across the Maryland countryside, rumors swirled that some of the locals had poisoned water wells hoping to fell Union troops moving south. While the regiment was setting up camp one evening, Corbett was dispatched with a few fellow soldiers to collect water from a nearby farmhouse. When the soldiers arrived and made their demand, Corbett pulled out his loaded musket and at gunpoint forced the farmer and his two sons to first drink the water. When they didn't keel over, he lowered his weapon and the soldiers filled their water carriers.[17]

Corbett and the rest of the Twelfth Regiment arrived in Washington on April 28, a Sunday. The city was in a bizarre state of flux as Union-sympathizing residents, fearing a Southern swell, fled north, and Southern secessionists fled south. Into the void were moving thousands of soldiers from the Union regiments, few of which had any real place to plant their flags. The firefighting Zouaves were deployed to the Capitol, where they made an ignoble mark by mockingly taking over the floor and holding their own congressional session. Some found Senator Jefferson Davis's abandoned desk and splintered it as souvenirs. Another regiment found quarters within the White House itself. It gave Washington the feel of a militarily occupied city, the streets filled with blue-uniformed soldiers.

Corbett likely felt conflicted about the Twelfth Regiment's assigned temporary quarters: a church. The day after they took over the building, President Lincoln and Secretary of State William H. Seward dropped in to welcome and thank the volunteers. "While W. H. Seward got in the pulpit and spoke encouraging words to us," Lincoln moved among the men offering his "thanks and blessing us for our response to his call for help" and shaking the hand of each soldier there—including Corbett's, a pregnant crossing of the paths of the man who would be the nation's first assassinated president and the obscure religious zealot who would kill his assassin.

The Twelfth moved from the church to hotels and boardinghouses for five days before being assigned to the new Camp Anderson, at Franklin Square, a spring-fed park a few blocks northeast of the White House. They quickly built wooden shacks for their barracks, and on May 2, the volunteers of the Twelfth were formally mustered in as soldiers. It wasn't until they reached Camp Anderson that their new blue uniforms caught up with them. They finally resembled a military unit instead of a guerrilla outfit.

The bulk of the unit's time was taken up with converting the mishmash of volunteers into a trained fighting unit, and it was a grueling, demoralizing process under the unrelenting Colonel Butterfield. "For a time I don't think I ever hated a man more in my life than I did General Butterfield," a soldier wrote well after Butterfield had risen through the officer corps. "It was 'double-quick' from morning until night, and then sometimes at midnight, to see how well we could do it."[18] The drilling was augmented by the addition of a handful of recent West Point graduates and became part of the evening entertainment for civilian Washington. "The huts and tents were gaily illuminated with lamps, and a crowd of well-dressed people never tired of the novelty of actual military life, strolled about among the lines,

The Twelfth New York State Militia and a troop of Zouaves in formation at Camp Anderson in Franklin Square, Washington, DC, on June 11, 1861.

Courtesy of Library of Congress, Prints and Photographs Division (reproduction number LC-DIG-ppmsca-19886)

and enjoyed the music of the regimental bands. There was no drunkenness, but a great deal of gaiety, and finally a dance before visitors were compelled to withdraw."[19]

Corbett was part of the daily militia life, but his name isn't singled out in any of the official reports. Among his fellow soldiers, though, he was cementing his reputation as an odd and deeply religious man, his conversation peppered with reminders to his colleagues that they should lead Christian lives, observe the Sabbath, and, in their few off hours, abstain from strong drink and carousing. Corbett found some support among fellow believers, but those less attached to faith openly mocked him.

Butterfield's strict leadership, and the response of his troops, was noticed up the command chain, and in May the Twelfth Militia was ordered to take the lead in the first Union movement into Virginia. The regiment was roused after 9 PM on May 23 and left a short time later, moving so quietly that neighbors awoke the next morning surprised to find the camp empty. The regiment marched through the deserted streets, past the White House and on southward to Long Bridge at the foot of Fourteenth Street, where they joined up with the Seventh and Twenty-Fifth Regiments from New York, the Third Regiment from New Jersey, and some engineers.

At 2 AM the order was given to cross the bridge, with the Twelfth leading the way, their rifle barrels glinting in the bright moonlight. Other troops followed over the aqueduct farther up the river near Georgetown, and by steamboat. Each regiment moved to assigned geographies, the Twelfth marching southwest to Roach's Mill near Alexandria. It set up camp in a mill building and the surrounding grounds, forming an instant village of military tents. Troops not assigned to security details at bridges and along roadways were drilled or sent out to forage for provisions.[20]

The Twelfth encountered no Rebel forces—in fact, most of the Confederate army had abandoned Alexandria days before the Union troops were ordered to move in. Some seven hundred Rebel soldiers remained, and at word that the Union forces were crossing the Potomac, they quickly packed up and left by train, pausing to burn wooden bridges once they crossed them. Members of the First New York Zouaves tried to pursue but didn't get very far, so reconciled themselves to making sure the bridges were sufficiently damaged to keep reinforced Rebels from chugging back into Alexandria.

It was not a gentle nor necessarily chivalrous occupation. A local woman appeared at the camp and complained to Butterfield that she "had been robbed of her all by some of the men." Further, she told Butterfield, she could identify them. Incensed by what he saw as behavior unfitting for a soldier, Butterfield ordered those still in camp, some nine hundred men, called out for inspection. Once the men were set, Butterfield appeared before them and railed about the breach in decorum and basic civility. "I will have no damned thieves in this regiment!" he thundered.[21]

Corbett took umbrage at his superior officer's language and stepped forward two paces. "I call the Colonel to order for swearing," Corbett shouted out. If Butterfield heard, he didn't let on, but Corbett's captain, William Raynor, witnessed the outburst and had Corbett arrested for disorderly conduct. Corbett was tossed into a makeshift garrison. He responded by going on a hunger fast, tossing out the window any food delivered to him and singing incessant hymns at the top of his lungs. "He was the most troublesome man in my company," Raynor later wrote. After two days, Corbett was released, unbowed and unrepentant.

Back in Washington, in an unforeseen bit of political pressure, neighbors near Franklin Square lobbied the Union military leaders to return the Twelfth, or some other regiment, to Camp Anderson to provide protection should the Rebels attack the capital. So on June 2, the Twelfth broke camp and returned to their parade grounds, where they continued to drill and play host to Washingtonians for whom the soldiers served as a communal distraction. Despite the war of separation, the Independence Day celebrations at Camp Anderson became a significant social event. "Franklin Square was thronged with the ladies and citizens of Washington, the whole scene presenting a fairy-like aspect, as the camp glittered with gaily painted Chinese lanterns, and blazed with lights, while dance after dance followed to the music of the regimental band." But the next day, the party mood faded as rumors swirled that the Twelfth Regiment would shortly be ordered to move out to western Virginia.[22]

The war itself was getting off to a soft start as both sides hurriedly tried to put together armies and military plans. Few people thought the war would last very long, and even though it had been a long time coming, when it came, it seemed to catch both sides by surprise. So the first few battles were more small skirmishes than the full-on engagements with thousands killed that would come to mark the nation's bloodiest war. And both sides struggled to figure out where to best place troops, and which pieces of ground would provide strategic advantages.

One such place was Harpers Ferry, the small village at the juncture of the Shenandoah and Potomac Rivers in the hills of western Virginia, where the federal army maintained a rifle-making arsenal. Just two years earlier, the fiery antislavery crusader John Brown had staged his infamous raid there, hoping to steal weapons to arm a slave rebellion that never materialized. Brown was hanged on December 2, 1859, an act witnessed by hundreds, including the actor John Wilkes Booth.

But now Harpers Ferry was in Rebel hands. On April 18, as Virginia was moving toward formal secession, several Rebel militias under the orders of Henry Wise—Virginia governor when Brown mounted his raid—had advanced on the arsenal. The forty-seven federal soldiers assigned to the fort got wind of the approaching Rebels, lit the facility on fire, and then fled north.[23] The fire damaged but didn't destroy the rifle works, so the Rebels settled in. It would prove to be a hard spot to defend, lying below three high bluffs that gave attackers a decided advantage. But its placement at the confluence of the rivers, as well as its proximity to the Chesapeake and Ohio Canal and a main line of the Baltimore and Ohio railroad, made Harpers Ferry strategically important. Control of the tiny village and arsenal would change eight times over the course of the war. In fact, the Rebels who took over in April abandoned it in mid-June as Union General Walter Patterson began assembling troops nearby.

On July 7, Butterfield received the anticipated fresh orders to move his men westward, where they would join up with Patterson. The Twelfth packed up and boarded a train for Baltimore, then marched through the city to a second station to take a train for Harrisburg, and on to Hagerstown, where they set up camp for several hours of rest. (Unlike the violence that had greeted the Sixth Massachusetts Regiment three months earlier, the Twelfth's passage through Baltimore went easily.)

Around 5:30 PM on July 9, the militia packed up and began moving on foot to Williamsport, crossed the waist-deep Potomac, and continued on to Martinsburg, where they arrived around 5 AM—a march of twenty-nine miles in under twelve hours, nearly all of it in the dark of night.[24] Butterfield reported in to Patterson, adding his regiment to the nearly thirty thousand soldiers already under Patterson's command. Butterfield also learned of a shuffle in the military organization that elevated him to brigadier general over a brigade consisting of the Twelfth as well as the Fifth New York Militia and the Nineteenth and Twenty-Eighth New York State volunteers. A Lieutenant Colonel Ward then took command of the Twelfth, encamped west of Harpers Ferry at Bolivar Heights.

The Twelfth wasn't operating in a vacuum. Both North and South were moving forces into western and northern Virginia, and they engaged in light skirmishes—until July 21, when after several days of troop movements and strategizing, a battle broke out in a shallow valley through which flowed Bull Run, a small river, and the Warrenton Turnpike. Just two days before, the Union forces under Brigadier General Irvin McDowell had a distinct advantage in men, but poor preparations and weak discipline slowed the start of the attack, allowing Rebel reinforcements, including a regiment led by Colonel Thomas Jackson, to move in. What the Union thought would be a relatively easy battle—picnickers from Washington came out to watch the fun—turned into a bloody rout that sent the Northerners, soldiers and day-trippers alike, fleeing back to the capital.

Jackson's performance in standing ground atop a hill, stifling a Union advance and turning the tide of the battle, earned him the nickname "Stonewall." But the most significant impact of Bull Run was as a harbinger of bloodshed to follow. The North suffered nearly 2,900 casualties, including some 460 killed, and about 1,300 men captured. The South reported some 2,000 casualties, including nearly 400 killed, but virtually no soldiers taken prisoner. The war, both sides now realized, would not be won quickly or easily.

The defeat at Bull Run came at a bad time for Lincoln. The Union army was facing a deadline. Lincoln's initial call-up was for volunteer stints of three months, which, for the Twelfth Regiment, would end on July 16.[25] But Butterfield had notified Washington that he would keep his militias in the field until August 2, three months after the day they were formally mustered in during a ceremony in Washington. It's not known how the men in the regiment took to Butterfield unilaterally committing them to a couple more weeks of service—with apparently no added pay—though Boston Corbett, for one, was not willing to go along. He had his own mustering-out date in mind, an assertion that would cost him. At midnight, while on picket duty, Corbett walked off his post. He was court-martialed on July 31 and docked two months' pay—a significant fine considering his stint was only three months.[26]

Most of the Union forces abandoned Harpers Ferry on July 28, and the Twelfth began making its way north to prepare for mustering out. The regiment camped near Knoxville, a mile down the Potomac River on the north bank, until fresh orders arrived dispatching the regiment home to New York City. The Twelfth made good time by train through Camden and Amboy, New Jersey, and then crossed by ship to Battery Place in lower Manhattan around dusk on August 2.

The return was nearly as boisterous as the departure more than three months earlier. A handful of wounded soldiers were the first to leave the pier, and then the healthy troops marched onto solid land and made their way to Broadway, then northward in an evening parade that drew thousands of cheering people. At Union Square, where they had first gathered as a regiment in April, the Twelfth was dismissed, the soldiers stepping into the arms of family and friends grateful to have them back alive and whole. But for most of the soldiers, the mustering out (formally done during a gathering at 10 AM August 5 at Washington Square) was only temporary, as the little revolt in the South grew into a massive war that would consume the nation.

Boston Corbett's role in all of this is hinted at through records and in reminiscences that trickled out in the decades after the end of the war and the end of Booth. Until that fateful moment, in fact, Corbett was just another soldier, albeit one whose motivations were never particularly clear. The devout Christian seemed to have no qualms about taking up arms intending to kill some of his fellow countrymen, with no way of knowing whether he was killing heathens or other faithful adherents. Eccentric beyond tolerance, he was viewed by his military colleagues—as he had been by many fellow Christians during his prewar prayer meetings—as an over-the-edge scold. His self-castration was widely known among his military peers. For many, it was inarguable evidence that Corbett was insane. But for a small coterie of fellow believers, it was a mark of devotion and faith.

After the Twelfth Regiment mustered out, many of its members reenlisted in a revamped Twelfth Militia, which in January 1862 was merged into the Twelfth Volunteers. Corbett wasn't among them. Though the regiment had ended its first deployment on August 5, it took the army another eleven days to pay the soldiers their back wages. In Corbett's case, that was only one month's worth because of the court-martial sentence, or about thirteen dollars.

It's unclear whether Corbett remained in New York after he mustered out, but on June 2, 1862, he was back in Manhattan, where he rejoined the Union army and the new incarnation of his old regiment, the Twelfth Volunteers, this time in K Company, at the rank of corporal. Within a couple of weeks, the Twelfth was again at Harpers Ferry, assigned to defend the small village itself and maintain a picket to monitor the crossings of Union soldiers.

On one Sunday afternoon, Corbett was among those assigned to picket duty, which must have chafed someone for whom keeping the Sabbath holy was not optional. Two soldiers from other regiments, a man identified only as JWB from the Twenty-Second New York Militia and Captain Herrick from an Ohio militia, decided to spend the afternoon picking blackberries when they were halted by Corbett, who was clutching a thick Bible a couple of feet from his rifle.[27]

Corbett asked the men where they were headed, and they told him. "Don't you know better than that?" Corbett replied, brandishing his Bible. "Doesn't this Holy Book teach you to remember the Sabbath day, to keep it holy?"

"I guess we know as much about the Bible as you," Herrick said as the two men resumed walking. In a flash, Corbett grabbed, cocked, and raised his gun, aiming it at his fellow New York soldier's chest. "If you go another step further," Corbett said, "you are a dead man."

The two soldiers turned back, and JWB wrote after the war (and it should be read with some skepticism, given the trajectory of Corbett's future fame) that he felt lucky to have lived. Word among the New York troops was that Corbett, for all his fervent Christianity, was eager to kill. "It mattered not who the victim might be, so long as he should have any justification of authority for firing."

By the time Corbett and his comrades returned to Harpers Ferry in the summer of 1862, the temperature of the war had changed significantly, and the river enclave was back in play. General Robert E. Lee dispatched

Stonewall Jackson and three columns of troops, complete with artillery, to recapture the strategic site, now defended by eleven Union regiments.

On September 12, the Rebel forces climbed naturally protected, and unguarded, slopes to the peaks overlooking Harpers Ferry and began routing the woefully inexperienced Union troops. The Twelfth—among the most experienced—was positioned within the village, and its artillerymen fired repeated rounds at the Rebel forces but with little effect. On the morning of September 15, with the Rebels manning artillery on all three ridges overlooking the river valley, Jackson unleashed a barrage that staggered the remaining Union troops, and followed it up with an infantry push from the West. Colonel Dixon S. Miles, in charge of the Union troops, surrendered, though not before losing a leg in the barrage, a wound that ultimately killed him, making him one of fewer than fifty men lost on each side.

The Rebels made easy work of it in part because Miles was slow and ineffective in defending the critical high ground around Harpers Ferry; he suffered from a lack of reinforcements. The surrendered forces totaled about twelve thousand men, constituting the largest single block of prisoners to be taken during the war. Jackson had few options for dealing with them. He was in a rush to join his divisions with those of Lee, who was headed for Sharpsburg, Maryland, and what would become known as the Battle of Antietam. So Jackson confiscated what Union weapons he could and "paroled" the soldiers, sending them home.

Corbett joined the paroled troops late on September 16 as they journeyed north, grabbing trains where they could. Despite the resounding loss at Harpers Ferry, when Corbett and the other men of the Twelfth arrived back in New York they were hailed as conquering heroes. And there Corbett's second tour ended: he mustered out on August 8, 1862.

Ten months later, the Twelfth was ordered back into service. It's unclear what Corbett was doing during that interval, but it seems most likely he was back working in James Brown's shop and taking part in street prayer meetings. The timing is uncertain, but during some of his wartime church appearances in New York he gave vent to a dark embrace of violence. He saw the war as not only necessary but also a just act to preserve the Union and to end slavery. Some of his fellow church members—particularly women in the congregation—took issue, seeing violence as immoral and sinful in any circumstance and fundamentally inconsistent with a Christian life. Yet it was said that Corbett was perfectly willing to "shoot men like dogs" and that "before shooting a Rebel he always prayed, God have mercy on your souls" and then would "pop them off." Pacifists among his fellow churchgoers sought to have him ejected for espousing un-Christian views, but apparently the storm blew over before any action was taken.[28]

When the call went out for the Twelfth to return to action, Corbett once again responded. The Twelfth was first ordered to Pennsylvania, leaving New York on June 20, 1863, for Harrisburg, and then moving a bit farther north to Marysville. Their orders were to defend roadways against northern incursions by the Rebel army, which was trying to move deeply into Pennsylvania as Lee pressed for what he hoped would be a resounding victory against the North, in the North.

On July 1, 1863, the first shots were fired in the Battle of Gettysburg, an intensely bloody affair that lasted three days, killed more than fifty-two thousand men, and sent Lee's forces into retreat. Though the war would continue for two more years, the battle marked a high point for the South; Lee's forces would never again be that ambitious or seek to move that far into Northern territory. And while the Twelfth was stationed to the north of the fighting, ready to repel Lee's troops had they continued on, Corbett ultimately was only lightly involved in that most critical of Civil War battles.

Ten days after the Gettysburg battle, however, murderous riots broke out in New York over the military draft, which quickly morphed into a race riot as poor whites (many of them Irish immigrants) blamed blacks for the war. The Twelfth and other New York troops were ordered back home to defend the city against itself. The riots had begun on the morning of July 13, and by the time the Twelfth Militia arrived on July 19, they had run their course but taken their toll in death and property damage. Corbett and the rest of the Twelfth headquartered at City Hall, though some were deployed to protect key parts of the city's infrastructure, such as the Gas Works. But in the end, they had relatively little to do and were mustered out of service.[29]

Corbett stayed on in New York, presumably returning to hat making. When the military compiled its list of draft-eligible men in May and June 1863, Corbett listed himself as living on Attorney Street a few blocks east of the Five Points neighborhood. Another man, Benjamin Cruger, a black laborer, also registered for the draft from the same address; they may have been roommates or merely fellow residents of a boardinghouse.

Yet Corbett didn't wait to be drafted. On August 4, he signed up for a three-year stint but changed outfits. This time he joined Company L of the Sixteenth New York Cavalry and was formally mustered in on September 5 in Washington as a private. The next day he was promoted to corporal, reflecting, no doubt, his experiences with the Twelfth Militia and Volunteers. But where Corbett's combat duties with the Twelfth were relatively light—the bombardment and surrender at Harpers Ferry notwithstanding—Corbett now found himself thrust into the middle of the raging war.

The Sixteenth Cavalry, commanded by Colonel Henry M. Lazelle, was based in northern Virginia, near Washington, part of a cavalry brigade under Colonel Charles L. Lowell. The troops were playing a deadly game of cat and mouse with the Forty-Third Battalion of the Virginia Cavalry, known more broadly as Mosby's Rangers. Unlike most other military commanders, Colonel John S. Mosby ran his troops as something of a guerrilla force, popping up here and there for surprise attacks on Union troops, then disappearing into the Virginia woods and fields and melting into the secessionist communities until the next call to battle.

The Sixteenth Cavalry lost one such encounter on February 21 while camping near Middleburg, Virginia. Around two o'clock in the morning, some 160 of Mosby's Rangers swept through the sleeping camp. "Surprised and confounded, with no time to form, they made but feeble resistance, and were perfectly overwhelmed by the shock of the charge," Mosby reported back to his superiors. "They fled in every direction in the wildest confusion, leaving on the field at least 15 killed and a considerable number wounded, besides 70 prisoners in our hands, with all their horses, arms, and equipments."[30]

Corbett survived, but five days later, his peculiar personality landed him in trouble once again with his superior officers. The details are lost, but at some point in the previous few days his behavior crossed a line and he was written up. The punishment, as meted out on February 26, was demotion, busting him back from corporal to private. Nearly three years after Corbett first volunteered to defend the Union against the secessionists, he was, in terms of his military career, right back where he had started.

He remained on active duty, and on May 1 the Sixteenth Cavalry achieved some revenge for the early-morning raid that had both embarrassed them and cost them men and materiel. While searching houses apparently identified by a spy, the Union soldiers confiscated a large number of guns and "contraband goods" and captured twenty-one of Mosby's men and two dozen horses, as well as an unrecorded amount of wool and tobacco. It wasn't a bloodless success, though. Two members of the Sixteenth Cavalry were killed and, unexplained in the records, they lost two others as prisoners.[31]

The records are also unclear as to what part Corbett played in these raids and skirmishes, but his battalion was clearly engaged in trying to counter Mosby's presence in northern Virginia as the tide of the war was turning in the Union's favor. But Corbett's role in the fighting was about to come to an end.[32]

3

ANDERSONVILLE:
A JOURNEY TO HELL

O n the evening of June 23, 1864, a group of ten Rebel soldiers patrolling near Centreville, Virginia, about twenty-five miles west of Washington, surprised a four-man scouting party from the Sixteenth New York Cavalry. The fight was brief and one-sided. Two of the Yankees were captured; the other two escaped and made their way back to the Sixteenth Cavalry's encampment at Annandale. The base commander, Colonel Henry M. Lazelle, quickly ordered one of his subordinates, Lieutenant Mathew Tuck, to lead a squadron of about forty cavalrymen in pursuit of the Rebels and the captured soldiers. Boston Corbett was among the pursuers.[1]

Tuck and his men rode westward, scouring the countryside as they went, but found no sign of the Rebels or the missing men. That had more to do with where they looked than with a lack of Confederate soldiers in the area. For the previous few days, Mosby—with a command of two hundred men and a small cannon—had been moving across the countryside at will. And it was a detachment of his men, under Captain James C. Kincheloe, that had captured half of the four-man Union patrol.

Tuck and his men had ridden most of the night, and by 11 AM, needing food for themselves and a break for their horses, the Union men descended on a plantation about one and a half miles north of Centreville, just a few miles from where the Battle of Bull Run had raged three years earlier. The cavalrymen turned out their horses to graze in a freshly mowed hay field and then scattered themselves around the farm, some relaxing in the house, others in the barn. A number of them climbed trees along the curving driveway, where they snacked on ripe cherries. A handful of the men went to a neighboring farmhouse to find food. Only one sentry was posted at the road, and he was doing a desultory job, draping himself over a wooden fence and, apparently, napping.

Some of Mosby's unseen scouts spotted Tuck's men and reported back. Easy pickings, Mosby thought, and sent one of his top aides, Captain William H. Chapman, at the head of a detachment of some sixty men to the plantation to capture the unsuspecting Union soldiers. The Rebels barreled down the roadway, revolvers drawn. The cavalrymen breakfasting at the neighboring farm fired off a few ineffectual rounds as Mosby's men clattered past, but otherwise the Rebels bolted onto the plantation unimpeded, shooting the lone sentry as they galloped past. Few of the other Union soldiers had their weapons within easy reach, and as the thundering horde of Rebels descended, the Union men scattered in a panic. The tree-sitters dropped to the ground and tried to hide in the tall grasses but were caught immediately. Those in the hay field—including, apparently, Corbett—ran for the nearby woods. Others in the house tried to steal away, too, but few succeeded. In clusters, the Union soldiers were quickly run down, except for the handful that made it to a stand of trees beyond a wooden fence.[2]

Chapman ordered one of his men, Bush Underwood, to lead a small detail into the woods to round up the escapees. Most gave up quickly in the face of the Rebel guns. But Corbett, slight of build, found a good defensive position in a shallow ditch protected by a persimmon tree, and made his stand. Armed with a seven-shot Spencer rifle, he opened fire whenever the Rebels neared. None of the bullets found a mark, but the gunfire was too persistent for Underwood and his men to get close. And Corbett was too well protected by the ditch and the tree for the Rebels to get a bead on him.

Underwood returned to Chapman with a handful of Union prisoners and reported that there was a lone resister out in the trees who "gave us some trouble." Chapman told Underwood to return to the woods and capture the gunman; Underwood came back a short time later with several more Union prisoners—but not Corbett. Chapman, with another detachment of eight men, joined Underwood as they went after Corbett a third time. By now, Underwood was seething. Instead of holding back to try to flush Corbett out, the Rebels rode their horses to the edge of the ditch, Corbett's bullets whizzing past as they neared. Underwood's horse hadn't

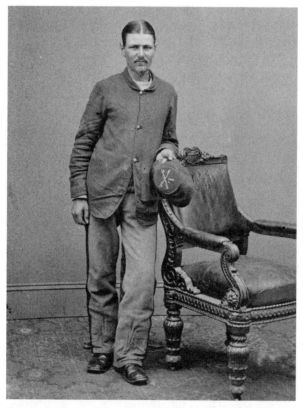

Boston Corbett of the Sixteenth New York Cavalry, 1865.

Mathew Brady, courtesy of Library of Congress, Prints and Photographs Division (reproduction number LC-DIG-cwpbh-03241)

fully stopped when Underwood leaped from saddle to ditch and knocked the rifle from Corbett's hands, then pulled his own revolver and pointed it inches from Corbett's head, ready to execute him. "Don't shoot that man!" Chapman barked out. "He has a right to defend himself."

Corbett related later to friends that the man who saved his life was Mosby, but the records and reminiscences of others at the scene put Mosby far from the plantation that morning. Regardless, Corbett went from being a Union soldier to being a prisoner of war, one of thirty-four from the rousted company of the Sixteenth Cavalry unit. Three Union men were killed and two wounded in the raid by Mosby's troops, and four or five—including Tuck—managed to escape.[3] Fourteen or so of the captured men, including Corbett, were sent to a prisoner of war camp at Richmond, Virginia, where they joined thousands of other captured Union soldiers. In a matter of days, though, they were dispatched farther south to Americus, Georgia, and the infamous Andersonville prison. Officially named Camp Sumter, the prison was only a few months old but already overfilled with Union prisoners. It was less a prison than a massive outdoor holding pen for men, and they flooded in by the thousands.

Prisoners were posing a problem for both sides. In the war's early days, there were regular prisoner exchanges and "paroles," the release of captured men without their weapons—as had happened to Corbett and his comrades at Harpers Ferry. But the exchanges broke down amid disagreements over who would be eligible—captured black Union soldiers were a particular sticking point—and how the exchanges would occur.

General Ulysses S. Grant had his own take on it, believing that releasing soldiers back to their armies would prolong the war. So the exchanges ended, greatly stressing the war prisons on both sides. The South already had a less charitable view of its prisoners than did the North, and as the numbers of captured Union men swelled, so did the prisons. At the same time, the South was losing the war, and in the process running short of provisions. Feeding Union soldiers was low on the list of priorities.[4]

The Confederate Army built the sixteen-acre Andersonville facility primarily to house Union prisoners who had been under guard on Belle Isle in the James River near Richmond, in the northern reaches of the

Confederacy. The Rebels feared Union forces would overrun Richmond and free the prisoners, bolstering their troop strength, though relatively few of the Belle Isle prisoners were in strong enough physical condition to fight. Disease was rampant; shelter was minimal—most of the men spent the winter sleeping out of doors with rags for clothes and only limited, low-quality food.

"Many of the men froze to death, and, instead of a burial, the hogs disposed of their remains," De Witt C. Peters, a Union surgeon imprisoned with the troops, reported later to his superiors. "There were hundreds of cases of frostbitten feet and legs, which, in a great many instances, had to be amputated in order to save their lives."[5]

With the spring, the Rebels began moving the survivors to the new stockade at Andersonville. It's uncertain whether Corbett reached the island prison at Richmond or was housed with fellow prisoners at nearby tobacco barns, but on July 1, 1864, he arrived at Andersonville, which quickly became an even more unimaginable hell than Belle Isle.

Built as an open stockade to hold ten thousand prisoners, by May it already was overstuffed with twelve thousand men. It soon expanded to twenty-six acres—work was in progress when Corbett arrived—and eventually held thirty-three thousand men, at a density of thirty-four square feet per prisoner. The camp had no permanent buildings, and inmates foraged for scraps, canvases, and tree branches to create their own shelters. Few had sufficient protection from the elements. A fifteen-foot-high wooden stockade fence enclosed the prisoners' space, with sharpshooters stationed along the perimeter. A "deadline" a few feet inside the fence, defined by a thin rail perched atop posts, served to keep the prisoners away from the walls. New arrivals unfamiliar with the deadline rule were routinely shot when they stepped over the line without permission; inattentive veterans were killed if they strayed over, or even, in some cases, reached an arm into the no-man's-land.[6]

"I used to make it a particular portion of my business when new prisoners came to show them the deadline, because when I went there at first myself I would have been shot if one of our own men had not dragged me back," Corbett said after the war. "The horrors of that prison were so great that one man went over the line and refused to leave it until he was shot dead. So great was the horror and misery of that place that I myself had thoughts of going over that deadline to be shot in preference to living there. But it immediately occurred to me that it was a Christian's duty to bear whatever was thrust upon me."[7]

Not all the atrocities were perpetrated by the Confederates. Violence by Union prisoners against their weaker comrades was a state of nature until the camp commander, Henry Wirz, had his men round up the ringleaders of the Andersonville Raiders, a gang of murderers and thieves working within the stockade. After a short military trial, the men were convicted of a series of crimes and the six leaders sent back to the stockade on July 11 to be hanged, in essence, by their victims, their fellow Union soldiers. The six bodies dangling at the ends of ropes had their intended effect.

"Good order has prevailed since," prisoner John L. Ransom recorded in his journal the next day.

The men have settled right down to the business of dying, with no interruption. I keep thinking our situation can get no worse, but it does get worse every day and not less than one hundred and sixty die each twenty-four hours. Probably one-fourth or one-third of these die inside the stockade, the balance in the hospital outside. All day and up to four o'clock P. M., the dead are being gathered up and carried to the south gate and placed in a row inside the dead line. As the bodies are stripped of their clothing in most cases as soon as the breath leaves, and in some cases before, the row of dead presents a sickening appearance. Legs drawn up and in all shapes. They are black from pitch pine smoke and laying in the sun. Some of them lay there for twenty hours or more, and by that time are in a horrible condition. At four o'clock a four or six mule wagon comes up to the gate and twenty or thirty bodies are loaded on to the wagon and they are carted off to be put in trenches, one hundred in each trench, in the cemetery, which is eighty or a hundred rods away. There must necessarily be a great many whose names are not taken. It is the orders to attach the name, company and regiment to each body, but it is not always done.[8]

Corbett's July 1 arrival fell the day after the hangings. The shipment of prisoners was split into three groups of about ninety each and then led into the stockade, where Corbett quickly recognized nine other members of the Sixteenth Cavalry. "Within two months' time, six of those nine men died," Corbett testified after the war. Including himself and four other captured men from Centreville, the Sixteenth Cavalry had fourteen members in the prison. "But two of us returned alive," Corbett said.

He found the conditions nightmarish. "The swamp which runs out of each side of the small stream that runs through the stockade was so offensive, and the stench from it so great, that I remember the first time I went down there I wondered that every man in the place did not die from the effects," Corbett said. "It was a living mass of putrefaction and filth; there were maggots there a foot deep or more. Any time we turned over the soil we could see the maggots in a living mass." Prisoners dug through the maggots to find pieces of root that could be dried, then burned to cook what

Union prisoners of war swarming for rations on August 17, 1864; view from Andersonville's main gate. Boston Corbett was among the prisoners.

Courtesy of Library of Congress, Prints and Photographs Division (reproduction number LC-DIG-ppmsca-34562)

little food could be foraged or bought from bribable guards. The camp food itself was often riddled with wriggling worms. "I have taken that food to the stream and washed the maggots from it," Corbett said.

The sick, those with open and maggot-infested sores, were driven off to the swampy area to die on their own. The sickest of the men were carried each morning to the deadline where doctors inspected them and the worst-off moved to a wood-frame hospital a few hundred feet outside the stockade. There they received limited and rudimentary medical care, including inconsistent meals of molasses and boiled beans, one of the few foods that men suffering from loose teeth and painful, bleeding gums could eat. Fellow prisoners who carried the sick to the hospital were rewarded with a few moments to scrounge for wood while outside the stockade, which they would then sell or trade inside the walls. "I had myself to carry out one of my comrades three times," Corbett recalled later. "The fourth time he was taken to the hospital, and he died a short time afterward." Most of the living suffered psychologically as well, and, to Corbett, their minds were affected by the hunger and horror.[9]

Corbett himself became gravely ill—scurvy and intestinal ravages were among his ailments—and his already slight build dissolved to a walking skeleton. Conversely, his feet and legs swelled, "contracting the cords of my legs so that it was crooked so I could not straighten. . . . I had to limp in walking." The only treatment his captors offered "was some sour meal-water," a kind of weak beer. "Twice they gave me that as belonging to scurvy patients. They called it vinegar. It was merely water laid on sour meal. Our own men made a better article inside the stockade, which they called sour beer." It didn't do any good. Corbett's gums bled, and he was constantly hungry and thirsty, the creek through the camp too contaminated to be used. One fellow prisoner walked past Corbett as he was spread out on the ground and called out, "Well, you old bag of bones, are you still living? I should have supposed you would have died a month ago. I swear, some men have more lives than a cat!"[10]

Like many others, Corbett had no shelter. He simply stretched out on the ground between two makeshift tents, leaving himself exposed to the sun (the scars on his shoulders would be visible more than a year later), the evening cool, and sporadic rains that turned the earth into a disgusting stew of filth and muck. "Those only can feel the extent of it who have seen their comrades, as I have, lying in the broiling sun, without shelter, with swollen feet and parched skin, in filth and dirt, suffering as I believe no people ever suffered before in the world," Corbett wrote in a March 1865 letter, as the war was winding down. "But, thank God, these things have come, I hope, to an end. May they never exist again in the good land!"[11]

Through it all, Corbett maintained both his faith and his eccentricities. He joined with Thomas J. Sheppard, a chaplain from the Ninety-Seventh Ohio regiment, and other devout Christians to lead alternate-day prayer meetings and religious services that drew hundreds of men, whether they gathered around for the prayers or for the distraction. But it was an evangelists' market: in the postapocalyptic setting, with men dying all around, religion was about the only affirmation of humanity. Fellow prisoner John McElroy recalled Corbett, Sheppard, and a couple other camp religious leaders gathering at a different spot each prayer session, drawing a crowd by bellowing out such hymns as "Come Thou Fount of Every Blessing." "They were indefatigable in trying to evangelize the prison," McElroy wrote. "In a few minutes they would have an attentive audience of as many thousand as could get within hearing. The singing was followed by regular services, during which Sheppard, Smith, Corbett and some of the others would make short, spirited, practical addresses, which no doubt did much good to all who heard them."

Corbett and his fellow self-appointed spiritual leaders also conducted funerals "as nearly like the way it was done at home as possible. Their ministrations were not confined to mere lip service, but they labored assiduously in caring for the sick, and made many a poor fellow's way to the grave much smoother for him."[12] The prevalence of death, and the fear of it, were strong motivators. "The prayer meetings are well attended now as the terrible death rate among us daily overawes us," Robert Knox Sneden, a captured private, wrote in his journal on September 10, 1864.[13]

Corbett made an impression—both good and bad—in the camp. He often was openly derided for his religious fervor, and he avoided the most aggressive of his antagonists, even if it meant going thirsty. Many of the prisoners banded together in small groups for protection and mutual ben-efit, which in some cases included digging water wells away from the pol-luted stream. "At times I would go to those who had wells dug," Corbett recalled after the war. "Sometimes they would give me a drink and some-times they would not. I received such rough usage and language from them that I have turned away parched with thirst, and drank the bad water from the stream, rather than beg it from the men who had the wells."

But Corbett also was received as something of an evangelical angel among the religious faithful and new converts seeking some sort of human-izing touch in a place of abject inhumanity. Corbett, despite his own ill-nesses, sought to alleviate some of the suffering of the hungry and the disoriented. "The prisoners seemed in many cases totally depraved and demoralized," he said. "Their minds in many cases were affected very much, so that they seemed . . . idiotic."

Illness, starvation, and lack of clean water will do that. In mid-August, though, the religious among them saw the hand of God alleviating some of the suffering. A massive thunderstorm swept over the area, unleashing violent lightning strikes and a sustained torrential downpour that left an indelible impression on prisoner John Maile.

> Crashes of thunder broke over our heads and flashes of lightning swished around us as if the air was filled with short circuits. The awful moving wall came towards us rapidly and we understood what was happening. As the mighty deluge swept through the clearing west of the prison, we bowed our heads in preparation of submersion in the advancing waterspout. When it came upon us the sensation was as if a million buckets of water were being poured upon us at once. The air was so filled with the roaring, hissing flood that we could not look up, but bent forward to protect our faces, covering our nostrils with our hands to preserve a little breathing space.[14]

The deluge flooded the befouled creek passing from west to east through the prison. It rose four or five feet into a raging torrent three hundred feet wide that had been dammed up by the eastern wall of the stockade. But with the riding waters pressing against it, the timbers groaned, then crumbled, opening the eastern wall, through which swept most of the accumulated festering earth and debris. Camp administrators and Rebel guards feared that the prisoners would rush through the openings and overwhelm them—a fear that proved unfounded, given the weak condition of the Union men. Just in case, soldiers fired bullets over the heads of the prisoners as a warning, and cannons trained on the gap; after the flood subsided, armed guards stood watch as slaves replaced the missing sections of stockade.[15]

The storm brought a gift, too: a fresh spring gushing from high ground. There are different versions of the story—one holds that a lightning bolt struck the ground just inside the western wall near the north gate, missing the prisoners but opening a crack in the earth from which poured sweet, uncompromised water. Another, probably more accurate version says the spring had emerged at a spot where a sagging section of the wall had recently been dug out and realigned, and that on top of the construction the deluge scoured enough earth away to give the spring a place to bubble to the surface. It seems likely that the spring already existed and its seepage had softened the ground beneath the stockade, which was why that section of the wall had weakened.

Regardless, the men who had been struggling for potable water now had a fresh source. There was one problem, though. The spring surfaced between the wall and the deadline, flowing southward within the dead zone until it joined Stockade Creek. In a rare act of humanity, camp officials sent in slaves, again under watch by the armed sentries, who crafted a wooden sluice and barrel basin to redirect the fresh water to a spot where the prisoners could access it.

One prisoner, Isaac N. Sutton, had his first encounter with Boston Corbett as the guards moved in a wagonload of timber and rumors spread that they were going to block off the spring. "When they commenced to unload the wagon, Corbett said, 'Boys, never fear. The first rebel that raises a hand to take from us that which God has sent, God Almighty will strike him dead in his tracks.'" Whether God had anything to do with Wirz's decision to give the prisoners access to the water is a matter of individual faith. Corbett likely saw Providence at play, as did many others, and the prisoners began referring to the natural fountain as Providence Spring.[16] (While the stockade is long gone, a pavilion marking Providence Spring is part of the Andersonville National Historic Site.)

Enduring such ordeals creates deep and lasting ties among the survivors, a bond forged in misery that cannot be adequately expressed or fully understood by those who have not endured it. Corbett made several such friends at Andersonville. One, Joseph H. Whitehead, was a dozen years younger than Corbett. Both men had been born in England and emigrated at young ages, though that's where the similarities ended. While Corbett grew up in teeming New York City, Whitehead's family settled in rural Illinois. Whitehead joined the Eighty-Ninth Illinois Infantry and was captured May 27, 1864—a month before Corbett—during the bloody battle at Pickett's Mill, Georgia. Like Corbett, he was a deeply faithful man. They met at the camp prayer meetings, and Whitehead, whose youth may have helped him better survive Andersonville's deadly conditions, watched as Corbett physically dissipated. "He was sick, and at times he was . . . unable to get around, had chronic diarrhea, scurvy, and his whole system became as if it were diseased. [He] was haggard and emaciated."[17]

About a month after Corbett arrived at Andersonville, Richard Thatcher, an eighteen-year-old drummer from the 111th Regiment of the Illinois infantry, walked through the gate as part of a group of new prisoners. Thatcher had been captured July 22, at the beginning of the Siege of Atlanta, and was wracked by fear. Corbett, noticing his young age, dropped by Thatcher's "dilapidated specimen of the dog tent" and introduced himself. They shared tales of their captures and backgrounds. For Thatcher, Corbett was a lifeline. "I found he had qualities that challenged my admiration, even more than the heroism he was capable of displaying in the battlefield. He read passages from the Scriptures to me, and spoke words of sound and wholesome advice, from which I began to learn that he was one who had the courage of his convictions."

Corbett's open-air sleeping spot was "near a narrow street some twenty steps west of my own tent," Thatcher wrote. *Street* was an exaggeration. The passages were two to five feet wide, like a temporary tenement neighborhood. Thatcher often walked past Corbett's spot "and found him stretched out full length on the ground, only his head and chest being sheltered by a shadow cast by his army blouse, which he had spread out and fastened" to two pieces of narrow board jammed into the ground. Thatcher noted that while others in the camp seemed overwhelmed by their circumstances, Corbett exhibited "wonderful composure" as "he passed through this fiery furnace of affliction." Rather than "sitting sullenly down and succumbing as a victim to his environments by brooding over his troubles," Corbett in effect made the camp a personal religious mission, trusting that God would protect him as he sought to minister to his fellow prisoners. "He was constantly moving around, like an angel of mercy, forgetful of his own sorrows, in trying to assuage the griefs and woes of his fellow mortals, especially the sick and the dying."

Thatcher, himself a man of deep faith, became a regular at Corbett's Sunday morning Bible-reading sessions. "If the aggregation of listeners increased to a fair-sized audience, he would deliver there a kind of service." In August, Corbett and his fellow preachers conducted a series of evening religious gatherings—tent revivals without the tents—that, Thatcher reports, drew a steady stream of Christian converts.

Still, Thatcher also recognized that Corbett was a bundle of peculiarities. On one occasion Corbett "looked me straight in the face, with as much composure as if he had been talking about the weather, and said, 'I tell you, comrade Thatcher, the Lord has given me his sacred promise that I shall never die in prison; he has promised me he will turn back my captivity, as the streams of the South.' The words astounded me. They seemed to be the words of a madman."

Thatcher came to realize that Corbett simply had no doubts about his faith. Corbett believed that it was possible to lead a Christian life "without committing any sin in thought, word, or deed, and that he had actually attained that condition. In consequence, he expected all his prayers to be answered." As a result, "he was often thrust into dilemmas and predicaments that would have embarrassed other men so seriously as to turn them infidel." Not so Corbett, though. One day, Corbett stopped by Thatcher's tent to tell him that 'the Lord has told me I shall be liberated from prison within twenty-four hours.' . . . I knew that the man was laboring under an hallucination."

Corbett was not released, but the failed promise didn't diminish his faith.[18]

There was another way out of the stockade besides death: escape. The prisoners dug dozens of tunnels, most of them destroyed before they could be used. Slaves under armed guard jabbed metal pikes deep into the ground around the outside of the walls, and as tunnels were discovered they were collapsed and filled in. Many caved in on their own, and occasionally the diggers would lose direction and emerge not far from the starting point—in one case, about fifteen feet from where the tunnel began. Most of the projects were done by groups of men who formed a "company" that would share the work, hiding the removed earth by scattering it around the camp, or mixing it in with the piles of earth built up by well-diggers. For most, the tunneling seemed to be an act of defiance and a way to pass the time while entertaining the dream of freedom.

In reality, few tunnels reached the outside, and at best a handful of men found their freedom that way. Nearly all of those who made it out via a tunnel were quickly hunted down by dog-handling guards. Others, though, blackened their skin with dirt and ash and slipped out by blending in with the slave work details. Some simply bolted for the woods when they found an opportunity. In August 1864, Andersonville held just under thirty thousand prisoners and recorded 3,061 escapees but 3,078 "recaptured"—the difference likely the result of tracking down runaway prisoners from the previous month. It also recorded 2,993 dead prisoners that month. The few who did manage to escape left a price to be paid by their colleagues: no rations for forty-eight hours for the remaining men in their assigned units.[19]

In October, as the weather began to cool, Corbett made his own plans to escape. (Thatcher had left on September 19 in a prisoner exchange.) During the hot summer months, the guards wouldn't allow the men, other than those carrying the sick to the infirmary, to collect firewood outside the stockade. But with winter settling in, they relented and each day, under guard, some of the prisoners were escorted to the woods to collect fuel for fires.

"I told some of my comrades that the first time I got outside the stockade I should try to escape," Corbett testified the next year. He soon got his chance as part of a group of about twenty prisoners who were led to the woods. Corbett, primed to take his chance, hobbled off at the first opportunity he saw and "got some short distance and secreted myself." There weren't many hiding places, but Corbett's short, slight, and now emaciated body proved to be an asset as he tucked himself like a rabbit into a hole. Guards tramped around his hiding spot and called out his name but didn't see him. Corbett said he "lay there perhaps an hour or two, when I heard the yelping of dogs in the distance. The man with the hounds evidently thought that I was further off, and he had taken them a considerable distance. . . . Then they came nearer and nearer, till they finally approached me, and one actually rubbed his nose against my face."

Corbett was ready to leap into the pack of dogs if they attacked, hoping a good and crazed offense might scare them off. But the well-trained hounds ran in noisy circles around his hiding spot until the dog handler caught up with them. The handler told Corbett that the camp commander, Wirz, had ordered him to let the dogs attack, but that the handler had been a prisoner himself at one point and "would not like to do that." Corbett was returned to the stockade; the records don't detail any punishment for the escape attempt, but his health continued to deteriorate. In late October, just a few days after the dogs found him, Corbett joined the daily parade from compound to infirmary, where he spent five days on a cot recovering from scurvy and diarrhea before returning to the stockade on November 2.

Corbett was soon to find freedom anyway. The Confederacy was on its heels, militarily and economically. Not wanting to continue spending scarce resources caring for Union prisoners, Rebel leaders decided to negotiate with the resistant North about a prisoner swap. At the same time, the Confederates built a new prison—Camp Lawton, near Millen, Georgia—to relieve the horrendous overcrowding at Andersonville. Nine days after he was released from the hospital, Corbett was transferred to the new Camp Lawton, about fifty miles east of Andersonville. Conditions there were fresher but not much better for the prisoners. They had reliable food supplies, but no shelter was provided within the forty-two-acre stockade, which, like Andersonville, was built along the banks of a small stream that was used for both water and sewer.

The good news for the inmates was that the prison was closer to where General William Tecumseh Sherman's Union troops were in the midst of their march through Georgia. For fear that the advancing army would free the prisoners, the Confederates renewed their efforts to swap the Union men for Rebels held in the North.

Knowing the conditions in Andersonville and other Rebel prison camps, the North began to relent, agreeing to limited exchanges. But the South wound up simply paroling many of the prisoners, including Corbett and Whitehead, giving them their freedom in return for a pledge not to fight until a Rebel prisoner had been exchanged for them. Not that Corbett and most of his fellow prisoners were in condition to resume the war anyway. "My right knee being so drawn up from the effects of scurvy, that I was compelled to go on crutches. At that time I had diarrhea and bloody flux combined," Corbett wrote later. "I was suffering greatly from fever rheumatism and piles. In fact, I was in a very bad fix." He would never fully regain his health.[20]

The prisoner trades and paroles began in mid-November 1864. Several thousand Union soldiers were moved to Savannah, where they boarded Rebel ships and steamed down the Savannah River to waiting Union ships. The vessels were maneuvered until they were side by side, and the transfer of the human cargo began. A reporter for the *New York Times* aboard one of the Union ships recorded a sobering scene conducted almost entirely in silence.

"Those of them who are able to move without aid pass to the protection of the old flag first. Then come those (alas! There are many of this class) who hobble on crutches, and the last few whose helplessness requires that they should be carried on stretchers. In all this operation the greatest formality is observed." The prisoners were accompanied by civilians wearing hats with bands identifying them as "committee for the wounded. But seldom on either side is a word spoken except on the subject of the matter at hand." Military guards quickly stifled side conversations, the *Times* noted, suggesting they feared an offhand comment might divulge a military secret. But as the Rebel ships disengaged and pulled away, the silence broke and "then rises hearty shouting and cheering. . . . There is the music of intense gratefulness in it."[21]

As the Union ships weighed anchor and moved down the river and out to sea, the former prisoners—skeletons in rags—began stripping and tossing their lice- and flea-ridden clothes over the sides, or took them in bundles to the ships' boiler rooms for burning, and in waves of nakedness began finding new clothes among supplies brought on the ship.

"Such is the condition of the men whom we are now receiving out of chivalrous Dixie," the *Times* reporter wrote acidly.

These are the sons, brothers, husbands, and fathers of the North. Men reduced to living skeletons; men almost naked; shoeless men, shirtless men, hatless men; men whose skins are blackened by dirt and hang on their protruding bones loosely as bark on a tree; men whose very presence is simply disgusting, exhaling an odor so fetid that it almost stops the breath of those unaccustomed to it, and causes an involuntary brushing of the garments if with them there is accidental contact. Imagine 25,000 of such wretched creatures penned together in a space barely large enough to hold them, and compare their condition with the most miserable condition that can be imagined. . . . Remember, too, that the men thus returned are the best specimens of the suffering. Only those are forwarded to us whom the rebel medical authorities decide to be strong enough to bear the fatigue of transportation. If those whose wretchedness I have vainly endeavored to portray are the best specimens of our sick and wounded, is it not awful to contemplate what must be the woes of the remainder?

Corbett was among those moving on crutches. Sailors helped him cross from the Rebel vessel to the *Baltic*, the same ship that had first carried him and his comrades in the Twelfth New York Regiment off to war nearly five years earlier. Now the *Baltic* served as something of a large marine ambulance. The ship put out to sea almost immediately on November 19 and made its way northward to the federal island Fortress Monroe off Hampton Roads, Virginia, arriving on November 24. Other ships ferried more paroled prisoners over the next few days, a flotilla of misery but also of relief. At the fortress, doctors assessed the prisoners to determine who needed what care. Corbett's condition earned him a spot in the 1,117-bed

USA General Hospital Division No. 1, a complex of interrelated hospitals built at the US Naval Academy in Annapolis, where the released men's arrivals made for an arresting sight.

"The first man who touched the wharf drew in a long breath, gave a shrill whistle, and a little leap into the air," reported the *Crutch*, a weekly newspaper published for the staff and patients at the complex. "Then he gave a look into the sky, but said not a word. . . . Directly on his steps came the victims of twelve, thirteen, eighteen month's imprisonment, in the most loathsome pens Southern ingenuity, and cruelty, could devise. Their skins discolored, their uncovered hair faded and worn, their long fleshless limbs purple, trembling, and calloused from exposure."[22]

Malnutrition had eroded Corbett's muscles, and scurvy tightened the tendons on his right leg, making it nearly impossible for him to straighten it. He hobbled about on a crutch, suffered from "bloody flux"—dysentery—and his gums bled. "I know that I suffered very much from hunger," he said later. "So much so that months after my release my appetite was constantly craving, and I could not restrain myself from eating, even after I had enough. This was a consequence of that slow process of starvation." A process from which, he noted, "many of my comrades died."[23]

Gaining his freedom must have provoked a heady mix of emotions for Corbett; now he needed to regain his health. He said later that he never contemplated the idea that he might die either in the war or in the prisons, because God watched over him. But he also remained remarkably unchanged by the experience and after arriving at the Annapolis hospital "was very soon marked as a young man of some peculiarities, and some genius. In person, small, and very delicate" with a "low, earnest voice in common conversation, but frequently . . . raised with so much power as to wonder that so small a man should make so large a noise."[24]

Corbett's faith remained unshaken. "The marked feature of his life among us . . . was his zealous Christian spirit. Every gathering for prayer found him present, and his voice was always raised in exhortation. . . . His nurse relates that the first time he left his room, hardly able to walk about, he borrowed a suit of clothes to go to a meeting in the Chapel."

Corbett slowly recovered, and in December, though still weak, he was released from the hospital on a furlough back to Manhattan, where his old friends in the church received him as a hero. He saw James Brown, his former boss and the man for whom he had substituted when he first went off to war, and made almost daily visits to the Fulton Street prayer meeting, where he "frequently spoke to those assembled there."[25] But his health remained severely compromised. "I hardly knew what was the matter with him except diarrhea and scurvy," Brown observed. "He was very weak and emaciated [and] appeared to be suffering with a complication of diseases."[26]

In early January 1865 Corbett reported in at Camp Parole near Annapolis, a holding base for released prisoners, where he idled for a few days before being sent on January 21 to Camp Distribution in Alexandria, Virginia, a way station for troops heading back to their regiments. On January 28, Corbett rejoined the Sixteenth New York Cavalry, which was still assigned to help defend Washington, and began spending some time at the offices of the US Christian Commission.

The commission formed in the early days of the war among activists in the Young Men's Christian Associations in New York who wanted to attend to the spiritual needs of Union soldiers. It quickly grew into a Union-wide organization coordinating religious support, but also relief for Union soldiers both on the battlefield and in the hospital. Hundreds of thousands of religious tracts were printed and distributed along with food, clothing, and other supplies. The "delegates," as they called their evangelists, filled in as nurses in medical facilities, built shelters in camps for the sick and wounded, and held regular prayer sessions for the faithful, some using large tents they carried with them across the countryside.

Had Corbett not joined the army, odds are he would have involved himself with the Christian Commission. As it was, his visits to the offices brought him in contact with Byron B. Johnson, a fellow Christian from Massachusetts who also was a strong proponent of temperance. Johnson, a returns examiner for the War Department's Ordnance Bureau, lived on H Street within view of both Ford's Theatre and Mary Surratt's boarding-house. He struck up a friendship with Corbett, whom he invited to dinners at his house, a relationship that would carry on after the war ended.[27]

Corbett maintained contact with his old friends, too. Three days after rejoining the Sixteenth New York Cavalry, Corbett wrote to Brown back in New York, telling him the news of his surprise promotion to sergeant, retroactive to the beginning of November.

"Thank God my health is improving, and I am now prepared to serve my country again," Corbett wrote. "I find things here favorable in general, and my old comrade, Sergeant Irvine, glad to see me in particular; in fact, they all seem glad to see me back from my Southern tour. May God grant that I may never be so favored again!"[28]

Corbett lamented that the unit's chaplain had left but "we expect that meetings will be carried on, as the Christian Commission have started a station here, and they now hold meetings on the Sabbath at the hospitals, brigade and regimental. But when the brigade tent is ready, I expect we will have meetings also through the week." He told Brown that he hoped to get acquainted with members of the Fifth Pennsylvania Artillery who "are here with us. . . . I hear they have a good many Christians among us." He wrote about the different regiments' bands and that they sometimes performed for the troops, "but I hope we will have a good revival by and by, and that will be better than brass bands." He also passed along greetings to mutual friends.

"Tell them I am still fighting the good fight of faith, and hope to enjoy eternal life in glory," Corbett wrote. "If you see any of the old Twelfth, tell them I will try and bring back a good report, if I come at all, and, if not, I hope to leave a good report behind."

Corbett's promotion gave him a few more dollars in his pay envelope and some authority over the lower-ranked men. With the war winding down, though, the work was light. The Confederate troops, while still fight-ing, no longer posed the formidable threat they once did, and a sense of inevitable victory for the North settled in.

But other dangers still lurked in the shadows.

4

THE ASSASSIN

Eight days before Boston Corbett returned to his cavalry unit, theatergoers in Washington, DC, filled Grover's New Theater on Pennsylvania Avenue, a few blocks from the White House, for a special presentation of *Romeo and Juliet*. The show was meant as a benefit for actress Avonia Jones, who was about to head off for a tour of the London stages. Jones played Juliet, and the other star-crossed lover was played by one of the most accomplished actors of the time, John Wilkes Booth.

It was, of late, a rare appearance for Booth. Throughout his career, the actor had traveled the country, his trunk of costumes in tow, to stage a wide range of shows. In 1860, the year before the war broke out, Booth had performed at least 128 times, mostly in Richmond, Virginia, and other Southern cities, and increased the pace across Maryland and mostly Northern states during the war. In 1864, he made ninety theatrical appearances through the end of May in St. Louis, Louisville, Nashville, Cincinnati, New Orleans, and, breaking out of the Midwest and South, Boston. Booth then stopped accepting theatrical engagements. But he still traveled. He went to Canada, where he did some solo dramatic readings intermingled with some clandestine meetings with expatriate Rebels, and to southeastern Maryland and northeastern Virginia as well as New York City, Baltimore, and Philadelphia. Ostensibly he was visiting friends and looking at various investment opportunities, including some farmland.[1]

In reality, he was plotting to kidnap Abraham Lincoln.

Booth was an unlikely criminal conspirator. Vain and spoiled, he was part of the most famous theater family of the day, led by his father, Junius Brutus Booth. One of the premier British actors of his generation, the father abandoned his wife, Adelaide, and son, Richard, in January 1821 for a Covent Garden flower-seller named Mary Ann Holmes. The couple traveled to France and then back to England briefly before Junius decided to ply his trade in the West Indies. He bought a piebald pony named Peacock and booked passage for himself, Mary Ann, and the animal for the Portuguese island of Madeira, where they spent several weeks before boarding the trading schooner *Two Brothers* on June 30.

Junius Booth had apparently changed his mind about the West Indies; they were the only passengers on the wares-laden ship headed for Norfolk, Virginia. By July 6, Booth was playing the lead role in *Richard III* at a Richmond theater, then played several other roles and theaters in the region until moving on to New York City in October, then back to the South for more engagements. The couple's first child, Junius Jr., called "June" by the family, was born in Charleston, South Carolina, on December 22, 1821, which means Mary Ann became pregnant shortly after the runaways left England.[2]

The Booths made their way to Maryland, where Junius bought 150 acres of farmland and wilderness about twenty-five miles northeast of Baltimore, and then bought and moved to the property a four-room log cabin, later added onto and called the Farm. (It would be supplanted a few years later by a Gothic Revival–style cottage the family called Tudor Hall.) And the Booth clan grew. The summer after Junius purchased the farm, Mary Ann gave birth to their second child, Rosalie Ann.

Around the same time, Junius's father, Richard, arrived from London and began living with his son and his son's concubine, though he was fully aware of the wife and child Booth had left in England. Richard eventually took over managing the farm and the slave labor rented from neighboring slaveholders while Junius traveled the country building his theatrical reputation as one of the top tragedians of the era.

For Junius, the property was less a farm than a sanctuary. He made his living on city stages; part of his decision to raise his family in rural isolation was to keep them safe from urban epidemics—Booth bought the land in the midst of a yellow fever outbreak—and provide a haven while he traveled for weeks at a time practicing his art.

Junius Booth was a mercurial figure, quick with a threatening letter or scathing rebuke to an audience he thought was insufficiently appreciative of his talents and performances. His skills were considerable, as were his quirks. "Booth was an actor of extraordinary power and extraordinary defects," the *New York Evening Post* once said. "His voice, figure, and gait were all against him, and yet the intensity and vehemence of his impersonations overcame the unfavorable impression which these created, and rendered him popular with even refined audiences. His Pescara, his Sir Giles Overreach, and his Richard were, at times, most vigorous performance; but Mr. Booth was so eccentric in his habits, that he never could be depended upon, so that at other times they were the most wretched."[3]

"Eccentric" understated it. Booth was an incorrigible drinker, and he seemed to lose sanity when in the depths of drunkenness, a condition in which he often performed, occasionally morphing lines from different shows. In one Boston performance he merged lines, then told the audience, "I can't read, I am a charity boy, I can't read. Take me to the lunatic hospital." At another performance, Booth climbed a ladder to the top of the backdrops and "crowed like a rooster until the stage manager lured him down by promising to let him go back up and stay there until the president of the United States was re-elected"—Booth's demand before he would resume the show. Another time, out of cash, he stood in a pawnshop window until a friend came by and bought his freedom.[4]

John Wilkes was born May 19, 1838, the ninth of ten children, three of them sons—June, Edwin, and John—who would follow their father into the theater, and a daughter, Asia, who would marry an actor. Four other siblings didn't survive childhood. Three, in fact, perished within a month of each other in 1833 during a cholera epidemic, a tragedy that turned Mary Ann into an overly doting mother by the time John came along five years later.[5]

By most accounts, it was an oddly idyllic upbringing at the Farm, where the young John had his chores to do but also plenty of time to roam the fields and woods and practice marksmanship with friends. The family was vegetarian—Junius the elder forbade even the killing of flies—but they were not particularly adept farmers, and they had difficulty managing life when the father was on the road. So the Booths spent winters in a rented house in Baltimore, where John began forging lifelong friendships, and where he and his older brothers took their first steps toward the theater by staging their own shows in barns, basements, and boardinghouses.

Booth's parents enrolled him in a local boarding school, Bel Air Academy, and then sent him off in 1849, at age eleven, to Milton Academy, about twenty miles west of Bel Air. It was a Quaker school with a rigorous academic regimen. Booth attacked his studies, particularly the classics: Cicero, Herodotus, Horace, Livy, and Tacitus.

While Booth was at Milton, his father's wife, Adelaide, arrived in America and set up house in Baltimore, where she created public scandals—including drunken confrontations with Booth's mother, Mary Ann—until she had lived in Maryland long enough to petition for a divorce, which Junius didn't contest. Once it was granted, Junius and Mary Ann married, putting a legal stamp on a relationship that had already lasted some thirty years and had begotten a brood of children, none of whom apparently had known about Adelaide and their half-brother, Richard, until her arrival in the States. In fact, Junius and Mary Ann possessed a marriage certificate dated January 18, 1821, but it was a fake, a revelation that must have shaken John Wilkes Booth to his roots. Michael Kauffman, among his most astute biographers, points to the shame and confusion the adolescent Booth felt from the scandal as a formative element of his character, an emotional crisis that he overcame but that left a lasting imprint. The young Booth etched a homemade tattoo of his own initials in the back of his hand, as though branding himself with his own identity.[6]

Three years later John was rocked anew by the sudden death of Junius. The father and two older sons, June and Edwin, had been touring the West together staging a series of well-received shows in such venues as the Jenny Lind Theater and the Adelphi House in San Francisco, where June was the stage manager.[7] Junius, tiring of the travel and time away from home, decided to head back East on his own.

On October 1, 1852, Junius Booth boarded the steamship *Independence* and traveled from San Francisco to San Juan del Sur, Nicaragua, part of Cornelius Vanderbilt's ingenious—and pre–Panama Canal—solution to getting from the West Coast to the East Coast. Called the Accessory Transit Company, Vanderbilt's network used interconnected routes of river and lake steamships and stagecoaches to ferry passengers between Nicaragua's Pacific coast and the Caribbean coast, where his oceangoing steamers collected the travelers and carried them on to New York. (Other carriers took passengers to Southern port cities as well.) Vanderbilt's route cut a week off the next fastest alternative of taking the ship-to-land-to-ship route across Panama.

While Booth traversed Nicaragua, robbers relieved him of all his gold. Penniless, he arrived in New Orleans on November 15 and performed for three nights to earn some cash, then booked passage aboard the river steamer *J. S. Chenoweth* up the Mississippi River to the Ohio River and on to Cincinnati to catch a train to Baltimore. (It's unclear why Booth didn't book a through passage on Vanderbilt's line.) Shortly into the Mississippi River trip, though, Booth fell ill with diarrhea, and over the next few days his condition deteriorated rapidly. By the time the steamer reached Louisville, Booth was dead.[8]

At the time of Junius's death, young John was studying at St. Timothy's Hall military boarding school at Catonsville, Maryland. It was a challenging school, but he thrived there, forging some deep friendships, practicing marksmanship, and excelling in the classroom. The death of his father, whom John idolized, brought that world crashing down, and at the end of the term he returned to the Farm to try to help out the rest of his family. With June and Edwin still in California, Booth saw himself as shouldering the masculine family duties.

But Booth also remained drawn to the stage, and in 1855 he made his professional debut at age seventeen as Richmond in *Richard III* at Baltimore's

Charles Street Theater, a secretive event he didn't tell his family about until afterward.[9] Two years later, acting became Booth's career when he signed up with Wheatley's Arch Street Theatre in Philadelphia, where he made near-daily appearances in a wide range of productions from August through the end of the year. Critics and audiences at first weren't very kind to the novice, but Booth developed his craft and grew with the steady experience. He was particularly drawn to works that romanticized struggles for freedom and against tyranny, a theme that seemed to take root in the young man.

As Booth devoted himself to his stage career, the United States careened toward war. The issue, of course, was slavery, and perceptions of where authority lay—with the federal government or with the state governments. Booth wasn't particularly politically engaged, though he evidenced a class-based disdain for workers and carried the predominant white world's dismissive view toward blacks as inferior. He saw himself as a Southerner and embraced the Southern view of the world—and rejected the growing calls by abolitionists to end slavery. But it was a back-of-the-mind issue for him. As an actor, he neither owned slaves nor depended (directly) on them for his livelihood. He was at heart a romanticist who loved the rigid codes and idealized chivalry of the South, and he ached to be accepted and loved by Southerners even as he made a lot of his living in the North.

The national frictions moved closer to crisis on October 16, 1859, when John Brown led his raid on the federal arsenal at Harpers Ferry. Brown and his small squad of men planned to spark an uprising of Virginia slaves that would then spread across the South, but they never made it out of Harpers Ferry. As the raid unfolded and a call was issued for federal troops, locals took up positions along the hills overlooking the town and kept the insurrectionists at bay until military reinforcements arrived on the morning of October 18. Brown and his men were quickly overwhelmed. Fourteen people were killed, including two of Brown's sons, and Brown and six others were captured. The survivors were tried for murder and fomenting slave insurrection, among other charges, and Brown and four others were sentenced to hang.

As Brown awaited the executioner, rumors swirled that fellow abolitionists would try to free him from the county jail in Charlestown, Virginia. To shore up security, the government dispatched the Richmond Grays militia.

Booth, who was about to open in *The Filibuster* at the Richmond Theater, instead hopped the train and inveigled a position with the Grays as a quartermaster. There was no abolitionist attempt to raid the jail, and the Grays stayed on as a security outfit. When Brown was hanged on the morning of December 2, Booth was in the crowd of onlookers, where he blanched as Brown twisted and writhed at the end of a rope. "He was a brave old man," Booth later reported to his sister. One has to wonder how deeply imprinted that image was on Booth: an extremist defending his beliefs to the point of violence and his own death.[10]

Brown's raid brought the simmering differences between the abolitionists and the proslavery factions to a full and raging boil. Proslavery voices blamed William Seward, an outspoken opponent of slavery who had infuriated the South with his 1850 Senate speech that a "higher law" than the Constitution proscribed extending slavery to new territories. Seward later, in an 1858 campaign appearance, warned of "an irrepressible conflict between opposing and enduring forces" over the issue of slavery, which would end with the United States "either entirely a slaveholding nation, or entirely a free-labor nation." To Southerners, and more than a few Northerners, Seward was introducing the specter of violence into the debate and, by extension, propelling Brown to act. Never mind that Brown had already established his violent abolitionism three years earlier when, in "Bleeding Kansas," he and his sons and supporters hacked to death several proslavery settlers. Considered a contender for the Republican presidential nomination, Seward saw his support dwindle after the Brown raid; he was now viewed as too radical. The beneficiary: Abraham Lincoln, who embraced Brown's antislavery views but disavowed the raid as indefensible "violence, bloodshed, and treason."[11]

Lincoln won the 1860 Republican nomination, but the Democrats were divided, North and South, and ultimately split into two parties, with Stephen A. Douglas running on the Democratic Party line and John C. Breckenridge running on the Southern Democratic Party line. A fourth candidate, John Bell, carried the flag for the new Constitutional Union party of conservatives who sought to put preservation of the Union ahead of the slavery issue.

Given how badly splintered the body politic was, the November victory was a minority one. Lincoln received only 40 percent of the popular vote but 180 votes of 303 in the Electoral College. Lincoln swept the Northern states except for New Jersey. Breckenridge won most of the South while the Tennessean Bell won his home state, neighboring Kentucky, and Virginia. New Jersey and Missouri were Douglas's only wins.

Five weeks after Lincoln's victory, South Carolina voted to secede from the Union. The die was cast.

As the politics played out on the national stage, Booth was sticking to regional stages. On Election Day, Booth had just finished a six-night run in Montgomery, Alabama, then was off the stage until late January in Rochester, New York, then on to Albany, then Portland, Maine, then back to Albany, followed by a break of several months. Booth, who had been loosely connected with the anti-immigrant Know-Nothing party in the 1850s, became more politically inclined and held a particular dislike for Lincoln, believing the president had become a tyrant and would destroy the country.

"He is made the tool of the north, to crush out, or to try to crush out slavery, by robbery, rapine, slaughter, and bought armies," Booth told his sister. "He is walking in the footprints of old John Brown, but no more fit to stand with that rugged hero—Great God! No. John Brown was a man inspired, the grandest character of this century! *He* [Lincoln] is a Bonaparte in one great move, that is, by overturning this blind Republic and making himself a king. This man's re-election which will follow his success, I tell you, will be a reign!"[12]

As the war went on, Booth resumed his acting schedule, largely keeping his pro-secession beliefs hidden. He held close friendships with many Unionists, including Julia Ward Howe, who was married to one of John Brown's backers, and Adam Badeau, a friend of his brother Edwin and a future aide to Ulysses S. Grant. In November 1863, Lincoln and the First Lady watched Booth perform in *The Marble Heart* at Ford's Theatre in Washington, just a few blocks from the White House. Booth reportedly

John Wilkes Booth.

Courtesy of Library of Congress, Prints and Photographs Division
(reproduction number LC-USZ62-25166)

gave an unusually subdued performance. He generally kept his acting career
separated from his political beliefs, but this was becoming increasingly difficult for the actor.[13]

The progress of the war frustrated Booth, for whom the South's looming defeat was personified by Lincoln—just the sort of figure, he felt,
against which many of Booth's characters were locked in romantic struggles
for freedom and dignity. With the secessionist states no longer part of the
US electorate, Lincoln ran for reelection in 1864 against Democratic Party

nominee General George B. McClelland, whose hesitancy in battle and military strategy had led Lincoln to depose him as general-in-chief of the Union forces. In running for the presidency, McClelland sought to appeal to the war-weary by pledging to negotiate an end to the fighting. Northern voters, though, smelled military victory and preferred to stick with Lincoln, who on Election Day won all of the Union's twenty-five states in good standing except for Kentucky, Delaware, and New Jersey.

Before the election, Booth was contemplating an audacious act: he would put together a group of fellow defenders of the South and kidnap Lincoln, spirit him away to Richmond, the capital of the Confederacy, and hold him as a bartering chip to gain the freedom of Rebel prisoners of war. In that one fell swoop, Booth believed, the battered Confederate army would get an infusion of fighting blood and be able to turn the course of the war. (Apparently he was unaware of the poor physical condition of the captured Rebels in Union prison camps.) The act seemed tantalizingly easy to achieve with the right group of men. Lincoln often went alone to political and social events, and he also frequently spent the night at a cottage on the grounds of the Soldiers' Home, about four miles northeast of the White House. The route took him along a wooded area where it would be a fairly easy task to waylay and overpower him. Spiriting the president out of the area posed significant hurdles, but none insurmountable. Booth became convinced he could pull it off.

A conspiracy needs conspirators, of course, and Booth slowly began collecting them. Biographer Michael Kauffman believes that Booth took a page from Brown's playbook and kept the details private while building the network of supporters. Part of it was smoke and mirrors. Or, more appropriately, stagecraft. Brown "built the appearance of a large conspiracy—one that created panic in the public mind, wrought havoc with investigators, and gave his followers a false sense of support," Kauffman wrote. "It was a brilliant move, and John Wilkes Booth would keep it in mind when forming his own plot."[14]

Booth turned first to two childhood friends from Maryland, trading on both personal loyalty and a sense of duty to the South. Michael O'Laughlen grew up across the street from the Booths' winter residence in Baltimore, and in late 1864 he was at loose ends. A member of the Confederate First Maryland Infantry (formed by Southern loyalists despite Maryland staying in the Union), illness had cut short O'Laughlen's war, and he was languishing out of work and out of the fight. Samuel Arnold was a friend from Booth's St. Timothy's military school days and a veteran of the First Maryland Infantry.

Booth drew the two men together at his room in the Barnum Hotel in Baltimore on an August evening, Booth supplying the cigars and wine. The actor sketched out his plan to nab the surprisingly lightly protected Lincoln as the president rode the streets of Washington. O'Laughlen and Arnold agreed to help. The records don't indicate exactly when he drew in David Herold, a pharmacist's clerk of no particular ambitions who had met Booth in April 1863 backstage at one of the actor's performances.

By all accounts, Herold was a pretty simple man, hungry for the companionship—and respect—of others and thus fairly easy to manipulate. He was taken with Booth's fame and the actor's democratic treatment of others—he spoke to Herold during that first meeting as he would have to any of Washington's elite. That relationship brought the young Herold into the conspiracy, but it would take more than the four men to pull off the kidnapping. So Booth began casting a wider net.

With the nation at war against itself, Confederate strategists and provocateurs—the Confederate Secret Service—migrated to Montreal to plot various actions in the North (few of which seemed to gel) and to arrange supply shipments in hopes of evading the Union blockade of Southern ports. Booth sought to tap into that Rebel underground to find men to add to his kidnapping plot and solicit help with the trickiest part of the plan: spiriting Lincoln away from Washington to Richmond amid what would likely be a massive manhunt.

On October 18, Booth, traveling with his acting wardrobe trunk, checked in for a nine-night stay at Montreal's St. Lawrence Hall hotel, considered to be the major meeting place for the Rebels active in Canada. Booth buttonholed a number of Confederate Secret Service members and sympathizers, though the details of what exactly he did, and with whom he spoke, are lost.

What is known is that Booth spent time with former Baltimore liquor vendor Patrick C. Martin, working now as a blockade-runner. Whether Booth and Martin knew each other before Booth arrived in Montreal is unknown, though it's possible, given Booth's time in Baltimore. Regardless, Booth was a guest several times at Martin's home in Montreal, and Martin helped Booth exchange some currency. Martin also agreed to take charge of Booth's wardrobe trunk and see that it was shipped to Richmond—a significant hint about Booth's future plans. In that era, an actor supplied his or her own wardrobe for playing different roles, and that Booth was willing to part with, in essence, the tools of his trade for weeks, if not months, suggests he had no intention of returning to the stage anytime soon. And the trunk's ultimate destination—Richmond, rather than Baltimore or New York, or even Washington—suggested that Booth planned to resume his career in the Confederacy.[15]

More significantly, Martin gave Booth letters of introduction to two men, Dr. William Queen and Dr. Samuel A. Mudd, living and working in Charles County, Maryland, a strong Rebel-supporting region south of Washington. Charles County also covered a peninsula defined by the Potomac River, separating the Union Maryland from the Rebel Virginia— the path Booth thought would be his best option for spiriting the kidnapped Lincoln from North to South.

Booth returned from Montreal in late October, stopping first in Manhattan, then moving on to Washington and the National Hotel, another popular spot for Southern sympathizers to meet. He continued writing letters to friends but also crafted a couple that he didn't post (he left them with his sister to be opened "should anything happen to me"), one a "to whom it may concern" manifesto of sorts and the other to his mother. The first letter was opaque but freighted with a looming unspecified act. Booth's letter to his mother was even more foreboding. After expressing his love for her, Booth wrote that he had "another duty," and that for four years he had felt a slave to the North.[16]

But I cannot longer resist the inclination, to go and share the sufferings of my brave countrymen, holding an unequal strife (for every human right & divine) against the most ruthless enemy, the world has ever known. You can answer for me dearest Mother (although none of you think with me) that I have not a single selfish motive to spur me on to this, nothing save the sacred duty, I feel I owe the cause I love, the cause of the South. The cause of liberty & justice. So should I meet the worst, dear Mother, in struggling for such holy rights. I can say, God's will be done.

On November 11, letters of introduction presumably in his pocket, Booth took a stagecoach to Charles County, intending to look up Queen. Booth told the curious—he was, after all, a famous and easily recognized actor—that he was scouting around for some land in which to invest. That ruse gave him a pretext to travel throughout the area and engage in private discussions while also explaining away what would become a series of visits, some lasting several days.

The day after he arrived, Booth tracked down Queen and spent the night of November 12 at his farm, where he outlined his plot to kidnap Lincoln. The doctor quickly agreed to help by introducing Booth to locals active in the Rebel underground. Among the first: Dr. Mudd. Booth accompanied Queen to church the next morning after Queen sent quiet word to Mudd that he should attend the same church service. Mudd showed up, and the first fateful meeting took place. Booth returned to Washington the next day but a month later was back in Charles County. He spent the first night with Queen and then the second, after meeting up with Mudd again at church, at Mudd's farm, where in the privacy of the doctor's house Booth enlisted Mudd's assistance. Mudd in turn brought Booth to Thomas Harbin, a Rebel river smuggler who was part of a network that could be tapped to move Booth and the kidnapped Lincoln to Richmond.

The plot was coming together, but Booth needed even more help if he was going to pull it off. Getting across the Potomac would be a hurdle, clearly, but getting *to* the Potomac would also be challenging. Booth knew of a Confederate-sympathizing family, the Surratts, who owned an inn and tavern, now leased to another proprietor, at a hamlet bearing their name. Surrattsville was along the route Booth hoped to follow. And he had heard that a son in the family, John Surratt, was connected with the Rebel underground and worked as a courier. But Booth couldn't just walk up to Surratt and enlist his aid; he'd need someone to introduce him and, by extension, vouch that he wasn't a Northern spy. On December 23, as Booth looked discreetly for someone who could act as go-between with Surratt, the actor providentially spotted Mudd, who knew the Surratts, outside the National Hotel. The doctor had come into Washington with his cousin, Jeremiah Mudd, to shop for a range of items, including a new stove.

Booth had a card showing John Surratt's name and the 541 H Street address of a boardinghouse operated by Surratt's mother, Mary, and he asked Mudd to go with him to make the introduction. Mudd tried to beg off, saying he was due at the Pennsylvania Hotel at eight o'clock to meet some friends. But Booth was persuasive, and as the two men walked along, they chanced upon John Surratt and a companion, Louis Weichmann, a Confederate sympathizer who, oddly, worked for the federal War Department. Surratt and Weichmann were former seminary students together, and through that friendship Weichmann had come to board with Surratt's mother. After Mudd made the introductions, Booth invited all three men back to his hotel for a little party and to talk about the lay of the land outside Washington, ostensibly to help Booth decide where to buy a farm. But Booth was hoping that he and Surratt could get each other's measure, the first step in drawing Surratt into the conspiracy.[17]

And so it grew.

5

A PRESIDENT
IS MURDERED

By the time Booth was done, his circle had expanded to five people. The late additions were Lewis Powell and George Atzerodt. Powell was over six feet, one inch tall and powerfully built. Born and raised in Alabama, he had served in the Confederate army, was wounded and taken prisoner at Gettysburg, and escaped and joined with Mosby's Rangers for a time before leaving the war, signing an oath of allegiance to the Union (to avoid future arrest) and settling in Baltimore at a boardinghouse frequented by Rebel spies and couriers. Atzerodt was similarly tall, though oddly built and misshapen by a curved spine. Atzerodt was born in Prussia, grew up in Maryland and Virginia, and settled as an adult in the Charles County town of Port Tobacco. After the war began, he put himself into the service of the South escorting spies, couriers, and others across the Potomac. John Surratt knew both men, and he brought them to Booth's attention—Powell for his strength, Atzerodt for his knowledge of the river.

In January, with Lincoln's inauguration coming up in March, Booth solidified his plan. He made several horseback trips along the route between the White House and the Soldiers' Home, scouting for the best spot at which to waylay the president. Surratt and Harbin had gone to Port Tobacco and bought a boat, and they enlisted the hard-drinking Atzerodt to be ready to help them when the time came. They also cached some weapons Booth had bought in Manhattan during one of his many trips north. All they needed now was a little advance word on when Lincoln would next ride out to the Soldiers' Home.

Then Booth changed his mind. Lincoln, he had discovered, was barely venturing out of the city anymore, which meant that the plan to nab him along the road to the Soldiers' Home was less viable. Booth, for obvious reasons, was drawn to the theater, and he knew that Lincoln attended regularly as an escape from the White House and the pressures of the war. Booth asked O'Laughlen and Arnold during a dinner meeting if it didn't make more sense to abduct Lincoln from Ford's Theatre; both men objected, so that plan soon fell away, too. Booth bided his time, rehashing his thoughts until he returned to something more like his original plot. He saw an item in the newspapers about Lincoln planning to attend a play at Campbell Hospital at Florida Avenue and Seventh Street. The president wouldn't be as exposed as he would have been if he were going to the Soldiers' Home, but it would be a lot easier to abduct him along the two-mile route to the hospital than it would be from Ford's Theatre, a few blocks from the White House.

Booth summoned his team, and they met in front of Mary Surratt's boardinghouse, where Booth told them the plot was on. They quickly split off to gather the weapons Booth had provided earlier, and then to their assignments. Herold took carbines to Maryland to await the arrival of the president and the kidnappers, who would change carriages and then head for the river. The others, now carrying sidearms, rode down Seventh Street to wait in a restaurant for the president's carriage to return from the hospital, at which point Arnold and O'Laughlen would overpower the driver and the president, Surratt would slip behind the reins, and they would take off for Charles County with Lincoln.

But the carriage didn't appear. Booth rode out to the hospital and returned a while later, reporting that the president had never arrived and the abduction was off. Herold was left dangling in Maryland and, after spending the night at an inn, he headed back for Washington the next morning, encountering Surratt and Atzerodt, who had gone in search of him, along the way. They explained what happened, and the men decided to stash the carbines in the Surratts' former tavern in Surrattsville, then return to Washington. Biographer Kauffmann believes the entire incident was a ruse by Booth to gain the return of his weapons and to implicate his conspirators in a public place with witnesses, giving him a hold over them should the need arise. Regardless, the kidnap plan died away.[1]

The war, meanwhile, was going poorly for the South. The previous September, Atlanta had fallen to Sherman, who continued his march to the Atlantic, capturing Savannah just before Christmas. A week earlier, Union forces prevailed in the Battle of Nashville, forcing the remnants of the Confederate Army of Tennessee to surrender. Across Virginia, the Carolinas, and Florida, Union troops were winning battle after battle. The Confederacy was in financial ruins, many of its people starving, and the tide seemed clear and unstoppable. In March, Grant's forces were arrayed against Lee's Rebels in northern Virginia, each army relying on trenches as their defenses, but with the Union pressing its advantage against Lee's thinned-out lines. On April 9, 1865, with his army surrounded and its supplies cut off, Lee surrendered.

The vanquishing of the South and Lincoln's March 4 inauguration for his second term (which Booth witnessed) led Booth to contemplate a different course of action. Nothing was to be gained now by kidnapping Lincoln. The Gray prisoners in the North were already being released, and there was no longer much of a Confederacy in whose name the kidnapping could be committed. But Booth's hatred of Lincoln didn't waver. If anything, it intensified as he saw the tall, high-voiced president as the cause of all the ills the South had endured.[2]

Booth's conspirators, though, began wavering. O'Laughlen and Arnold wanted out. Atzerodt was too much of a drunk to be trusted; in fact, Booth had begun dropping misinformation when he was around the river man so that if Atzerodt did start talking, he'd have nothing dangerous to say. Surratt was fading away, too, resuming his courier work, and was soon in Canada.

But Booth remained committed. Though the nature of the crime was changing.

With the end of the war, Washington, DC, hastily planned a "grand illumination," an evening celebration involving massive amounts of candles, torches, and lanterns. Planners scheduled it to coincide with a rare visit to Washington by General Ulysses S. Grant, who would arrive by boat on April 13, four days after accepting Lee's surrender at Appomattox Court House in Virginia. By now, Booth had firmly decided that kidnapping the president would be pointless. But he could still avenge the South. So the plot evolved into something more heinous.

Booth decided that he would kill Lincoln and, through his conspirators, direct the assassinations of Vice President Andrew Johnson, living at the Kirkwood Hotel, and Secretary of State William Seward—who had warned that slavery would lead to war—convalescing at home from severe injuries incurred nine days earlier in a carriage accident.

The best place to kill the president, Booth decided, was at the theater. Booth had stopped by Washington's two popular theaters, Ford's and Grover's, and chatted up the managers, asking if they planned to invite the president to any upcoming performances. Both managers assured Booth they intended to do just that, and Booth, easily gaining access as an actor, reacquainted himself with the layout and exits of both theaters. In one of them, if all went right, Lincoln would die.

On the evening of April 13, with the grand illumination celebration roaring on the street below, Booth met with Powell, Herold, and Atzerodt in Powell's hotel room, where he handed out the final assignments. On whatever night and at whichever theater Lincoln attended, Booth would kill the president. At the same time, Herold would lead Powell to Seward's home and help him escape after the secretary of state had been murdered. Atzerodt would kill Johnson. (Atzerodt would say later this was the first he heard that the kidnapping plot had become a murder plot, but Booth had boxed him in as a conspirator.) Booth had been carefully mapping out strategies, including riding a horse from each of the theaters in different directions, trying to pick the most sensible escape route. Killing the president would shock the theater into inaction, but that wouldn't last long, and Booth would need to get free of the neighborhood as fast as possible. A carriage would be better than on foot, but a lone horse was best.

As it turned out, the Lincolns did not watch the grand illumination with Grant and his wife as planned; the president had taken ill with a severe headache. Mary Lincoln hoped she and her husband could make it up to the Grants by taking them to Ford's Theatre to watch a performance of the popular comedy *Our American Cousin* the next evening, Good Friday. Before hearing back from the Grants, she sent a messenger to Ford's the morning of the performance that she would like to reserve the President's Box for that evening. Another message reserved a seat for the Lincolns' son, Tad, to watch *Aladdin! Or His Wonderful Lamp* at Grover's that same evening.[3]

Knowing a marketing opportunity when they saw it, theater managers posted ads in the Washington newspapers that afternoon about their esteemed guests, a common practice in hopes that a big name in the audience would spark ticket sales. And that indeed was the effect of the Lincoln-Grant announcement. Ticket requests flooded in to Ford's, though by showtime those making reservations in hopes of seeing Grant would be disappointed to learn that the general and his wife had already left Washington. Instead, Major Henry Rathbone and his fiancée, Clara Harris, last-minute substitutes for the Grants, accompanied the Lincolns.[4]

By the time the newspapers came out, Booth already knew of the president's plans for the evening. He happened to be at Ford's Theatre around lunchtime to check on his mail—the theater served as a mail drop for many in the acting community. He spoke with the manager, who mentioned in an aside that luck had fallen his way: Lincoln and Grant would attend that night's play, which likely meant a run on tickets and a full house. Booth had no memorably visible reaction. But it was time, he decided, to put his plan into action, though with the curtain scheduled to go up at eight o'clock, he would have to hurry. Booth alerted Powell, Herold, and Atzerodt, then stopped at Mary Surratt's boardinghouse, catching her as she returned from a day trip to the old tavern in Surrattsville. He asked her to return to the tavern and drop off a package that included field glasses. And as the evening progressed, the wheels began to turn.

Atzerodt met a friend for a drink at a tavern a block from the Kirkwood Hotel, where he had taken a room, and where Vice President Johnson was living, and drank until the hour neared ten—the time at which the killings were to take place. Herold and Powell loitered near Lafayette Park, which was also near the Seward house. Booth stopped at a couple of saloons on his way to Ford's Theatre. He knew exactly when he wanted to strike—at a point in the play in which a gag on the stage would make the audience erupt in laughter, which he hoped would obscure the explosion from the single-shot derringer in his pocket.

Powell's assignment was the trickiest. Atzerodt had an excuse to be in the hotel in which he rented a room, so could easily make his way to Johnson's suite. Booth was a familiar face at Ford's Theatre, so would not arouse any suspicions. But Powell had to talk his way into Seward's home, then get to the injured man's room. The conspirators had hit upon a stratagem in which Powell would knock on the door and announce that he was a messenger bearing medicine sent by Seward's doctor. Powell and Herold waited near the house, watching a flurry of guests that made them balk. Herold ran off to the hotel to warn Atzerodt about the delay, but didn't find the fellow conspirator and would-be killer of Johnson in his room, where he was supposed to be. Atzerodt was still at a bar pounding drinks to fuel his bravery for the murder he was supposed to commit, a strategy that backfired. Atzerodt lost his nerve and never approached the vice president's door, choosing instead to move from saloon to saloon.

Herold, confused by not finding Atzerodt, hurried back to Powell, and the two waited until the traffic of guests at the Seward house stopped, which happened a little after nine o'clock—plenty of time with the killings scheduled to happen just after ten. At the appointed time, Powell walked to the door and knocked. When a servant opened it, Powell said he had a package of medicine to deliver to Seward and pushed his way in and began mounting the stairs. On the third floor, which held Seward's room, Powell encountered Seward's adult son, Frederick, an assistant secretary in the state department. The son told Powell, the medicine messenger, that his father was sleeping and was not to be disturbed; he asked Powell to hand over the delivery and leave. Powell turned in the hallway as if he were leaving, then spun around quickly, pressed his revolver to the young man's head, and pulled the trigger. The gun failed to fire. Powell then used it as a club, striking the son over the head. The tumult drew the attention of Seward's daughter, Fanny, and Private George Foster Robinson, an army nurse, who were in the room with Seward. They opened the door to see the stunned and bleeding Frederick, and Powell, now armed with a large knife, which he used to slash Robinson, sending him crumbling to the ground.[5]

Powell then leaped to Seward's bed and began stabbing wildly. Seward, despite being injured and roused from a deep sleep, wriggled and writhed. The knife found its mark several times, gashing Seward deeply in the face. As Powell reached back to swing again, Robinson caught him from the

David Herold.

Courtesy of Library of Congress, Prints and Photographs Division
(reproduction number LC-DIG-ppmsca-35251)

rear, and in the struggle Seward managed to slip from the bed and roll to the floor. Fanny's screams and the sounds of the violent encounter echoed through the house; another Seward son, Augustus, who'd been sleeping in a room next door, entered and together he and Robinson wrestled the powerful Powell away from the bed. Augustus broke away to retrieve a gun from his room, and Powell, too strong for Robinson to hold, bolted, pushing past servants and stabbing a departmental secretary in his race for the door, then galloped off on his waiting horse. (Herold, hearing the screams from inside the house, had already run off.)

As Seward was writhing for his life under Powell's knife attack, Booth was slipping into position at Ford's Theatre. As he hoped, the comedy unfolding on stage drew the packed theater's attention, giving Booth cover as he made his way to the President's Box, the upper-level private suite that Lincoln always used when he attended performances. Booth had been there earlier in the day and quietly laid out some of the tools he would need. The President's Box was separated from the hallway by a small vestibule that led to two doors, one to box 7, the President's Box, and one to the adjacent box 8, which, through the removal of a temporary wall, had been merged with box 7 for the evening's performance. Booth had drilled a small peephole in the door to the President's Box. He also quietly gouged out a space in the plaster wall inside the vestibule, and left behind a length of pine lumber to fit into the groove.

As the play reached the comedic high moment, Booth—carrying in his pockets the single-shot derringer and a large knife—slipped into the vestibule and quietly forced the piece of wood into place, jamming the hall door closed from the inside. He peered through the hole in the door to the box and saw Lincoln sitting in front, slightly to the right, with his wife on his far side. Rathbone and Harris were still farther to the right in box 8. Booth couldn't have asked for a better setup.

With the audience's eyes focused on the stage, Booth quietly opened the door, stepped inside, raised the derringer, and as the punch line was delivered on stage, pulled the trigger. The lead bullet, a half-inch in diameter, struck Lincoln just behind the left ear and came to a stop in his brain behind the right eye. The president sagged forward, instantly unconscious and mortally wounded. Rathbone rose from the sofa and ran at Booth who, anticipating the moment, swung the knife at the major. Rathbone raised an arm to absorb the attack, suffering a deep and painful gash. As Rathbone recoiled, Booth vaulted over the rail, catching his boot on the bunting and landing awkwardly and painfully on the stage floor some ten feet below, but standing.

Turning to face the stunned audience, some of whom presumed the actor's sudden appearance to be part of the performance, Booth yelled out, "*Sic semper tyrannis!*" then limped quickly across the stage and out an alley exit to where he had arranged with stagehand Edmund "Ned" Spangler to have someone wait with his horse. (Neither Spangler nor the stable boy to whom he delegated the task knew what Booth had planned.) The actor mounted the horse, smacked the stable boy with the knife handle, and galloped off into the night, leaving behind a theater erupting in confusion, anger, and shock.

The assassination of President Lincoln at Ford's Theatre, Washington, DC, April 14, 1865.

Currier & Ives, courtesy of Library of Congress, Prints and Photographs Division (reproduction number LC-USZC2-1947)

Booth's knife had cut deeply into Rathbone's arm, severing an artery and spurting blood across the president's box. Weakening rapidly and fighting off shock, Rathbone managed to get to the barricaded door and knock loose the pine board Booth had used to jam it shut. At least a dozen men flooded into the small space to find the dazed Rathbone, his stunned fiancée, and the near-hysterical First Lady propping up the slumped-over president, begging him to answer her. The throng grew quickly; one doctor, Charles Leale, managed to get inside through the door; another, Charles Taft, was helped up and over the railing that Booth had hurdled just moments before.

Lincoln wasn't bleeding very much, so the wound wasn't evident at first. It took a few minutes before the doctor's experienced hands found the hole in the back of the skull, and he knew immediately that the president would soon be dead. The best they could do was to make him comfortable and, maybe, let him die in more dignified surroundings than in a public theater box.

Leale enlisted some of the men packed into the box to help move the president. They carried him gently, feet first, down the stairs and out onto the street, where a large crowd was gathering. Leale looked around for a place to take Lincoln, opting against a saloon. He sent a soldier bounding up the steps of a brownstone across the street but no one answered the knock. A man emerged on the stoop of a nearby three-story townhouse—he was a boarder in the home of William A. Petersen, a German tailor—and hollered that they could bring the president there. The bearers carried Lincoln up the steps and through the first floor to a bedroom near the back of the house, where they had to place the tall president diagonally on the bed.

And the deathwatch began.

News flashed through the city, by word of mouth and telegram, that the president had been shot and that Seward had been attacked in his sickbed. No one knew of the plot against the vice president, but fears spread of a Confederate coup. Former Wisconsin governor Leonard Farwell, who had been attending the play at Ford's Theatre, heard the chatter of the assault on Seward and thought immediately of Vice President Johnson, a fellow guest at the Kirkwood. Farwell, an examiner for the US Patent Office, went to the hotel and pounded on Johnson's door, rousing the vice president from sleep, and delivered the news that the president had been shot and Seward stabbed. After a few moments of emotional confusion, the two men calmed down, and Farwell arranged for a guard to be posted in the hallway outside Johnson's door, then returned to the theater to gather whatever news he could of the president's condition. Learning that Lincoln was across the street, Farwell went to the Petersen house and, amid the crowd and turmoil, spotted Major James R. O'Beirne, the provost marshal for Washington. Farwell told the chief of the military police that Vice President Johnson was alone and with little protection at the hotel. Soon a contingent of detectives stood in the hallway outside Johnson's room while others, under the direction of O'Beirne's chief of detectives, John Lee, searched the hotel. Johnson eventually went to the townhouse but then returned to his rooms at the hotel in the early hours of the morning.[6]

O'Beirne's men questioned the hotel staff about whether they had seen anything suspicious, questions that reminded the bartender of the furtive and odd-looking patron who drank heavily. It was an upper-class establishment, patronized by the rich and the powerful, and this man—shifty and ill-clad—stood out as neither. The man was staying at the hotel, the bartender told Lee, who soon tracked down George Atzerodt's name and room number. Atzerodt had taken his room key with him, so Lee and his men broke through the door and in short order found a loaded pistol and a knife in the bed. There were some papers, too, and in a jacket pocket a Canadian bankbook in John Wilkes Booth's name. The patrons and cast at Ford's Theatre had already identified Booth as the man who had shot the president. Now Atzerodt was added to the alert of wanted men.

Washington was in utter pandemonium, a reign of confusion that only worsened as news spread of the attacks and then, after seven o'clock on the morning of April 15, that the president was dead. Johnson was sworn in as president at his hotel a short time later. Tips, leads, and accusations flooded into official Washington, and investigators tried to sift the wheat from the chaff, with middling success. They cast a wide net and arrested scores of people with potential, but usually tangential, connections with the assassinations, including the owner of the stable at which Booth kept his horse. One woman passed along word that her niece, an African American servant in Mary Surratt's boardinghouse, had noticed a lot of suspicious activity and a churn of visitors who talked quietly and in secret, usually outside the house.

A detachment of military police under Major Henry W. Smith showed up at Surratt's boardinghouse while Lincoln was still alive, intent on taking Mary Surratt and anyone else they found at the house into custody. While they were inside questioning Surratt and searching the rooms as they awaited a carriage to carry away the prisoners, heavy feet pounded up the front wooden steps, and then the bell rang. When the soldiers opened the door, a disheveled Lewis Powell stepped into the vestibule. He looked around and then told the soldiers he must have arrived at the wrong house, but they detained him. Powell then said that rather than arriving at the wrong house, he was a workman who, despite the late hour, had come to see Mary Surratt about a job she wanted him to do. Major Smith had Surratt brought to the front of the house and asked her if she had ever seen the man before; Surratt, though she knew Powell by another name, said no, exposing the lie but not the truth, so Powell was arrested too. It would be some time, though, before the investigators discovered just how lucky they had been that Powell had walked into their arms.

Most of the other arrests came quickly, though again, it was some time before investigators untangled who exactly had done what. Sam Arnold and Michael O'Laughlen, Booth's old friends and conspirators in the kidnapping plot, were caught on April 15, the day Lincoln died. Atzerodt was traced to an uncle's house in Germantown, Maryland, and dragged from his bed on the night of April 19. But they found little trace of John Surratt, unaware that he was not involved in the murder plot and was in Elmira, New York, and then Canada.

As for Booth and Herold, it seemed as though they had disappeared with the wind. In fact, they were quite near.

6

THE HUNT FOR BOOTH
AND HEROLD

Booth's escape plan was simple. After Booth, Atzerodt, and Powell carried out their assassination assignments, they, along with Herold, were to flee the city. Booth planned to loosely follow the path he had mapped out for spiriting Lincoln away to Richmond, stopping at the tavern in Surrattsville to pick up weapons that Herold, Atzerodt, and John Surratt had stashed a few weeks prior and the field glasses that Mary Surratt had dropped off earlier in the day.

But Booth almost didn't get out of the city. The quickest route was over a military-manned drawbridge near the Navy Yard across the Anacostia River and on into Maryland. The bridge closed at nine o'clock nightly; Booth approached on horseback around ten thirty, about fifteen minutes after he shot Lincoln and before word had spread. The gate was down, and an armed sentry halted Booth. Sergeant Silas T. Cobb, in charge of the bridge that night, emerged from the guardhouse and started questioning the rider, who told him his name was Booth and he was trying to get from the city to his home in Charles County, Maryland. Booth proclaimed that he knew nothing about the rule closing the bridge, and cajoled Cobb into letting him pass. Cobb, unaware that Lincoln had been shot and sensing nothing suspicious about Booth, decided to let him through.

About ten minutes later another rider, Herold, arrived at the drawbridge's northern gate. His flight from Washington was a bit more dramatic than Booth's. The horse Herold was riding had been checked out of a livery and was hours overdue. As Herold fled Seward's neighborhood, the livery manager, out looking for his overdue horse, spotted and tried to stop him. Herold evaded the effort and rode off to the south. The liveryman returned to the stable and mounted another horse and went off in pursuit, but Herold had outdistanced him.

At the bridge, the sentry stopped Herold and summoned Cobb, who repeated his admonition that the bridge was closed. Herold lied and told Cobb that his name was Smith and that he was heading home. "He made use of a rather indelicate expression and said he had been in bad company," Cobb later testified, meaning that Herold told him he had spent the evening with a woman, probably a prostitute. Cobb let him pass, too. A few minutes later the livery manager arrived at the gate, but when Cobb told him that if he let him pass out of the city he would not be allowed to return until morning, the manager wheeled his horse and returned to Washington, where he reported that Herold had stolen a horse. Compared with conspiring to murder a president, it wasn't much of a crime, and at that point no one had connected Herold with the attacks. So the clue dangled, unused.

Booth and Herold met up on the road to Surrattsville and arrived at the tavern to find a drunk John M. Lloyd, the man to whom Mary Surratt had leased the property when she moved into Washington. As Lloyd retrieved the stashed guns and the field glasses, Herold nabbed a bottle of whiskey. Booth, whose awkward jump from the President's Box to the Ford Theatre stage had fractured a bone in his leg, was in considerable pain. He stayed on his horse; Herold handed the whiskey bottle up to him, and the actor took several swigs to dampen the hurt.

After a few minutes, Lloyd emerged from the tavern with the weapons and field glasses. As Herold mounted his horse, Booth asked Lloyd if he wanted to hear some news. Lloyd was noncommittal but Booth, ever eager for an audience, was not to be stopped. "I am pretty certain that we have assassinated the president and Secretary Seward," Booth told Lloyd before the two men rode off. (Oddly, he didn't mention Vice President Johnson.) The next day, soldiers in search of the killers stopped at the tavern with the same news. Lloyd, fearing he might be tied to the assassination, withheld the detail that Booth and Herold had been at his tavern just the night before.[1]

Tracking Booth and Herold became a consuming manhunt, with Booth vilified by a bloodthirsty North and cheered on by many in the vengeful South. Rebel leaders, though, including General Robert E. Lee and Jefferson Davis and his cabinet, sought to distance the assassination from the Confederate cause by condemning Booth's act. Given the mood of distrust, the disavowals were ignored, and by the time the furor died down, new president Johnson would issue arrest orders for at least six Rebel leaders, beginning with Davis.

Johnson was in charge of the nation, but Secretary of War Edwin M. Stanton was in charge of the search, and he attacked it with vigor. The flood of tips that came in was assembled and analyzed, with the likeliest checked out as quickly as men could be dispatched. (Some, such as the suggestions from psychics, were probably given a lower priority.) Scores of homes were searched, and scores of suspects, or the merely suspicious, were detained, often in violation of the Bill of Rights. Wild geese were chased hither and yon. One detachment went to Canada to get a bead on John Surratt, even though there was no extradition agreement they could invoke to return him to the United States. And with more than $100,000 in reward money on the line seeking the capture of a list of conspirators, the public reported every little bit of suspicion in hopes that it might be the right detail to lead to Booth and the cash.

Yet those with the best information were not swayed by money. The presumption was that Booth would head for familiar territory, where he might count on friends and Confederate supporters to help him hide. So the spotlight was focused on Baltimore and the northern reaches of Maryland. Old friends were hunted down and interrogated. Relatives were hounded. The theater world was subjected to intense scrutiny, actors, managers, and stagehands plumbed for their political beliefs on the war and their connections to Booth. But no definitive leads surfaced. And as the days passed, the mystery, and the frustration, deepened. And the search broadened.

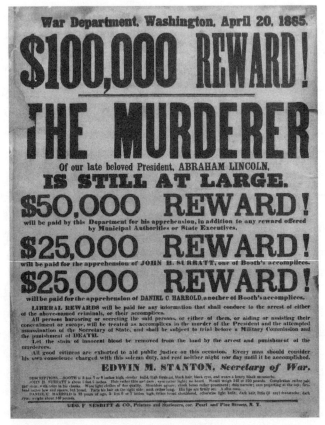

Poster broadcasting the hunt for John Wilkes Booth, kept
by the National Park Service Ford's Theatre National
Historic Site, Washington, DC.

Carol M. Highsmith, courtesy of Library of Congress, Prints and Photographs
Division (reproduction number LC-DIG-highsm-04756)

The hunters, it turned out, were looking in the wrong place. Booth had fled
south, not north, though he was indeed hoping to eventually find help and
cover among friends within the disintegrating Confederacy. After leaving
the tavern in Surrattsville around midnight, Booth and Herold continued
south to Samuel Mudd's farm, arriving around four in the morning on

April 15—about three hours before Lincoln died and well ahead of the search parties.

Dr. Mudd answered the knock at the door to find one man on his porch and a second man sitting on his horse, getting soaked by a spring rain. The man at the door said his friend had injured a leg falling from his horse and needed a doctor's attention. Such calls were not that unusual an occurrence for doctors of the era, and with the help of the man at the door, Mudd managed to get the injured rider through the darkened house to a second-floor bedroom, where he cut off the boot and examined the injury. A simple break of the fibula, he concluded, with no dislocation of the bone. It would heal. Mudd splinted and bandaged the limb and all three men went to bed.

Mudd contended later, not convincingly, that he did not recognize the injured man as Booth; Herold had introduced himself as Henson and Booth as Tyson. Herold came down for breakfast the next morning and Sarah Frances "Frankie" Mudd, the doctor's wife, sent a tray up to Booth's room. A gardener was put to work fashioning a set of crutches for the injured man.

Historian James L. Swanson argues that Mudd recognized Booth and that he traveled into Bryantown that next day, leaving Booth and Herold at his farm. When Mudd learned that Lincoln was dead, he returned, angry that Booth had not told him of the danger he had brought to Mudd and his family. He ordered Booth and Herold to leave. But he also provided the names of other Confederate sympathizers who could help them reach Virginia.[2]

There have been many interpretations of the uneven and sometimes contradictory details of Booth's stop at the farm, and of the extent of Mudd's involvement in Booth's plots. It seems most likely that Mudd had signed on with the kidnapping plan and would have helped Booth move Lincoln along the Confederate underground but was unaware of the assassination until that day's visit to Bryantown. But it's also clear that Mudd knowingly abetted Booth and Herold in their escape.

While Mudd was off to Bryantown, Herold tried to rent or buy a carriage in which Booth could ride, but none of Mudd's neighbors would part with theirs. So it would be horseback again. Booth and Herold left around

7 PM and rode deep into the night, eventually hiring a black tobacco farmer named Oswell Swann to lead them through a swamp to the home of Samuel Cox, a former colonel in a Maryland militia that disbanded when the state decided not to secede. Cox displayed his loyalties by joining the Rebels' version of the Underground Railroad, moving people, documents, and information. With Swann's help, Booth and Herold arrived at Cox's house a little after midnight and, after rousting Cox, were taken about four hours later to a hiding spot in a pine thicket. Cox sent word to a nearby farm that he wished to speak with the owner, Thomas A. Jones, a noted river man who, Cox hoped, would be able to get Booth and Herold across the Potomac and into Virginia.

Jones arrived about nine o'clock that morning and Cox took him a bit away from his house to tell him about the assassination—Jones had heard the news from Union soldiers the night before—and that the two men who had stopped by his house needed help crossing the river to Virginia. Cox gave Jones the whistle code he had told Booth and Herold to listen for, and directions to where the fugitives were hiding in the pines. Jones went directly to the woods, giving the whistle as he neared. Herold emerged from the brush and after a brief conversation led Jones to Booth.

"He was lying on the ground, with his head supported on his hand," Jones wrote later in a memoir. "His carbine, pistols and knife were close beside him. A blanket was drawn partly over him. His slouch hat and crutch were lying by him. He was dressed in dark—I think black—clothes, and though they were travel-stained, his appearance was respectable." Jones described Booth as handsome but "exceedingly pale and his features bore the evident traces of suffering. . . . His voice was pleasant and though he seemed to be suffering intense pain from his broken leg, his manner was courteous and polite."[3]

Jones said he would help but that the two men would need patience. It made the most sense, he advised, for them to not move until the intensity of the search had died down. Jones said he'd stop back daily with food and updates and recommended that the two men get rid of their horses, since their sounds and meanderings would likely attract attention. After Jones left, Herold took the horses to the swamp and shot them.

As Union troops scoured the countryside, Herold and Booth remained in their thicket, Jones bringing them fresh food and news as he played his own game of cat and mouse with family, friends, neighbors, and soldiers, who had been conducting daily searches of houses and farms, including Jones's. They also talked to Mudd, and the soldier in charge of that interview, Lieutenant Alexander Lovett, felt Mudd was being evasive. Mudd gave a loose description of the men who had stopped at his residence, saying that one had a broken leg, which he set and then sent the injured man off with crutches. But he also lied and said the injured man had asked for a razor with which to shave his beard, and that the two men had ridden on to the home of a Union supporter. Lovett intuited that the doctor knew more than he was letting on. He made a mental note to come back after their first cursory investigation—they were looking for men more than information—and arrest Mudd for more thorough questioning. (Lovett, in fact, returned three days later and arrested Mudd as the doctor's story crumbled, in part with the discovery of a monogrammed boot Booth had left behind at Mudd's house.)

Jones didn't dare enter the thicket in view of anyone, so he had to time his visits. He also directed his helper, a former slave who now worked for him, to take one of his two boats from a place called Dent's Meadow out onto the river every morning and fish with his gillnets—an attempt, it seems, to accustom people to the presence of the boat. And then Jones watched and waited for a time when the Union troops weren't around and he could lead Booth and Herold to the Potomac and across to Virginia.

The break was slow in coming, and Booth and Herold grew increasingly impatient. Left alone in the thicket, they had few distractions and plenty of time to stew. Finally, a week after the assassination, rumors ran through Charles County that Booth had been spotted in St. Mary's County to the southeast, and many of the troops were diverted from Charles County. That gave Jones the opening he needed to get Booth to the river. At dusk on April 22, he went to the pine thicket and told the fugitives it was time. Jones provided a horse for Booth to ride and directed Herold to walk along beside. Jones would stay ahead of the duo, who would await a signal from him that they could proceed. In that slow, stop-and-go fashion, they made their way unnoticed through the dark, stopping at Jones's house as he slipped inside to grab some food for the two men to take with them, and then continuing on to the river and the boat.

Jones helped the two men to their places, Booth at the stern with the steering oar and Herold at the bow, where he could paddle them across the river. Jones gave Booth a compass and a small candle, told him the heading to follow, and then pushed the boat out into the river. Herold paddled and Booth steered late into the night, unknowingly carried by the tide far from their intended spot on the Virginia shore. In fact, after hours of work, they landed back in Maryland and spent the next day secreted until they could try again.

Early on April 23, Booth and Herold finally crossed the Potomac River and arrived in Virginia, near Mathias Point in King George County. After hiding Booth, Herold went to the nearby farmhouse of Elizabeth Quesenberry, long part of the Confederate underground. Suspicious, she declined to help but sent word to Thomas Harbin, with whom Booth had talked of the kidnapping plot. When Harbin arrived, Herold took him to Booth. After a brief conversation, Harbin agreed to move them along and took them to another house.

The dragnet was tightening. An unsigned telegram went out to Lieutenant Commander Thomas H. Eastman at St. Inigoes, Maryland, about eighty miles down the Potomac from Washington, stating:

> Booth was near Bryantown last Saturday, where Dr. Mudd set his ankle which was broken by a fall from his horse. The utmost vigilance is necessary in the Potomac and Patuxent to prevent his escape. All boats should be searched for and destroyed and a daily and nightly patrol established on both shores. Inform the people that more than one hundred thousand dollars are offered for him. Allow none of your boats to leave except for search elsewhere.[4]

Booth had no way of knowing but must have presumed that the pursuers had picked up his trail. Still, the fugitives had no option other than to move slowly, trying to stay out of sight while simultaneously searching for sympathizers who would help them, an act that exposed each abettor to possible hanging under a decree issued by President Johnson. One contact, a Dr. Richard Stuart, gave them food but refused them a night's rest. Booth and Herold moved on to the shack of a former slave named William Lucas and at knifepoint forced the man to let them sleep in his house. Interestingly, Booth relied on wits and charm when he was dealing with white Southerners, but when he needed to force an issue with a black man, he resorted to physical threat. But he also was becoming more desperate.

Booth had little idea how close the federal authorities were. Jones had brought him newspapers so he was aware of the uproar, the manhunt, and the arrests of Atzerodt, Powell, Mary Surratt, and the others. But he likely didn't know that key figures along his escape route were being rounded up behind him. Mudd, Jones, and Cox were already in custody, though not cooperating (Jones and Cox were eventually released, and it would be twenty years before Jones's involvement was known, and before the world learned how Booth and Herold had spent those days immediately after the killing). As time passed, speculation over where Booth was hiding filled the newspapers and kept saloon tongues wagging. Still, the search focused on Maryland, not Virginia, so Booth had managed to escape beyond the outer edges of the dragnet. But he knew he needed to keep moving deeper and deeper into the South.

On the morning of April 24, Booth and Herold forced Lucas's son, Charlie, to drive them in a wagon to Port Conway, on the north bank of the Rappahannock River, which they would need to cross to reach Richmond. The ferry was on the other side of the river, but they met local store owner and fisherman William Rollins, who accepted ten cents each to row them across in his fishing boat. Before Rollins was ready to leave, however, three other men on horseback appeared on the rise above the small port, then descended to the landing. They were soldiers, their uniforms tattered and hard to place. Booth and Herold eyed them warily as they approached, Herold reaching inside his coat for ready access to his gun. Herold asked what command they belonged to. "Mosby's," came the response, and the tension melted considerably. These were Rebels, not Union soldiers: Private Willie S. Jett, Lieutenant Mortimer B. Ruggles (son and aide to Confederate general Daniel Ruggles), and his cousin, Private Absalom R. Bainbridge, all heading from Fauquier County to Caroline County for a social visit.

The soldiers rode down to the riverbank and the wharf, where Herold followed. He asked if the soldiers would help them get farther south. They were Confederate soldiers themselves, he said, brothers by the name of Boyd, and the brother back in the wagon had been wounded in fighting near Petersburg. They wanted to link up with another Rebel company to keep fighting the North once the brother had recovered. Jett was skeptical; he told Herold they couldn't help. They were just going a few miles farther on for a visit anyway, not heading deeper south to join up with remaining fighting units. Herold returned to the wagon, and the soldiers moved back up the bank, tethered their horses at Rollins's stable, and sat down to await the ferry.[5]

Herold was back a few minutes later and, after some small talk, he asked Jett if he could have a private word with him. The two men moved back down the riverbank to the wharf, where Herold again beseeched Jett to help them get farther south. Jett still resisted. "I cannot go with any man that I do not know anything about," Jett told Herold, who "seemed very much agitated, and then remarked, when we got down on the wharf, 'We are the assassinators of the president.'" Jett was stunned; after a few moments he called Ruggles to join them at the wharf, where Jett shared the news. Booth, curious about the conversation, lowered himself from the wagon and hobbled over, his face drawn with pain and exhaustion, his clothes dirty from a week in hiding.

"I suppose you have been told who I am?" Booth asked. When the men told him they had, Booth pulled out a revolver and said, "Yes, I am John Wilkes Booth the slayer of Abraham Lincoln, and I am worth just $175,000 to the man who captures me." He overstated the price on his head, but it didn't matter: the Rebels told Booth they had no intention of turning him in. Booth put his gun away and after a few more minutes of conversation they helped him onto the back of Ruggles's horse and, when the ferry arrived, all five men boarded and set out for Port Royal on the southern bank of the Rappahannock.[6]

At Port Royal, Jett—in familiar territory—went to the home of Randall Peyton, a lawyer who also kept a farm nearby, where he had gone for the day. Jett asked Peyton's two unmarried sisters if they could house a wounded Confederate soldier named James Boyd for a couple of days. At first the women agreed. But after Booth was ensconced on a sofa in the parlor, one of them pulled Jett aside and said that they had changed their minds out of a sense of propriety. It would be unseemly for the two women to house a man while their brother was away. Jett understood and moved Booth on, but a neighbor across the street had the same issue—a woman home alone unwilling to invite scandal. One of Peyton's sisters suggested Jett go out of town a ways and try the farm of Richard Garrett, who had several sons and likely would be willing to take in the wounded soldier.

Booth, Herold, and the three Rebels arrived at the Garrett farm by midafternoon, and Garrett quickly agreed to take in Booth, introduced to him as Boyd. The actor was helped from the horse—his swollen and blackened leg useless—to the covered porch, where he settled in for a talk with Garrett. Herold rode off with Ruggles and Jett to the next town, Bowling Green, where Herold said he wanted to buy some new shoes and planned to spend the night. (It seems he went to a brothel.) Booth dined with Garrett's large family, which included the two Confederate veteran sons, John and William. That night, Booth slept in the bed of one of the sons, the first bed he'd used in more than a week. He didn't awaken until late morning, the comfort of the bed and the exhaustion from traveling, hiding, and healing catching up with him.

Booth spent the day mostly in the Garretts' yard, and at first left his guns in his belt draped across a chair in the bedroom in which he had slept. But the sound of horses riding fast along the road in front of the farm spooked Booth, and he demanded that one of the Garretts retrieve his weapons for him. The sharpness of Booth's demand caught the Garretts by surprise, and a suspicion began to grow in John Garrett that the traveler named Boyd might be something more than a wounded soldier seeking a place to heal. Booth also spent time with a map, taking notes of different roads to the south.

In late afternoon, with the elder Garrett away from the house, Herold returned. Booth introduced him to John Garrett and asked if Herold—his cousin David Boyd, he said—could stay the night as well. John demurred, saying it was his father's decision and they would have to wait. In truth, the young man had grown suspicious of Booth and didn't want him in the house.

As if to affirm his fears, two riders barreled up the road on their horses, then banked and turned in to the farm. It was Ruggles and Bainbridge, and they had a hurried and hushed conversation with Booth and Herold. Word was, they said, that a detachment of Union cavalry was heading that way.

Booth and Herold gathered their weapons and walked to a nearby wood, where they hid for a time. When no soldiers came they emerged and asked John Garrett if he thought the news of Union troops was credible. As they spoke, an African American named Jim came walking along the road. One of the Garretts went to question Jim, returning with the news that yes, indeed, the cavalry was in Port Royal. As they talked, thunder rose from down the road, and before Booth and Herold could determine a course of action, a squad of some two dozen Union soldiers galloped past the farm.

They were safe. For the moment.

Herold gave one of the Garrett sons some money and asked him to find the two men a horse. Garrett went to a neighboring farm, but the farmer wasn't home. His wife told Garrett that the Union troops had stopped and asked if two traveling white men had been seen in the area. It was clear they were on a search, and while Garrett didn't know what the Boyds had done, he presumed they were the men the soldiers were looking for. Suspicions elevated further at the dinner table that night when Herold spun a web of lies about his nonexistent Confederate service, lies with details that conflicted with what the Garretts knew about some of the regiments with which Herold claimed to have been affiliated. The father agreed with the sons; there was much to be suspicious about these two men. He wouldn't have them in the house.

Late in the evening, after idling on the porch, Booth and Herold announced they would be turning in. The Garretts barred them entry. Herold said they'd be happy to sleep under the porch, but the Garretts said no, the farm dogs slept there. They finally agreed to let the two strangers sleep in an old tobacco barn now used to store hay. As Booth and Herold made themselves comfortable, the Garrett brothers quietly locked the door from the outside, fearing the strangers might sneak off in the night with the family's horses. And then they set themselves up in a nearby corncrib where they could maintain a watch over the barn through the night.

On Good Friday, the night Lincoln was shot, Sergeant Boston Corbett and his Sixteenth New York Cavalry were based across the Potomac in Vienna, Virginia. Saturday morning the regiment was sent out to scour the northern Virginia countryside between Vienna and the Potomac looking for signs of the assassins. They entered houses and barns, storerooms and businesses, "every place that would be likely to afford shelter to the fugitive." At first, they were chasing suspicions—looking for anyone acting furtive and limping. It wasn't until they were already in the field that a message with the name of the assassin caught up with them: John Wilkes Booth, the actor.

The cavalrymen returned empty-handed, as did other searchers, but Stanton and the other top figures directing the manhunt still planned for an eventual capture. Gideon Welles, the navy secretary, sent a telegram to Commander J. B. Montgomery at the Navy Yard on the day Lincoln died advising him that

> if the military authorities arrest the murderer of the president and take
> him to the Yard, put him on the Monitor and anchor her in the stream
> with strong guard on vessel, wharf and in Yard. Call upon Cmdt.
> Marine Corps for guard. Have vessel prepared ready to receive him at
> any hour of day or night with necessary instructions. He will be heav-
> ily ironed and so guarded as to prevent escape or injury to himself.[7]

The next morning, Easter Sunday, another order directed a detachment of two dozen men from the Sixteenth to join the search in Washington itself. Somewhat surprisingly, considering it was the Sabbath, Boston Corbett asked and received permission to ride with the detachment. The rest of the unit followed shortly thereafter, decamping Vienna for Seventeenth and I Streets in Washington, just a few blocks from the White House.[8]

By then, Lincoln's body had been moved to the White House, where the autopsy was conducted, and then prepared to lie in state in the East Room. The doors opened at 10 AM Tuesday, April 18, to a mostly silent and grieving parade. The line measured four to six people wide and stretched a half mile from the White House. Lincoln was the first president to be murdered in office, but not the first to die—William Henry Harrison in 1841 and John Tyler in 1850 preceded him. So there were protocols for handling large numbers of visitors, a routine that also applied to happier events, such as the annual New Year's Eve celebration. The mourners, some twenty-five thousand in all, entered the White House through the main door and on into the Green Room, then into the East Room, where they shuffled past to pay their last respects before being ushered out a portico doorway.[9]

The next day an invitation-only funeral was held in the East Room, followed by a solemn two-hour procession down Pennsylvania Avenue to the Capitol building. Corbett and the rest of the Sixteenth New York Cavalry formed part of the parade, joining other regiments leading the horse-drawn hearse the one-and-a-half miles to Capitol Hill, where the eulogies and prayers that had been offered in the White House were repeated for the masses. The body was to remain there until Friday.

The city—the entire North—was in mourning, but the hunt for Booth didn't slow down. Corbett and his fellow cavalrymen had barely left the Capitol after the funeral parade when orders caught up with Lieutenant Doherty to gather twenty-five men and join some carriages of detectives to pursue a lead about Booth and Herold being seen in southern Maryland. They followed Booth's flight across the bridge over the Anacostia River and then on into Maryland. But again they returned empty-handed, and they seem to have had no other search orders issued for the next few days.

Corbett took advantage of the time to request permission to attend night meetings at McKendree Chapel, a Methodist church on Massachusetts near Tenth Street. "One night while there the leader of the meeting said, 'Brother Corbett, lead us in prayer.' It was only a few days after Mr. Lincoln's death, and feeling, as we all did, deeply about the event, I prayed." It was a brief supplication. "O Lord, lay not innocent blood to our charge, but bring the guilty speedily to punishment."

On the afternoon of April 24, ten days after Lincoln was shot, Doherty was sitting on a park bench across from the White House, talking with a friend, when a messenger approached him. The War Department had asked Captain J. Schneider, then commanding the Sixteenth New York Cavalry, to appoint a "reliable and discreet commissioned officer" to lead a detachment of twenty-five men, who was then to report to Colonel Lafayette C. Baker at the War Department at 217 Pennsylvania Avenue, across the street from the Willard Hotel. Schneider had picked Doherty to lead the troops; the lieutenant returned to camp and ordered the bugler to blast out "Boots and Saddles," the military summons to troops to fall in line. He told his men he needed two dozen of them for a special mission. Boston Corbett was among the first to volunteer, and one of two sergeants. Though the order was for twenty-five men, an additional soldier insisted on going too, and Doherty assented.

Doherty led the volunteers to the War Department, arriving around four o'clock. While the men waited outside, Doherty met inside with Colonel Baker, who despite his rank had a tenuous connection with the government. Unpopular and self-promoting, he had been summoned to Washington after the assassination by Stanton, who was among the few who thought Baker possessed skills and integrity. True to his character, Baker had overheard the arrival of a telegram in the war wire room and commandeered it: the wire said that two men had been spotted crossing the Potomac. While most of the manhunt for Booth and Herold was focused on Maryland, this new information, if true, meant the fugitives were actually in Virginia. As it turned out, the details in the telegram were wrong, but by coincidence they were close enough to the truth to set in motion the final play of the manhunt.[10]

As Doherty arrived, he likely already presumed the mission was related to the all-consuming search for Booth and Herold, but also was likely surprised at the orders. Baker "informed me that he had reliable information that the assassin and his accomplice were somewhere between the Potomac and the Rappahannock rivers." Baker gave Doherty photographs of Booth, Herold, and John Surratt and introduced the lieutenant to his own nephew, L. Byron Baker, and Everton Conger, both former Union soldiers now working for the War Department as detectives. Baker ordered Doherty and his men to help the detectives, search as they saw fit, "forage upon the country, giving receipts for what was taken from loyal parties," and stay in the field as long as Doherty thought useful. It was a free rein to try to run Booth to ground. Colonel Baker had already arranged for the steamer *John*

S. Ide to take the troops and their horses to Belle Plain, Virginia, where the search was to begin.[11]

The men loaded themselves aboard the boat at the foot of Sixth Street, where Baker and Conger joined them, apparently taking a different path to the river than the cavalrymen. Corbett was the senior of the two sergeants, and he took down the roster of the cavalrymen aboard. They were armed, naturally, but had no time to provision themselves so were traveling light, without food or camping gear. Once aboard the boat, Doherty gathered the men and passed around the photographs of Booth, Herold, and Surratt, "telling us that these were the men we were in pursuit of, and that if we took them, each man would share in the reward offered for their apprehension."

The boat pushed off and steamed in darkness down the river, arriving at Belle Plain before midnight. The troops started off toward Fredericks-burg but "after going a few miles in that direction, our course was changed towards the Rappahannock." Ignoring the late hour, the troops stopped to search houses, rousting the sleeping inhabitants, and questioned everyone they encountered on the roads. They picked up no leads as they worked through the night and well into the next day, stopped for breakfast at a farmhouse, then continued on. Early in the afternoon, Conger separated with a handful of soldiers to explore a different route while Doherty and the rest of the men, including Corbett, continued on to the Port Conway ferry dock. And there the trail heated up: they found Rollins, the riverside shop owner and fisherman, who told them about the man with the bad leg, his friend, and the three Confederate soldiers they met and then traveled with across the river farther into Virginia.

Doherty sent one soldier for Conger and ordered three others to take a small boat across the Rappahannock and return with a scow they could see on the other side, one large enough to ferry the men and their horses across the river. It was a slow process, with room for only eight horses and men on each crossing. "It took four trips to take us all," Corbett said. "I was in the first party that crossed, and heard from those who followed that rebel troops were seen on the heights of the back of Port Royal who disappeared rapidly when we approached." As the ferrying continued, Rollins's wife told Doherty, Conger, and Baker that she recognized the three Rebels—Jett,

Ruggles, and Bainbridge—who had crossed with Booth and Herold. She speculated that they were headed for the village of Bowling Green, where Jett had a girlfriend whose father owned a hotel. The soldiers ordered Rollins to go with them.

Trying to be thorough, the soldiers worked their way westward, picking up bits of the fugitives' trail from people they met on the road and in houses they stopped to search. Baker, Conger, and Doherty became convinced that Jett, at least, was at the hotel in Bowling Green. They galloped with their men past the Garrett farm—the horde Booth and Herold heard—and on toward the village, stopping about a half mile short. Doherty ordered fifteen of the men to proceed with him and the detectives on foot to the hotel, which the men surrounded as the leaders banged on the door. After some delay in getting a response, Doherty, Baker, and Conger were directed to a room where Jett was sharing a bed with his girlfriend's brother. They ordered Jett, half-dressed, to a front room, where Conger, sitting in a chair as though the man in charge, demanded of Jett, "Where are the two men who came with you across the river at Port Royal?" There was no room for Jett to maneuver; the tone of the question made it clear the Union men knew Jett had helped Lincoln's assassin escape.

Jett asked Conger if he could speak with him privately. After Baker and Doherty left the room, Jett, still wearing only pants and an undershirt, reached out a hand to Conger and said, "I know who you want, and I will tell you where they can be found." They were at a farm, he said, "on the road to Port Royal, about three miles this side of that." Jett offered to escort the soldiers—preempting what was likely to be an order. "At whose house are they?" Conger asked. Garrett's house, Jett said. "I will go there with you, and show where they are now, and you can get them."

They saddled Jett's horse and began the trip back eastward along the road to Garrett's farm, remounting their horses and reuniting with the soldiers they had left behind. After a slow and quiet ride, Jett riding ahead with Doherty and the detectives, they found the cut in the road-edge bushes and pulled up at the gate. Doherty quietly told his men they believed Booth was at the farmhouse and asked Corbett "to deploy the men right and left surrounding it completely, which was done." After Baker persuaded the

Garretts at gunpoint to take him to the tobacco barn, Corbett and the other soldiers arrayed themselves around the perimeter with "each man cautioned to see that no one escaped." Baker demanded that Booth and Herold give themselves up, and Herold eventually complied while Booth refused with "much defiant language."

Corbett stood near a crack between two boards. The gap was about the width of a hand, and he feared that as the sky was lightening, Booth could see, and shoot, the soldiers while remaining hidden from them in the dark of the barn. Better, he thought, to enter the barn and try to subdue Booth. He walked over to Doherty and offered to go after Booth alone. If the actor shot him, Corbett argued, the other soldiers could overwhelm the assassin before he had a chance to reload. (Corbett was unaware that Booth had a seven-shot carbine and several revolvers.) Doherty rejected Corbett's suggestion, and the sergeant moved back to his position along one side of the tobacco barn. A few minutes later, Conger came from around the front of the building and past Corbett to the rear, where he began igniting clumps of hay and slipping them through the cracks in the wall, hoping to burn Booth out. The actor hobbled to the flames, assessing whether he could put out the fire.

"While he was advancing toward the fire he came very near to where I was standing and I took aim on him with my revolver, keeping my eye on his movements," Corbett later said. "I could have shot him very easily when he was so near but kept my fire reserved until I thought it was not safe to trust him any more." Booth hobbled back toward the front of the barn, Corbett watching through the wide cracks.

"I saw him in the act of stooping or springing, and concluded he was going to use his weapons."

Corbett raised his own gun in his right hand, steadied it on his left forearm, and fired.

7

CELEBRITY, AND INFAMY

Corbett's bullet hit Booth just below the left side of the skull, then traveled across the top of the neck and on out into the barn. Corbett would later note a sense of poetic, or cosmic, justice in that Lincoln and Booth were each shot around the same spot of the head. And the damage to Booth was no less severe than that to Lincoln: the bullet shattered vertebrae and severed the spinal cord, leaving Booth alive but paralyzed and in great pain.

As the flames spread with a fury, Doherty, several of his soldiers, and Conger rushed into the barn and carried the momentarily unconscious Booth to the grass outside. The fire grew so quickly that they soon moved the wounded assassin a second time, ultimately placing him on the Garretts' porch, his head on a thin, rolled-up mattress fetched from inside the house.

At first there was confusion about what had happened. Conger presumed Booth had shot himself, though Baker was certain he had not. "Lieutenant Doherty and the detective officers who were in front of the barn did not seem to know that I had shot him," Corbett said later. "I informed Lieutenant Doherty of the fact, showing him my pistol which bore evidence of the truth of my statement, which was also confirmed by the man placed at my right hand who saw it." Doherty, Baker, and Conger all questioned Corbett, who said he aimed at Booth's shoulder, hoping to wound the assassin, but either his aim slipped or Booth moved at the moment Corbett pulled the trigger. Doherty and the detectives' first statements after Booth's capture and death make no mention of Corbett having violated any orders, nor do they suggest that he should face disciplinary action for shooting Booth.[1]

Mortally wounded, Booth drifted in and out of lucidity. In a weak voice, he asked the detectives to "tell my mother I died for my country." He asked Baker to raise his paralyzed hands so he could see them, then mumbled, "Useless, useless." Doherty dispatched a soldier to find a doctor who, after a cursory exam, concluded Booth would live. A subsequent closer examination of the wound led to a change in prognosis. The actor, in fact, was dying, and quickly. The sun was low in the morning sky when Booth took a last, short breath.[2]

As Booth lay dying, the soldiers raced to save the rest of the Garretts' farm buildings. A small shed connected the burning tobacco barn to the

The capture and shooting of Booth in the barn at the Garrett farm.

Kimmell & Forster, courtesy of Library of Congress, Prints and Photographs Division (reproduction number LC-USZ62-4352)

corncrib and some other storage shelters, and as the flames raged the men dismantled the shed to contain the damage to the tobacco barn. The effort worked: the building in which Booth and Herold were found burned to the ground but the other buildings survived.

That job done, Doherty turned his attention to his men. They had left Washington two evenings before and had yet to sleep, and so far on this day they'd had nothing to eat. Doherty told Corbett to ride to some of the neighboring farms and try to find breakfast for the men. Corbett mounted up, but made a personal detour before carrying out his orders. "I rode off to a spot where I could be alone and pray, and when I had gone through my usual morning prayer, I asked the Lord in regard to the shooting. At once I was filled with praise, for I felt a clear consciousness that it was an act of duty in the sight of God."

In the months and years that followed, a number of versions of what Corbett said and did that morning emerged, some reliable, others less so. One often-noted detail is that Corbett professed Providence had guided his actions and the path of the bullet. Yet his initial statement, and those by Baker, Conger, and Doherty, don't mention Providence. Several of the later statements and testimonies do, but those details came long after the shooting itself, amid the swirl of rumor and conjecture and considerable lobbying over the reward money. Perhaps casting Corbett as an erratic zealot could tip the scales in favor of others. It's possible that Corbett had mentioned divine guidance during those first conversations with Doherty and the commanding officer dismissed such talk as just more religious fanaticism by Corbett, whom he knew well. But Baker and Conger had just met Corbett. Had the sergeant issued such an unusual proclamation of faith, it's hard to imagine the detectives leaving it out of their initial affidavits and reports. And if Corbett already believed God had guided his actions there at the tobacco barn, would he have then gone off to pray for some sort of affirmation that he had, in fact, done the right thing?

Believing his prayer for guidance had been answered, Corbett remounted his horse and began following his orders to forage for breakfast. He found supplies for about half of the men, and they finished their meal before Booth died. By then, the wrangling for credit—and a piece of the

$75,000 reward set aside for Booth and Herold—was already underway. Conger announced that he would take the contents of Booth's pockets back to Washington and present them to Colonel Baker, his boss and the man who had sent him and the colonel's nephew out with Doherty's men to find the fugitives. Using his handkerchief, Conger bundled up Booth's small pocket diary, its pages filled with the actor's pinched scrawl, some bills of exchange on banks in Canada, and a compass flecked with small bits of wax as though it had been used at night and illuminated by a dripping candle. He picked Corbett to ride with him, and they set off to the north, retracing their path to the Potomac, where they waded their horses into the river and flagged down a passing steamship, the *Keyport*, with a single gunshot. The ship's captain dispatched a small tender boat to fetch Conger from the shallows near the riverbank, and once the boat started back for the steamship, Corbett returned to shore. Leading Conger's horse, he rode off to the ferry dock where the *John S. Ide* was awaiting the arrival of Doherty and the rest of the troops, the prisoner Herold, and Booth's body.

At Garrett's farm, Doherty sewed a horse blanket around Booth's body as a shroud. He commandeered a wagon from one of Garrett's neighbors, a black farmer, and the men loaded Booth for the trip to the Rappahannock and then on to the Potomac. Baker took off first with the body, two cavalrymen, and Jett, still held as a prisoner. The rest of the troops, with Herold as their captive, caught up with them at Port Royal, where they encountered the same logistical issue they faced on the pursuit: moving that many horses and men across the Rappahannock would take several trips and several hours.

Baker and the wagon carrying Booth's body crossed the river first. After the second load of men and horses reached the north bank, Baker, tired of waiting and anxious to get his prize back to Washington, sent word to Doherty that rather than waiting he would start off and the faster cavalry could catch up with him. Doherty was incensed. On the next crossing, he dispatched one of his men to catch up with Baker and pass along Doherty's order that the detective was to wait for the rest of the squadron. Baker, who was not under Doherty's command, replied that, given the wagon's slow progress, Doherty should be able to catch up before Baker reached the

Belle Plain ferry dock on the Potomac, and the *John S. Ide*. But then "by a mistake of the negro [wagon owner], we made the creek about three miles above the Landing," well off the mark and with no easy way to move the wagon along the river to the ferry landing.

Because of the wrong turn, Doherty and his men reached Belle Plain before Baker, which sent a jolt of fear and anger through Doherty: Where was the body? Doherty was about to seek permission from his superiors for a special detachment to go find Baker when the detective rode up alone on horseback and explained the problem. They dispatched a small boat down the river to retrieve the body, and a short time later, all, including Corbett, were loaded aboard the *John S. Ide* and steaming for Washington. All except Jett, who had escaped from Baker during the ride.

Conger, meanwhile, reached Washington and Colonel Baker's office; he and the colonel went to see Stanton, the war secretary. It had been a frustrating twelve days, and newspapers were beginning to openly mock the search. How hard could it be to find a man with a broken leg in the Maryland countryside? Stanton was napping when they burst into his house, Colonel Baker shouting out, "We have got Booth!" Stanton covered his eyes with his hands for a moment, not moving, as though trying to compose himself, then slowly rose from the sofa and put on his coat as Colonel Baker laid out on a table the cache of Booth's possessions that Conger had brought as proof. Conger told Stanton what had happened, that Booth was dead and Herold alive, and the body and the prisoner were en route to Washington aboard the *John S. Ide*. Stanton ordered his aide, Major Thomas Eckert, and Colonel Baker to steam down the river on a gunboat to meet the *John S. Ide* and move the body and prisoners to the ironclad *Montauk*, at anchor off the Navy Yard.[3]

Over the next couple of days Corbett, Doherty, Conger, the younger Baker, Herold, and others were interrogated aboard the *Montauk* as an autopsy determined that the dead man was indeed Booth. The face was his, the tattooed initials on the back of his hand were his, the broken leg matched the injury Mudd had treated, the papers confiscated from the pockets were his, and Herold identified the man shot in the tobacco barn as Booth.

There was no question: the assassin was dead.

As the man who killed the man who killed Lincoln, Boston Corbett found himself cast in an unaccustomed role: celebrity. Newspapers had closely followed the search for Booth, and after his death they tracked the transport of the body, the autopsy, and the burial. (Though Baker conducted a charade of sinking the body with weights in the Potomac, the remains were secretly buried at the Old Arsenal at Greenleaf's Point to avoid sympathizers using the corpse for propaganda purposes.) Most of the spotlight, though, swung to the surviving suspected conspirators, led by Herold, Powell, Atzerodt, Mary Surratt, and Mudd. But the newspapers also wrote about Corbett, the odd little "Glory to God man" who had avenged the martyred Lincoln.

"He has been greatly lionized, and, on the street, was repeatedly surrounded by citizens who manifested their appreciation of his services by loud cheers," the Associated Press reported in a widely reprinted article from Washington the day after Booth's death. The wire service also reported that Corbett "is said to be a man of deep religious feeling, who has at prayer meetings, lately, prayed fervently that the assassin of the late President might be brought to justice."

On April 28, the *New York Herald* published a short story detailing Corbett's birth in England, immigration as a child, his work as a hatter, and his conversion and baptism, along with the assumption of the name Boston. "His religious faith would in the present age almost be called fanaticism," the paper reported. "On Friday night he visited McKendry [*sic*] chapel and prayed with great earnestness that God would not lay innocent blood to our charge, but bring the guilty to punishment. He feels assured that Booth was delivered into his hands in answer to his prayers. He appears a very intelligent young man, and, aside from a most reserve [*sic*], converses with much intelligence and interest."[4]

The *New York Tribune* described Corbett as "modest as he is devoted" to his religion, "and his Lieutenant pronounced him a most worthy soldier." The paper reported that the government offered Corbett one of Booth's pistols as a memento "but he declined it, saying he desired no reminder of the sad duty he has performed, and desired to have it banished from his mind as soon as possible."[5]

Someone also offered Corbett cash for the gun he used to kill Booth, an overture he rejected. It wasn't his gun to sell, he said; it belonged to the government (though someone stole the gun shortly afterward and it remains unaccounted for). Reporters also asked Corbett whether he thought he

Sergeant Boston Corbett, left, and Lieutenant Edward Doherty.

Courtesy of National Archives, Washington, DC (record group 111: Records of the Office of the Chief Signal Officer, 1860–1985; series: Mathew Brady Photographs of Civil War-Era Personalities and Scenes, 1921–1940)

deserved a share of the reward money that had been offered, $50,000 for Booth and $25,000 for Herold. Corbett replied that he had acted as a function of his duty, so no, he didn't deserve part of the reward—a position he would soon reverse. But he said he would like to keep his cavalry-issued pony. And he accepted an invitation by photographer Mathew Brady to visit his studio, where he posed for several portraits, alone as well as in a dual scene with Doherty. The latter is an odd photo, with both men in uniform, Corbett on the left and Doherty on the right. Each leans on a sheathed sword and gazes off into the distance as though looking past each other; Corbett, in knee-high riding boots, is by far the slighter of the two men, barely coming up to Doherty's nose.

Corbett seemed to reap some social rewards from the spotlight. He stayed for a time at the Clarendon Hotel in Washington, though it's unclear who picked up the tab. Byron Johnson, his friend from the Christian Commission, brought him home for dinner a few days after Booth's death, and Corbett's presence attracted a crowd on the street outside Johnson's house. In his memoir of Corbett and Lincoln, Johnson wrote of a meeting among Stanton, Doherty, an unidentified newspaper reporter, and himself in which Stanton absolved Corbett of any official sanctions stemming from the killing. "The rebel is dead, the patriot lives," Johnson quoted Stanton as saying. "He has saved us continued excitement, delay, and expense. The patriot is released." The problem is, no other source mentions such a meeting, and if a newspaper reporter had been a witness, he didn't appear to have written about it, which seems unlikely. It's doubtful the meeting happened, and Johnson's memoir, which came out a half-century later, is just another part of the lore.[6]

The newspaper articles in the weeks after Booth's death seemed to have captured the essence of the cavalryman, albeit thinly crafted and peppered with wrong details. Reporters depicted him as a simple and humble man devoted—perhaps excessively so—to his faith, a man who had eccentricities but who also did his duty at the moment it mattered and avenged Lincoln's murder. Over the next few months, though, darker themes would slip in as the jockeying increased for the reward money. There were insinuations that Corbett had acted willfully and against orders when he shot Booth. (Not true; no orders were issued on whether Booth should be taken alive.) That

Corbett had credited "Providence" with guiding his hand and the bullet. That Corbett was crazy. And so the legend of Boston Corbett began to spread.

Booth's body was barely in the ground when claims for the reward money began filtering in. Corbett wrote his on May 6 to Secretary of War Stanton, apparently as part of a passel of correspondence Doherty coordinated among his men who were directly involved in the pursuit of Booth and Herold. Later critics saw that as an act of self-interest by Doherty, but it seems like the role one would expect of a commanding officer looking out for his men. Doherty would eventually compete with Conger and Baker over credit and, ultimately, a share of the reward, but he never downplayed the role of his men, other than to feed the public perception that Corbett was somehow mentally unbalanced.

In his letter, Corbett struck a gracious tone and complimented all who were involved in the pursuit and killing of Booth and the capture of Herold. He didn't hold himself up for any special consideration and told Stanton he was putting "in my claim for any portion of the reward . . . that it may seem right for me to receive."[7]

I do not put forward this regardless of the rightful claims of others for I am aware that I am only one of 26 enlisted men who were engaged in the capture of the criminal, and my own commanding officer on the occasion I place before all others. There were also the boat crew of the government steam tug *John S. Ide*, who conveyed us safely to Belle Plains, and also sent a small boat ashore to carry the detective officer [Conger] to a steamboat (*Keyport*) by which means he was enabled to reach Washington ahead of the party—bringing the news. And their Captain Henry Wilson of the *J. S. Ide* brought us and the body of Booth, and the live prisoner Harrold [*sic*] to Washington for which services I think all are entitled to share the reward. But as their accompanying letter will better explain to you my own position than I could otherwise do, I hope sir it may meet your approval.

Stanton already knew how the chase had unfolded. Doherty had sub-mitted his formal report as the officer leading the detachment within two days of returning to Washington, preceding it with copies of the orders he received. He detailed the events in matter-of-fact tones, weighting the language a bit to give himself the pivotal role in the hunt. The wording presaged arguments to come. Doherty had been ordered by his commander to assemble twenty-five men and report to L. C. Baker, "special agent, War Department," for an assignment. Baker had separately summoned Conger and his own nephew, Byron Baker, and determined to have the three men pursue the lead about Booth and Herold having been spotted crossing the Rappahannock. Yet the orders lacked specificity about who was in charge. And each man at different times asserted authority and decision making that was obeyed by the others. Within the moment, the arrangement worked. The detachment of soldiers and two detectives covered a remarkable amount of ground, without sleep, and ultimately cornered Booth and Herold.

Corbett's statement reflected the hierarchy of the military and his pre-sumption that Doherty was in charge. Doherty's statement seems to agree. Yet Conger later intimated that he was specially deployed by Colonel Baker to get Booth, with the aid of the soldiers, as did Byron Baker, saying he had "commenced the pursuit of Booth a week ago . . . under the direction of Colonel Baker." Those conflicting visions of their personal roles in the ultimately successful capture of Herold and the killing of Booth would spin off into their own long-running tale of intrigue, one that would slow the doling out of the reward money and eventually involve competing factions within the House of Representatives.

With the suspected conspirators in custody, President Johnson had to figure out what to do with them. A trial, obviously, but what kind? Was it a case for the civilian criminal courts? Or since the commander in chief had been assassinated at the tail end of a brutal war, should a military commission handle the trial? Security entered into it, too. The administration distrusted the Rebels—Johnson and others incorrectly placed Jefferson Davis, the embattled president of the Confederacy, at the top of the conspiracy to kill Lincoln. It wasn't beyond imagination that loyal separatists might try to rescue the conspirators. Stanton, the war secretary who oversaw the search for Booth, viewed the assassination as a war crime, and Johnson found his argument persuasive.

On May 1, five days after Corbett shot Booth, Johnson issued a special order that the conspirators' fate be determined by a military tribunal of nine "competent officers" who would oversee a trial in which Judge Advocate General Joseph Holt would serve as prosecutor. They didn't dally; the trial opened with an introductory session by the commission on May 9, eight days after Johnson's order and less than a month after Lincoln's assassination. The accused were arraigned May 10 and testimony began May 12. Though the nation followed developments through newspapers, secrecy shrouded the specifics of the trial. At the end of each day Holt decided which portions of the testimony could be distributed, and the courtroom journalists filed their reports under the constraints of a military censor. It was a remarkable usurpation of constitutional protections, though consistent with Lincoln's suspension of habeas corpus and other civil rights— even though the war was now over.

The eight accused conspirators were held in third-floor cells in an old penitentiary at the US arsenal on Greenleaf's Point, at the confluence of the Potomac and Anacostia Rivers. This junction forms the southernmost point of the broken-diamond-shaped District of Columbia. With the outbreak of the war, the government had decided to expand the Navy Yard and absorbed the penitentiary, sending the existing prisoners off to another penal complex in Albany, New York. Given the secretive nature of the trial and the security concerns, the government decided to hear the evidence in the same building, so it carved the courtroom out of open space in the northeast corner of the penitentiary's third floor, just feet from where the prisoners were being held, their ankles and wrists manacled even while in their cells. Powell and Atzerodt, the two largest men, had the added encumbrance when they were taken to court of large iron balls chained to their legs, carried by soldiers as though they were personal valets. While in their cells, each of the men had a heavy canvas bag over his head to preclude him from seeing or communicating with the other prisoners, a precaution ordered by Stanton. Powell's head bag carried extra padding, added after he tried to kill himself by banging his head against his cell wall. In a nod to her gender, Surratt was allowed to go without the head covering, though she remained as tightly manacled as the men.[8]

The courtroom was outfitted specially for the trial. The spare, intimidating space measured about thirty feet by forty-five feet. Four high windows covered by iron grates opened on one wall. The room had been freshly whitewashed; new gas-jet stanchions ensured even lighting. The members of the commission sat at a long table with their backs to the windowed wall, facing the witness chair and, beyond, the table of newspaper reporters. Holt, the judge advocate general, sat at the end of the commission's table facing two tables for the defendants' lawyers. The defendants themselves sat, interspersed with military guards, in a specially built prisoner's dock filling the wide wall, perpendicular to the commission's table, elevated one foot above the floor and separated from the room by a wooden rail.

The prisoners for the most part did not impress some of those who attended the trial. Though Surratt, "a belle in her youth," had "rather pleasing features," and the burly Powell "was very tall, with an athletic, gladiatorial frame, the tight knit shirt which was his only upper garment disclosing the massive robustness of animal manhood," the latter was said to display "neither intellect nor intelligence . . . in his unflinching dark gray eyes." Herold was "a doltish, insignificant-looking young man" and Atzerodt "a short, thick-set, round-shouldered, brawny-armed man, with a stupid expression." Another observer described Atzerodt as "a vulgar-looking creature, but not apparently ferocious. . . . He is just the sort of man to promise to commit a murder and then fail on coming to the point."[9] To Horatio Nelson Taft, a US Patent Office examiner who kept a fairly detailed diary of the war years in Washington, Mudd stood out as "the most inoffensive and decent in appearance of all the defendants," while Ford's Theatre stagehand Ned Spangler had "an unintelligent-looking face, evidently swollen by intemperate use of ardent spirits . . . and anxious-looking gray eyes." On the other hand, Arnold, one of Booth's school chums, "had a rather intelligent face, with curly brown hair and restless dark eyes." O'Laughlen, the other schoolmate conspirator, "was a rather small, delicate-looking man, with rather pleasing features, uneasy black eyes, bushy black hair, a heavy black mustache and imperial, and a most anxious expression of countenance shaded by a sad, remorseful look."[10]

Despite the military censor, the trial allowed space for a certain number of daily watchers. Taft went to the Navy Yard on the morning of May 22 "and visited the Military Court in session there trying the conspirators. I had a fair opportunity to view the prisoners who all sat on a raised platform which ran across one side of the room. The room was not very large perhaps 25 or 30 feet square. There was nothing very striking about any of the prisoners excepting [Powell], the one who attacked Mr. Seward. He is a splendid specimen of a man, 6 feet 1½ inches, but his countenance indicated the desperado which he probably is. Herold looks rather weak minded or silly. Atzerodt like a low villain. Spangler has an Italian look. Dr Mudd is a very ordinary looking man with red hair or (rather Sandy hair and beard). Sam Arnold does not look like a bad man. [O'Laughlen] might be one. Mrs. Suratt sat at the end of the row by herself draped in deep black and veiled. Genl Hancock was there as a spectator."[11]

Corbett played a bit role in the trial. One of 450 witnesses called, he was subpoenaed to testify on May 17, a Saturday, about the capture of Herold and the killing of Booth. Because of the order in which the prosecutor presented the case and the evidence, Corbett followed Conger on the stand, and in turn was succeeded by John Fletcher, the livery man who had chased Herold as far as the Navy Yard bridge the night Lincoln was killed. Corbett took his place in the witness chair facing the tribunal, with the array of defendants to his left. Holt told Corbett that Conger had testified about the pursuit and there was no need to duplicate that. What the court wanted to know, he said, was what happened once the soldiers arrived at Garrett's farm.

Corbett laid out the story, beginning with Doherty ordering him to deploy the cavalrymen around the house to ensure no one fled, the shift of focus to the tobacco barn, the discussions among Booth, Doherty, and the detectives, and the actor's refusal to give himself up. Corbett described the snatches of conversation he overheard between Booth and Herold from inside the barn, and Herold's emergence, then Conger's igniting the back wall and Booth's movements inside, which Corbett watched through the wide gap between the wall planks. Then, Corbett testified, Booth raised his rifle and "I supposed he was going to fight his way out. . . . My mind was upon him tentatively to see that he did no harm. And when I became impressed that it was time, I shot him."[12]

The trial continued on through June 27, when the last of the witnesses finished. Three days later, the military commission returned its verdict. Seven of the eight defendants were convicted of being part of the conspiracy; one, Edmund Spangler, who had arranged to have Booth's horse waiting for him outside Ford's Theatre, was convicted of helping the assassin escape. (The historical record raises some doubt about whether Spangler was a witting accomplice.)

Four of the defendants—David Herold, Lewis Powell, George Atzerodt, and Mary Surratt—were sentenced to hang. The rest were sent to prison for sentences of varying durations. On July 7, in front of a large crowd on the penitentiary grounds, the four condemned conspirators were simultaneously dropped at the end of thick ropes through the trapdoors of a gallows specially built for the occasion.

By then, Corbett was back in the hospital.

Corbett's celebrity life had its dark undercurrents. Some condemned him for acting in what they presumed to be haste and against orders to take Booth alive—orders that didn't exist. Because of the secretive methods the government used to bury Booth, doubts were raised about whether Corbett had, in fact, shot Booth, doubts that would grow and echo over the years.[13]

For some of the backers of the South, Booth's assassination of Lincoln had been a dramatic and welcome extraction of revenge for the devastated Confederacy, with its economy in shambles, its workforce—former slaves—now free, and with no clear sense of the future. Booth became a martyr and Corbett a pariah. Southern sympathizers sent letters threatening to kill Corbett. He kept a gun nearby at all times, ready to defend himself should

The Lincoln conspirators moments after they were hanged on July 7, 1865.

Alexander Gardner, courtesy of Library of Congress, Prints and Photographs Division (reproduction number LC-DIG-cwpb-04230)

any of the mailed threats to avenge the death of Booth turn out to be real. In early May, rumors swirled that Booth had been avenged with the gunning down of Corbett at the Relay House, a rail stop near Baltimore, which caused a stir until Corbett proved to be quite alive—if not healthy.

The threats, usually anonymous, stayed with Corbett and left him edgy. On May 21, four days after Corbett testified against the conspirators, he and other members of the Sixteenth New York Cavalry were dispatched to Bladensburg just east of Washington "in haste to make some arrests. We returned from the scout pretty late in the evening and thoroughly wet through from a heavy rain and fording a stream." They dropped the arrested men at the Central Guardhouse, then rode on to the K Street Stables—the Sixteenth was assigned to one half of the horse barn; the 243rd Company of the Veteran Reserve Corps Cavalry used the other half—to feed their horses.

Having not eaten, Corbett and his comrades went to the Soldiers Rest on G Street to eat supper, and when they returned to the stable received some good news: another unit would cover the remainder of the night patrol.[14]

Corbett looked around for a place at the stable to sleep. Ever since his ordeal in Andersonville prison his health had remained fragile, and he feared sleeping on the cold, wet stable ground would exacerbate his illnesses. "I looked for a dry spot to lie down in" but found nothing suitable in the Sixteenth Cavalry end of the stable. So he walked down the open central area, passing stalls on the left and the right, and crossed the midway point, an invisible dividing line between the two cavalries, and apparently into an area from which soldiers were barred. Quartermaster Sergeant P. L. Mason, on watch at the stable for the 243rd Company, hailed Corbett and asked what he was doing. Corbett told him he was part of the Sixteenth patrol, and Mason replied that "your patrol is not in that direction," and offered to lead him to the stables assigned to the Sixteenth Cavalry. Corbett said he knew where his comrades were, and Mason turned his attention to another matter. Corbett, though, kept going, unnoticed by Mason. He stopped when he found a stall with a suitably thick stack of hay to insulate him from the cold, damp ground, stretched out, and covered himself with his overcoat.

Mason, who had stepped out of the stable presuming Corbett had left, circled back and saw the mound on the hay. He rousted Corbett, repeated that the patrol wasn't in that part of the barn, and accused Corbett of lying to him about being attached to the Sixteenth. Corbett, by then on his feet, bristled. "I haven't told a lie in seven years," Corbett said, referring to the day he was baptized in Boston. Mason grabbed Corbett by the shoulder to escort him out, telling him, "It's best you get out of the stable." Corbett didn't react for several seconds, then pulled his revolver from his pocket and pointed it at the sergeant's chest. He told Mason in a quiet voice to remove his hand. Mason stepped back a few paces, then went to rouse fellow soldier Private A. W. Johnson, who was sleeping in the granary, as a backup.

Corbett left. Mason later testified that Corbett, when Mason accused him of lying, said, "What is that you say, young man? Do you know who you are talking to? I am the man that shot Booth." Corbett, though, denied invoking Booth's name. Regardless, Mason complained to his superior officers.

Corbett was summoned for a court-martial on June 3, which was postponed until June 22 because Corbett's illness had sent him to the hospital. The hearing stretched over two days, with Corbett cross-examining the prosecution's witnesses himself. The charges were "conduct prejudicial to good order and military discipline," "forc[ing] a guard post," violating orders by entering the off-limits section of the stable, and pointing his loaded revolver at Mason. He was found guilty only of pointing the gun at Mason and sentenced to a reprimand by his regimental commander during "general orders" before his comrades. "The court is thus lenient in view of the excellent character given the accused by his commanding officers," the court said, "and also in view of the extenuating circumstances." Presumably, the circumstances were Corbett's health, his quest to find a dry place to sleep, and his fame.

That fame had drawn a steady stream of visitors to Corbett, some seeking autographs, others just wanting to hear from Corbett's own lips what had happened at Garrett's farm that night and what Booth's last moments were like. Some of those who looked Corbett up were old friends, including Richard Thatcher, the young drummer from the 111th Regiment of the Illinois infantry whom Corbett had befriended at Andersonville. After Thatcher was released (he later asserted that he escaped but apparently was part of a swap), he joined up with Sherman's army and stayed on through the March to Savannah and the war-ending victory in the Carolinas. By mid-May he was in Washington and soon caught up with Corbett. "I spent a full day with him in his regimental quarters. But it took only a few moments for the 'avenger of the great Lincoln' to satisfy my curiosity with the simple narrative of the details of the tragic shot that ended the life of John Wilkes Booth." They swapped stories of their time since each left Andersonville, and Thatcher noted that Corbett's health still seemed precarious. Yet Corbett's religious faith was unflagging. "Amidst all these dire disasters, Corbett never despaired for a moment of his life."[15]

Thatcher had come to Washington with Sherman's army to take part in a national celebration. With the war over and the conspirators on trial at the Navy Yard, three of the main Union military divisions—the Army of the Potomac, the Army of the Tennessee, and the Army of Georgia—descended on Washington for the Grand Review of the Armies, held May 23 and 24.

The Army of the Potomac, to which Corbett's Sixteenth New York Cavalry was attached, had been based just over the Potomac River in Virginia, so had little distance to travel. But Sherman had marched sixty thousand members of the Army of the Tennessee and the Army of Georgia 250 miles from their final victorious campaign in the Carolinas to take part in the review, which preceded the dismantling of the armies just a few weeks later.

After the deprivations and fears of the war and the assassination of Lincoln, the Grand Review was something of a communal catharsis for the city and the soldiers. Washington's streets and taverns were filled with celebrants. Train schedules were doubled, overland routes were jammed, and steamships made their way to the Potomac River landings. "It is estimated that each train since yesterday morning has brought in over one thousand passengers. Three hundred is the average number on ordinary occasions," the *Evening Star* reported. "Such a concourse never assembled before in Washington. Thousands were turned away from the hotels, and hundreds spent the night in the open air; and at sunrise this morning occupied points along the [Pennsylvania] avenue, commanding favorable views of the column."[16] Workmen erected a viewing stand outside the White House, at the edge of Pennsylvania Avenue, where President Johnson, General Grant, and other top Union officials watched the pageantry; another stand on the opposite side of the street was reserved for wounded soldiers and newspaper reporters. Two public viewing stands cropped up to the east. Most viewers, though, crowded the sidewalks and open spaces along the route that stretched from Capitol Hill to the White House, with cavalrymen shutting off intersections to keep horse and carriage traffic from interfering with the marchers.

And then they came, tens of thousands of people, mostly soldiers, some in units in tight drill formation, others slipping into the revelry of winning, and surviving, a four-year-long war. Corbett's Sixteenth New York Cavalry was based at Lincoln Barracks, about a mile east of the Capitol, and took part in the first day parade, which the patent examiner Taft recorded on May 24 in his diary:

> There was a great deal of prancing and dashing to and fro of officers on the Avenue. The Sidewalks, the Doors, and windows and the House

tops were crowded with spectators who were cheering constantly as some favorite officer or Regt was passing but more than all when some of the "Colors" blackened and tattered and hanging in shreds from the Staff was held aloft by the proud color bearers. The Artillery of each Division followed in the rear. In Shermans Army hundreds of negroes with axes and shovels on their shoulders marched after each Corps. In the rear of all came the "Bummers" or foragers, without any pretension to order but gave on[e] something of an idea of a Caravan of the Desert, only there were no Camels. They were black and white. Many mounted, mostly on mules, some on Jacks, and a few on poneys. Others walking, leading their mules which were loaded down with every conceivable thing in the way of baggage or cooking utensil. Huge bags and Bundles tied on and across the back of the beast. I wondered whether the contents of some of those bags might not have once graced some of the palatial Mansion[s] at the south, or even the persons of some of the fair dames of the "Palmetto State." Besides this kind of loading there were living specimens of the country which the Army had passed through in the form of cats and dogs, Coons, oppossums, fighting Cocks and other fowls, all perched on the backs of the mules (or rather on the bags and bundles). Then the frying pans, the kettles, the buckets, and tin dishes garnished the sides hanging nearly to the ground. These were the camp followers, the "Bummers," and numbered hundreds. Some females rode in the Review yesterday and today who I was told had been "through the War." Some officers and soldiers wives and some "Daughters of the Regiment," who had followed their Brothers or Fathers or husbands, and shared their dangers, taking care of the wounded, and nursing the sick.[17]

The females included Clara Barton, whose aid to the wounded during the war was already the stuff of legend. Taft, who knew Barton, described her as "highly educated and refined, and few ladies ar[e] as inteligent as She is."

Two days later, Corbett was overcome with a crippling bout of diarrhea and went on "sick report," apparently remaining off duty at the barracks and under the care of the regimental surgeon at least through late June.[18]

While he was recovering, Corbett met a young man from Indiana, George A. Huron, who had spent most of the war as a sergeant, then quartermaster sergeant, for the Seventh Regiment of the Indiana Infantry, which took him through some of the more brutal battles of the war. He mustered out in October 1864 but stayed connected with the Union army as a "sanitary agent" for the Army of the Potomac, stationed at City Point, Virginia, the base point for the Siege of Petersburg, which in effect was the tightening noose that helped force Lee's surrender at Appomattox Court House.

With the war's end, Huron migrated to Washington, like many soldiers without a farm to return to, uncertain what his future would be. Having just turned twenty-seven years old, he began making the rounds of different offices looking for an appointment, which he eventually found in December as an auditor's clerk at the Treasury Department. Over the next few years, Huron also studied law at the newly formed Columbian College law school; he was part of its second graduating class in 1868. (It later became George Washington University Law School.) It's uncertain how Huron first met Corbett, but the two ran into each other at different points while they were both in the capital. Huron didn't share Corbett's ecstatic embrace of faith, the common thread coursing through most of Corbett's friendships, but he found Corbett memorable, no doubt in part due to the "Glory to God man's" celebrity as the killer of Booth. The relationship ended with Huron's departure from Washington, law degree in hand, to open a practice in Valley Falls, Kansas, about twenty-five miles northeast of Topeka. But their paths would cross again more than twenty years later.[19]

In the following weeks, the health of the "avenger of Lincoln" took a turn for the worse. He had been under the care of the regimental doctor, but in July, Surgeon General Joseph Barnes ordered Corbett to the 2,575-bed Lincoln United States General Hospital, adjoining the Lincoln Barracks and more commonly called the Lincoln Hospital. The hospital was mostly a series of log-and-canvas-walled structures connected by open-sided walkways, with fourteen-foot ceilings and a window placed between each of the sixty or so beds in each of the buildings. Though open dormitory-style for the patients, each structure had four rooms at one end for the baths, sinks, nurses, and clothing storage.[20]

Now that the fighting was over and the troops were mustering out, Washington sought to move quickly from war footing to something close to normalcy. Military camps began closing as the soldiers left for home, and the Lincoln Hospital shut down shortly after Corbett was admitted. He was transferred to the Armory Square Hospital at the edge of the National Mall, which closed shortly afterward as well, sending Corbett on to the Douglas Hospital at New Jersey Avenue and I Street.

On August 17, Corbett's service in the US Army came to an end. He had signed up on four different occasions and was in uniform just three months short of four years, including nearly five months as a prisoner of war. In the end, he was released because of his health: military doctors recommended he return to New York City to get away from the fetid summer atmosphere in Washington. "One of the doctors told me the sooner I could get back to New York the better for me, as fever was one of my complaints," Corbett wrote in 1880 as part of a pension application. "The climate of New York was better for me than Washington."[21]

Yet Corbett couldn't leave right away. On July 29, while still a patient at Lincoln Hospital, a subpoena had arrived ordering him to appear as a witness at the trial of Henry Wirz, accused of war crimes over his management of the Andersonville prison.[22]

Much like the trial of the Lincoln conspirators, the case against Wirz was more about extracting revenge than seeking justice. Wirz was born in Switzerland in 1823 and, abandoning a wife, immigrated to the United States in 1849—fleeing, according to most accounts, unspecified legal trouble in his home country. He worked as a weaver in Massachusetts before moving in 1854 to Kentucky, where he studied medicine and married a widow with two young daughters. In 1856, Wirz moved the family to Louisiana, where he tried to establish a practice as a homeopathic physician. When the war broke out he enlisted in the Confederate army and slid into a bureaucratic role assisting General John H. Winder with tracking captured Union soldiers.

Wirz advanced quickly, overseeing prisoners of war in Alabama and Virginia before being transferred in March 1864—four months before Corbett arrived—to Andersonville. The rudimentary prison was already filled far past capacity. Records indicate Wirz and other prison officials complained about the continued influx of prisoners, but as the commander of the facility at its peak and at its closure, Wirz became synonymous with the crimes against humanity that occurred within the stockade. Federal troops arrested him on May 6, 1865, two days after the prison closed, then ferried him to Washington.[23]

The Wirz trial began on August 23 and featured a steady parade of witnesses describing the atrocious conditions at Andersonville. Corbett was near the head of the parade, taking the stand on August 28. He detailed what he had seen and experienced. The undrinkable water and lack of food and medicine. The ground teeming with maggots. Men shot by guards for straying over the deadline, and other men dying from illness and injuries, their wounds filled with bugs and pus. And Corbett testified about the day he escaped, and the dogs that hunted him down but didn't attack him. "I believe that the only reason why the hound did not tear me was because the same power kept him from doing it that kept the lions from tearing Daniel—that God in whom I trusted. Undoubtedly the hound did smell me when he rubbed his nose against me, and I believe the Almighty prevented him from biting me."[24]

Yet Corbett notably never witnessed Wirz committing or commanding an atrocity, so his evidence was of limited use. But then, Wirz's guilt was a forgone conclusion.

Corbett's last commitment to the government over, he packed up and left Washington. On October 18, the military tribunal convicted Wirz of acting "in violation of the principals of war" and he was hanged November 10 at the Old Capitol Prison, site of the present-day US Supreme Court building. By the time Wirz died, Corbett had already resumed his life in Manhattan: attending prayer meetings, preaching, and trying to save the souls of sinners.

8

Citizen Corbett, Preacher

Before he went off to fight and during his brief returns to New York, Boston Corbett had rented a room at 91 Attorney Street in lower Manhattan. With the war behind him, Corbett returned to the same address, and to his old routine. Pursuing the same kind of work he had left four years earlier as a finisher of silk hats in James H. Brown's shop, Corbett went to work for Nicholas Espenshied at 118 Nassau Street, later for Robert Beck on Fulton Street in Brooklyn, and then on to a few other shops. At one point, Corbett went to Boston to work, but he returned to New York; when he left the Attorney Street address, it was to move to 192 Rivington Street, just around the corner.

Despite his war experiences, Corbett was essentially the same man he had been when he left New York.

In mid-September 1865, the *New York Observer*, which focused on religious news, reported that Corbett had returned to the daily prayer meeting at which "he was regular in attendance before the war, and during the progress of it he has occasionally been present. He led in prayer, and afterwards remarked that he was glad to return to this place of prayer." Corbett apparently was circumspect about his ill health and recent hospital stays. "He has been wonderfully preserved through the war, and he thanked God for it. He had been where the bullets flew swift and thick about him, but they had no power to harm him." Corbett's stay at Andersonville and its "horrors" were touched on, as well. "He had always felt, in war and everywhere, that God was his protector. He had performed his duty to his country to the best of his ability and had been honorably discharged, and was now determined, more than ever, to devote himself to the cause of his Saviour. He related several touching incidents in army life."[1]

Now a celebrity—a national hero in the eyes of many; an avenging devil to others—Corbett received regular invitations to speak before other religious gatherings, and incremental changes in his life were reported in the nation's newspapers. Fans wrote to him seeking autographs, and some sought Corbett's personal recollection of the killing of Booth, seemingly with an eye toward procuring a memento they might be able to sell.

But the mail also continued to bring occasional death threats. And as conspiracy theories grew that Booth was, in fact, still alive and that Corbett had killed a stand-in, Corbett found himself defending his actions that day—and, in his mind, defending his honor, for if the dead man at Garrett's farm wasn't Booth, then Corbett was a liar. Corbett would be dogged by the conspiracy theorists, and the suspicions, for the rest of his life.[2]

He was still plagued, as well, by the ravages of his incarceration; he was often overcome with debilitating intestinal problems. "He was much emaciated, pale and weak, and appeared very much broken in health," noted Thomas Brown, a friend who also lived at the Rivington Street address. "[He] had the appearance, of many other Andersonville prisoners, his skin was yellow and of a smoked appearance." He also was suffering from scurvy and rheumatism. "During all this time I was a great sufferer, yet I had to work enough to earn my bread, although I was wholly unfit to do so," Corbett wrote years later. But the faith that Corbett believed once protected him during battle and the torturous conditions at Andersonville propelled him still.[3]

Corbett slipped back into the religious world with ease. He became active in the Young Men's Christian Union, stepping forward as an inspirational speaker when needed.[4] He went out alone, or with fellow evangelists, to spread the Word of God, with mixed results. Edward Kirk, a fellow veteran of the Twelfth New York State Militia, visited New York after the war and stumbled across Corbett as "he was preaching temperance and religion to a crowd on a Sunday morning on a pile of ship timber in a shipyard on the East River. . . . He saw me and at once, excused himself, and joined me and my little daughter on an adjoining pile of timber. We had a long talk about the shooting, and in answer to my criticism as [to] the propriety of his act, he said, 'God commanded me to, and it was necessary to save the lives of some of my comrades.'" The former soldiers spent a half-hour catching up before Kirk and his daughter left and Corbett returned to his preaching.[5]

In Washington, the reward money promised for the capture of Booth was drawing a small flood of applicants. To bring some order to the process, the War Department announced on November 24 that those who felt they were entitled to a share of the money needed to file a claim by the end of the year. A special panel headed by Joseph Holt, the judge advocate general, would weigh the claims and the details of the capture and recommend who would receive what share of the money. It was to be a difficult decision, involving rewards for Booth ($50,000) and Herold ($25,000) as well as separate cash offers for the captures of Lewis Powell ($10,000) and George Atzerodt ($25,000). It seemed that anyone who had an even tenuous connection to those events tossed in claims as though buying a lottery ticket. Several members of the Sixteenth New York Cavalry who were deployed elsewhere that day and uninvolved with the capture sent in claims, hoping that mere membership in the unit was enough to warrant a piece of the prize.[6]

Corbett had filed his claim on May 6, 1865. Doherty wasn't far behind, submitting his on May 9; he also arranged for that series of affidavits by his men detailing the actions leading up to Booth's death and Herold's capture.

The bulk of the supporting affidavits were submitted over the last few days of May 1865. They vary in depth of detail but are unequivocal that Doherty was commanding the troops during the sixty hours the cavalry pursued Booth and Herold. Several of the affidavits establish that while the troops rode and searched without sleep, Conger—who suffered the painful legacy of battle wounds to his hips—pulled off for a few hours of sleep and was summoned by Doherty to rejoin the hunt once Doherty picked up Booth and Herold's trail where they had crossed the Rappahannock. The reports also detailed the detention of Jett, the arrival at the Garrett farm, the cavalry's actions surrounding the house and barn, the discovery of Booth and Herold, the negotiations, Herold's surrender, the torching of the barn, and the gunshot that dropped Booth. Interestingly, none of the affidavits identified Corbett as the gunman.

On Christmas Eve, Conger and Baker filed their claim, and the story they told was subtly, but significantly, different from what they had said aboard the *Montauk* hours after Booth's death. In the first statements, Conger said Colonel Baker summoned him and sent him off with orders to procure a boat from the quartermaster. When Conger returned, the colonel said he had a lead on where Booth and Herold had gone. "I want you to go to Virginia and get Booth. The cavalry will go with you." Baker's statement was even less detailed, just that "I commenced the pursuit of Booth one week ago last Sunday, under the direction of Colonel Baker." Neither mentioned the colonel appointing anyone in charge. But in the men's reward claim, which was drafted at the colonel's request and written in the third person, the history acquired some details.[7]

They [Conger and Baker] were important actors in the pursuit and capture of those parties, and themselves did, and saw others do, every thing that went to make up that enterprise, from its inception in the brain of its projector and master spirit [the colonel], until the bodies of the two fugitives, living and dead, were delivered into the hands of the Department of War; and it is that this narrative may, in some degree, help to the proper appreciation of the services of the parties to whose hands the chief of the Detective Bureau committed the execution of his plans.

Based on the ensuing narrative, top credit went to the colonel, secondary credit to Conger and Baker, and a much lesser share for Doherty and the Sixteenth Cavalry. In reality, all those involved played a role in the pursuit and capture, and their actions were so intertwined that it's hard to make an objective assessment that one player was more responsible than another.

Doherty reacted with an aggressive second campaign, which appears to have been effective. Holt's recommendation followed the military tradition of divvying up the spoils of war based on rank and command. Holt's commission recommended $3,750 to the colonel, but $7,500 to Doherty and $4,000 apiece to Conger and Baker. Boston Corbett and another sergeant were to receive $2,545 each, seven corporals were recommended to receive $2,291, and the privates were each allotted $2,033.[8]

Less than a month after Holt's recommendations were submitted, a movement arose in Congress to reassess them. A Committee of Claims was convened to investigate the process Holt and his colleagues had followed, and it upended Holt's recommendations. It put the shares for the colonel and Conger at $17,500 each, with $5,000 going to Baker and $2,500 to Doherty, and lesser amounts for Corbett and the rest of the lower-ranked men. By the time the measure reached the floor of Congress, though, backroom dealing had changed the payouts once again. In the final version of the payouts to the miliary men, the politically connected Conger received $15,000 and Doherty, the top military officer involved in the capture of Herold and death of Booth, received $5,250. Colonel Baker, who never left Washington, received $3,750 and his nephew, Byron Baker, $3,000. Doherty's men—including Corbett—received $1,653.85 apiece.

Corbett kept trying on his own, though, to reap more reward money. He enlisted—or perhaps he was recruited by—agents who would keep a percentage of whatever money they could recover on Corbett's behalf. In the days after Lincoln's death a wide range of organizations and governmental bodies, including city councils, had pledged rewards, and Corbett's solicitors queried the different sources to procure whatever they could.

Key among the claims agents was Byron Johnson, the man who'd befriended Corbett and then entertained him at his home in the days after Booth's death. In October 1866 Johnson mailed Corbett an update from his firm, identified on the stationery as "Johnson, Brown and Co.: Solicitors of Army and Navy Claims," with offices in the *National Intelligencer* building at the corner of Seventh and D Streets in Washington.

> I am very glad to learn of the pleasant and profitable manner you have been enabled to spend your time of late. Time thus occupied is valuable to your own soul. Should be glad to write a long letter but Mr. Brown being absent I must refrain. Have received replies from Penn. and Ills. The authorities of the later state never offered a reward. Penn. offered one if Booth was captured on her soil. We have nothing definite from the other sources yet but will push in investigations and write soon. Have not seen Doherty.[9]

Two years later, though, Johnson would send Corbett a check for $100, asking him to remit $10 back to the firm as commission, which Corbett did. The source of the cash was one Major A. D. Robinson, but the records don't indicate why Corbett was owed the money.

Meanwhile, far across the Atlantic, in the town of Edgware about ten miles northwest of the heart of London, a landlady by the name of Mrs. Allen noted that it had been a few days since she had seen or heard from one of her tenants, Bartholomew Corbett, Boston's father. After he returned to England in the 1850s, his career aspirations as a taxidermist and naturalist apparently unfulfilled, he and his son had maintained a sporadic correspondence but apparently had never seen each other again.[10]

Bartholomew, like his son, was an odd figure. He rented a single room from Allen at the back of the top floor, a space that included a small alcove on one side, "a recess not much larger than the interior of an ordinary-sized portmanteau," where the old man curled up to sleep. A recluse, Bartholomew for seven years had denied entry to his room to anyone, including Allen, who was content to leave the old man alone. But when he didn't appear for several days, she began to fear the worst, and on October 24, 1865, she summoned J. L. Beale, a "divisional surgeon" for the police.

Beale tried to enter Bartholomew's room but couldn't get the door to budge; it was blocked by stacks of refuse. Beale summoned two constables and together they managed to force the door inward enough to gain entry. There was barely room to breathe; the room was crammed to the ceiling with books, papers, stuffed animals, and a wide range of other possessions. The only clear space was a tunnel three feet high and two feet wide that led to the small alcove. Beale and the constables crawled in on their hands and knees and found the old man unresponsive but alive in his sleeping alcove. It took some effort, but they finally pulled Bartholomew through the collection of junk, and he was taken to the Marylebone Workhouse, a combination infirmary and poorhouse.

Officials from the Workhouse showed up at Bartholomew's rented room the next day to examine the collection of items, seeking, no doubt, some clues as to the state of the still unconscious man's mind and health. It was a lifetime collection "with cases of stuffed birds, books, and papers. The latter were carefully covered and labeled, and many of them appear to be of value." Some of the letters suggested a relationship with John James Audubon, according to the newspapers. But everything was coated with the dust and grime of years of nonuse. And the reports noted that Bartholomew's son, Sergeant Boston Corbett, was the man who had killed the man who killed Lincoln, and that he was expected to return to England shortly, though where that expectation came from was not established.

When Bartholomew was found, he was described as suffering from erysipelas, or a severe swelling of the skin from an infection. He was unconscious, or in a state of delirium, and he wasn't expected to live for long. The initial reports were off, though. Bartholomew had suffered a stroke, and he lingered on at the Workhouse for nearly four months. He finally died on February 19, 1866, without reuniting with his son.

As the postwar years unfolded, Corbett moved further into organized religion. In July 1868 he was among the featured speakers at a Methodist camp meeting in Northport, Long Island, a session that lasted for several days and drew a substantial crowd. Camp-goers alighted from the train, then walked a short distance to a grove that rose gradually to a hillcrest on which the organizers erected a small tent village.

"The place is a very beautiful one, with thick oaks and elm woods covering many acres of ground, and pleasant shady paths extending in all directions into pleasant quietudes and shady nooks, in which it is quite delightful to tarry," the *Brooklyn Eagle* reported. More people turned out than the tents could hold, forcing late arrivals to seek out space in local boardinghouses and hotels. The temporary gathering of the faithful "presents quite a lively appearance, and forcibly brings to mind collections of camping during the late war, only that there is more of ease and comfort to be found."

The organizers invited Corbett to speak on July 22, a Wednesday, at the close of afternoon services. He "got up a little excitement by haranguing the crowd. He related his experience while fighting a whole column of rebels, spoke of his capture and imprisonment at Andersonville jail, and said the Lord had delivered him."[11]

In August Corbett attended another camp meeting in Ossining, on the Hudson River north of Manhattan, and in September he took part in a religious gathering in New York City. By early 1869 he was apparently living in Connecticut, presumably working for one of the Danbury hat manufacturers. He was affiliated there with the Methodist Bethel Church in New London and, it seems, was undergoing some level of Bible study in preparation to become a minister. In May, he landed a job running a Methodist mission in Camden, New Jersey, earning $250 a year, which he augmented with hat-finishing work across the Delaware River in Philadelphia. While Corbett had gained fame and a certain amount of notoriety when he killed Booth, his time in Camden was likely the peak of his aspirations—a man of God in charge of his own flock of the faithful.[12]

The Camden mission building was small, measuring thirty-two feet by forty-eight feet, and named the Broadway Methodist Church after the address, 831 Broadway. Corbett shared a nearby home with a teamster named Isaac Boggs and his family, and he ran the church for a couple of years. The records don't indicate why he left, but Corbett moved a few blocks away and established the Siloam Mission Church in his rented house at 828 Pine Street. His church isn't included in local history books, suggesting his brand of faith and preaching style wasn't particularly resonant. A pocket diary for the years 1870–1872 listed eighteen members and thirty-one probationers for 1870. An 1872 entry notes that he made a hat for a Dr. Marcy for seven dollars.[13]

The flock apparently was neither large nor wealthy enough to support Corbett, and he continued working as a hatter in Philadelphia to make ends meet. He remained a figure of significant public interest, often queried by strangers for a personal retelling of the moment when he shot Booth, popping up in the occasional newspaper article, most mentions blandly reporting that the avenger of Lincoln had become a preacher. A few reports, though, continued the vitriol that marked the Civil War itself.

Under the headline "The Tool of a Conspiracy in the Church," a Chicago newspaper called *Pomeroy's Democrat* updated readers on what had happened to key figures caught up in the arc of the Lincoln assassination. The piece sought to hold Lewis Powell, hanged for the assault on Seward, as a martyr:

> Boston Corbit [*sic*], the skulking blood-thief who for a reward shot to death Wilkes Booth, has turned preacher. . . . Another of that gang of cut-throats turns up in the role of a preacher of the gospel! We pity that congregation of helpless and deluded beings for whose salvation he may be called upon to minister and shall keep an inquisitive watch upon his course. But, to save trouble and much religious scandal, we would advise his select flock to a course specially suited to the special merits of this bloody wretch. Let them pass a resolution in church meeting, and with a donation of ten dollars, appoint him a chaplain to the wondering Jew of Radicalism, whose steps, weary though they

may be, can know no rest because he is haunted by the ghost of a man hanged on his account.[14]

Another news account in February 1872 in the *Troy Whig* misreported that Corbett had died, news that quickly was reprinted around the country and then just as quickly corrected, with the added detail that Corbett was writing letters in support of General Ulysses S. Grant's campaign for the presidency, a race the war hero went on to win. Where Grant established himself as a motivator of fighting men and an agile and daring strategist during the war, he proved to be remarkably ill equipped to run the country. He was trusting and supportive of his friends and staff, some of whom were more than happy to take advantage of that faith, leading to a series of political corruption scandals against the backdrop of an unfolding national economic and financial corruption crisis that remains one of the most severe in US history. And it would have a profound effect on Boston Corbett's life.

In the years after the end of the Civil War, the United States returned to its core pursuit: capitalism. With peace at hand, railroad firms resumed their rapid expansion, fighting and sometimes colluding with each other to connect the heart of the American economy—agricultural production—with major urban markets and ports. All that building took a lot of money, and the railroads borrowed heavily by selling bonds to be repaid through the income generated by passenger tickets and freight fees once the railroad lines were laid down and the trains were moving. It takes prudent planning and a delicate balance to control that kind of growth, but with the scent of riches wafting across the nation, prudence went out the window.

A microcosm: in upstate New York, the New York Central Railroad already connected the northern tier from Buffalo eastward to Albany, roughly following the line of the Erie Canal. The Delaware, Lackawanna & Western Railroad cut two paths through the southern and central tiers of counties from Binghamton westward to Buffalo, and the Lehigh Valley line followed a similar route. But there were thousands of highly productive farms in the central part of the state, from northwest of the Catskills through the Leatherstocking District, made famous by the prewar frontier novels of James Fenimore Cooper, to just east of Syracuse.

The New York, Oswego & Midland Railroad sought to fill that void. Capital investors—including people and local governments who would be served by the new rail line—put in about $6.5 million and the company issued bonds to raise another $8 million to build the four-hundred-mile railroad. By early 1873 all but about twenty miles between the towns of Walton and Liberty in Delaware County was built, and trains were running on the completed sections. But without the middle, the trains were only good for local or regional transit, and the anticipated revenues that would come from a line connecting the Great Lakes port of Oswego, north of Syracuse, with the markets and ports of New York City didn't materialize. The railroad was running out of money, credit was tightening, and the company defaulted on $1 million in interest payments. The line failed.[15]

Jay Cooke, one of the key Wall Street moneymen propelling the growth of the railroads (and who had raised most of the money for the Union war effort), was heavily invested in the bonds of the Northern Pacific Railway. Cooke shared the vision of rail lines stretching eastward from the Pacific Northwest to Duluth, at the western tip of Lake Superior, where lake shipping would take over, then returning to land and rail lines in New York. But the conservative view toward investing and aversion to risk that had made him such a successful banker and wealthy man deserted him just when he needed it most; rather than serving as a middleman for bonds for Northern Pacific, he heavily invested his bank's assets. The railroad encountered significant delays, slowed in no small part by sporadic war with the Sioux whose lands the train would transect.

Because agriculture was still a driving force in the nation's economy, credit was routinely tight and cash scarce in April and October, when farmers either withdrew their savings or took out loans, in the spring to plant and in the fall to pay for the harvest. That meant the banks had to have more liquidity—cash on hand—in those months than at other times of the year. Cooke's bank, though, had low liquidity because of his interconnections with the railroads: the bank was oversubscribed with bonds, which offered fixed interest payments but could not be converted to cash when farmer depositors demanded their savings to pay their seasonal expenses.

The missed interest payments by the New York, Oswego & Midland rail were part of a financial shifting of the ground that brought down Cooke's financial house of cards. Northern Pacific also became insolvent, and with it, Jay Cooke & Company. With American cash and credit pinched tight, Cooke tried to sell bonds to European investors to raise enough cash to meet the bank's liabilities. He failed, and the bank abruptly closed.

Much like the collapse of Lehman Brothers 135 years later, Cooke's collapse dovetailed with other financial weaknesses, creating a financial panic and a run on banks, freezing credit—with banks collapsing, no one dared loan money—and sending the economic systems in the United States and Europe into tailspins. The Wall Street stock exchange closed for ten days; tens of thousands of rail workers lost their jobs and, since many lived in company buildings, their housing. The rail expansion had propelled the steel industry, and factories now cut back production or went completely idle. Fear led people to stop spending and instead hoard what little cash they could obtain. The economy seized up like an engine out of oil, casting as much as half of the nation's willing workforce out of jobs at a time of few safety nets. The depression would last for six years and was, until the Great Depression, the worst economic crisis in the young nation's history. Its ripple effects to Europe, which had an even deeper credit crisis just two years after the end of the Franco-Prussian War, signaled the changing and interconnected nature of the world's economies.[16]

With the nation's economy off the rails, Corbett, like millions of other Americans, had trouble finding and keeping work, a problem that was exacerbated by his continuing poor health. In 1874, Corbett packed up his bags and headed to Cleveland, joining about a dozen men at a boardinghouse at 95 Lake operated by a woman named Mary Sullivan. Most of the renters were printers or, like Corbett, hatters. Corbett and two fellow boarders worked for Richard C. Barrett's small wholesale hat factory at 225 Superior Street. How Corbett learned of the job is unclear—in fact, why he chose Cleveland is unknown—but Barrett, like Corbett, had been a Union soldier and prisoner during the Civil War. Though Barrett had been held at the Libby Prison, the two could well have crossed paths during their post-imprisonment convalescence.[17]

But God was never far from Corbett's mind. On May 16, Corbett delivered a sermon before the congregation of a Methodist church at the corner of Bridge and Taylor Streets, an appearance that was duly noted in the *Plain Dealer* newspaper. "Mr. Corbett's notoriety as an historic character, and his reputation as a zealous and devoted Christian of the Methodist persuasion, attracted a large audience, the church being crowded. He conducted the usual Sabbath evening service in a simple, earnest, and unostentatious manner, greatly interesting his audience."[18]

Corbett's "notoriety" also gained him an invite as one of the main figures at a soldiers' reunion and encampment in September 1874 at Caldwell, Ohio, that drew more than twenty thousand Union veterans, including General William Tecumseh Sherman. Local veterans around Caldwell raised the money to pay Corbett's transportation, and he stayed for a week as the guest of James Dalzell, a former Union private and the main organizer of the reunion.

While the gathering was a resounding success for the Union veterans, the reaction in the South was predictably rancorous. Dalzell decided to hold another reunion the next September and invite the veterans of the Confederate army as well. Corbett again was a central figure in the events, a function of his celebrity. Another Union veteran, R. B. Hoover, was assigned the night of the reunion to share a first-floor, single-bed hotel room with Corbett, whom he described as "a nervous, excitable man, always the center of attraction, with a keen, but wild, look in his eyes, and an interminable restlessness of body and limb."[19]

Corbett traveled as he lived, with two guns always at the ready in case he was attacked. "He got into an exciting argument with several men one afternoon over the question as to whether Booth had really been killed at all. Hot words ensued, a rush was made towards Corbett, and in an instant the gleaming barrel of his revolver flashed in the faces of his opponents. It was with considerable difficulty that they were separated and peace restored."

Corbett also began to exhibit some of the paranoia that would eventually come to frame his worldview. Hoover reported that Corbett told "those of us whom he considered his friends that he had been hounded for years by men who were high in authority at Washington at the time of the assassination, and that they caused him to lose several important positions after he went into civil life, and had refused to shake hands with him or to answer his salutation on the streets." That night in the room at the hotel, Hoover asked Corbett about the killing of Booth. Corbett maintained that his actions "had deprived the Washington authorities of an opportunity to make a grand display in the execution of Booth." Hoover said Corbett seemed ill at ease. "It was a close, hot night . . . with the window raised. Corbett walked the floor for ten minutes after I was in bed. He would frequently clasp his hands and exclaim: 'The Lord have mercy on my soul!' At last he knelt down and offered a fervent prayer, after which he placed a large revolver under his pillow and went to bed."

The two men talked for a while; Hoover said Corbett recounted the night he killed Booth. Corbett went to sleep, and "I followed later on, with a restless, troubled sleep, in which I dreamed of something which made me awaken Corbett. He sat up in bed, drew out his pistol, and covered me with it. I assured him it was all a dream, and he calmed down again."

Corbett's stay in Cleveland wasn't long. There's one unconfirmed report in Chicago's *Daily Inter Ocean* newspaper that Corbett had settled in the city, but if true, he didn't leave much of a mark. Regardless, by August 1876, Corbett was back in Camden, now at 328 Pine Street, sermonizing at camp meetings and getting whatever work he could in Philadelphia. It was at best a hand-to-mouth existence. Apparently seeking a human interest story to draw readers to the new *Philadelphia Sunday World*, a reporter dropped in on Corbett at his home.

He is about 40 years old and is very plain in dress, and his principal boast appears to be his devotion as a Methodist. He lives alone in his little house, doing his own cooking and housekeeping, and seeing nobody but the members of the little flock of Methodists which meet nightly at his house, and of which he is the head. Heaped together in one corner of his kitchen are half a dozen rough benches for the use of his congregation. He preaches and exhorts himself, and uses a Windsor chair for a pulpit.[20]

Corbett kept up his traveling card as a member of the Hat Finishers' National Trade Association, which he had joined in 1873, and that gave him access to union hat shops. But access to shops that aren't hiring doesn't do much good. Corbett did manage to find a short-term job as a $1.50-a-day janitor for the Centennial Exposition in Philadelphia in 1876, but then he evidently moved into a position as a guard, and he appears as such in a photograph that was part of his work identification card. The gathering was the first world's fair on American soil, and it coincided, as the name suggests, with the one-hundredth anniversary of American independence.

But the exposition only lasted six months. Corbett soon was out of work again, and his health was deteriorating—a subject of interest for the newspapers, which often published one-paragraph updates about Corbett's destitute condition and his bad health. Most were accurate; some were not. Several papers picked up an erroneous wire report that Corbett had left Camden and was homesteading in Nevada. In fact, Corbett was still trying to get by in Camden. Attempting to trade on his notoriety as the killer of Booth, and as a Union army veteran still suffering from his war experiences, Corbett wrote on January 12, 1878, to President Rutherford B. Hayes hoping to land a job.

I take the liberty of appealing to you in my own behalf to see if you will think it beneath your notice to do something for one who has risked his life, and in a measure lost his health, by four months imprisonment at Andersonville, to serve that government of which you are now the head. For a testimonial in my behalf, please read the Words of Solomon, in the Ninth Chapter of Ecclesiastes, and the fifteenth verse. They are the words of a wise man! A great ruler! And a close observer of human events.[21]

The request went nowhere. Desperate, Corbett again began contemplating a move to a place with better prospects and apparently discussed his predicament with friends. A letter arrived in early February from a church leader in Cawker City, in north central Kansas, that opened by noting, "I am informed through one who has listened to you that you are unsettled." The congregation offered Corbett a position teaching Sunday school, though there was no mention of money. Corbett wrote to an old friend from his days in Troy, New York, a man named Thomas Kirby, who had settled in Troy, Kansas, in the northeast part of the state. Corbett's letter is lost, but Kirby's response implies Corbett had asked about life on the far side of the Mississippi. "Times is very hard hear [*sic*]," Kirby wrote on February 17, 1878, apparently referring to the previous harvest season. "We have not raised more than half a crop this summer. Corn is eighteen cents a bushel and everything is very low."[22]

The records contain no details, but somehow Corbett learned of an eighty-acre homesteader's plot that remained unclaimed in Center Township, near Concordia, Kansas, about 150 miles west of Kirby's place in Troy. No letters survive to hint at a connection, but it's reasonable to wonder whether Corbett's war experiences once again came into play. Joseph Whitehead, who was a regular attendee of the prayer sessions Corbett had helped lead at the Andersonville prison, settled after the war near Concordia. It was a place of open countryside ripe for farming, and it seems most likely that Corbett heard from Whitehead about the unclaimed homestead adjacent to Whitehead's farm.

Sometime during the summer of 1878, Corbett apparently made a trip west to Kansas, presumably to scope out the potential. While he was in the area, a man named George Strickler invited Corbett to speak at an Independence Day celebration in Delphos, a small farm community in Ottawa County, just north of Cloud County. The locals, Strickler wrote, wanted Corbett to "deliver an address for us relating somewhat of your experiences in the killing of Booth the assassin. We are anxious to see you. The Concordia band will attend and make our music." Strickler offered what must have been good bait for Corbett. "You will be entertained while here, and all expenses paid . . . and if possible will have our committee donate you something." It's unclear whether Corbett obliged.[23]

He also was invited to take part in a quarterly religious meeting by the Reverend Lemuel Faulkner in mid-August, but it's most likely Corbett had left Kansas by then, and was now either in Camden or on his way there. Despite the westward foray, Corbett still seemed more interested in remaining in Camden, which had been his home for nearly a decade and where he had his flock of fellow Methodists, as small as it might have been.

In early September Corbett wrote to the postmaster general of the United States asking for an appointment to any job available in the Camden post office. Somehow, the job application reached the newspapers and was duly noted around the country. Yet even that appeal for work drew fire from defenders of the Old South. From Georgia, the *Columbus Daily Enquirer* noted briefly, and with sarcasm, on September 10 that

> ex-Sergeant Boston Corbett, who shot John Wilkes Booth, has written to the Postmaster-general asking employment in Camden, (N.J.) post office. He stated that he has never been in any Government position, although he thinks he has earned some consideration for his services. He says a very modest situation will satisfy him. If murdering a wounded maniac in a barn constitutes a claim upon the government, Boston Corbett should be provided for. We have no doubt that the Erring Brothers will render favorably the application of this modest and meritorious individual.

Whether the postmaster replied is unknown, but Corbett finally gave up on Camden—and hat finishing. Packing up his few belongings, Corbett left the little house-church on Pine Street on September 14, 1878, and, like so many others before him, headed west.[24]

9

CORBETT GOES WEST

By 1878, the United States was a rapidly industrializing country, and despite the 1873 financial collapse and railroad crisis, it was still a place of relatively easy travel. The surviving railroads consolidated and expanded as they built out the growing national system. Steamboats still connected cities and villages along navigable waterways, and horse-drawn coaches and wagons moved in intricate networks among smaller towns and settlements. But travel took money, of which Boston Corbett had little. So Corbett, notwithstanding his compromised health, decided to walk to Kansas. He left his house on September 14 and took about a week to cover the one hundred miles to Harrisburg, Pennsylvania, all but sixteen miles of it on foot.

There, he gave up on the idea of walking. In the state capital, he finagled a half-fare train ticket to Pittsburgh, where he stopped in at the *Commercial-Gazette* newspaper offices hoping to drum up public interest in his plight, some short-term work, or maybe patronage for the rest of the trip. The newspaper was happy to oblige. The story of the Andersonville survivor and avenger of Lincoln now down on his luck and hoofing it to what he hoped would be a personal promised land was too good to ignore.[1]

It was a short article but it covered the basics of Corbett's past few years, his economic hardship, and the lack of job prospects in the East. "During the Centennial Exhibition he served as one of the guards, but since then he has not been regularly employed. He applied for appointment to the government service [but had no] success and finding it impossible to get work in Philadelphia or elsewhere in the East he determined to go West to Kansas. . . . He was endeavoring during yesterday afternoon to identify transportation further west . . . riding as opportunity offered, to his destination."

The publicity worked. The next day, Corbett received a pass from R. C. Meldrum, a freight agent, to ride for free on the Pennsylvania Company rail line, and an endorsement letter to other freight agents to offer the same accommodation on other lines. Pennsylvania rail officials also came up "with a purse of money" to help him on his way. Corbett stopped in Chicago briefly, staying with a friend and telling the *Chicago Journal* that he thought he still had a good enough eye to shoot buffalo. But Corbett shortly moved on, reaching Concordia in early October.[2]

The eighty acres to which Corbett staked a claim were up for grabs for a reason. Rocky and uneven, the land wasn't particularly promising for farming, which is what Corbett, who had spent most of his life in cities, planned to take up. "Farming was the last thing in the world that he should have undertaken, for he had no equipment and he knew nothing about that treacherous and slippery art," wrote Albert T. Reid, a Concordia native who was a child when Corbett arrived and whose father, the county treasurer, recorded Corbett's homestead claim. "But here, on those eighty acres, he built himself a house, planted a few lone cottonwoods, and stuck a plough in the prairie. But the plough rusted and only weeds grew on the rich soil."[3]

The land did have a spring, and a separate small creek wound through the property. Corbett decided to build his home in both an unusual fashion and an unusual place. He selected a spot on the north side of a rise, which meant he would get limited benefits from the sun during the long and hard Kansas winters. But that's where the spring emerged from the ground, and

Artist's rendering of Boston Corbett's dugout home near Concordia, Cloud County, Kansas.

Albert Reid, Scribner's, copy in Kansas Historical Society archives, Topeka (item number 305820; call number FK2.C7.75.C *2; KSHS identifier DaRT ID: 305820)

Corbett wanted ready access to a consistent and reliable source of water. He soon hired a man named Grigsby and three laborers to carve away the low hillside on either side of the spring, then use sod and hewn limestone to build his low-roofed, single-room home. He had the spring itself framed with stone, like a fireplace, then laid a wooden floor—a rare component in a prairie dugout—over the rivulet that trickled out the front of the house and down the slope to the creek about fifty yards away. The doorway stood between two small windows, through which Corbett could look across the shallow valley to the road that transected it.

Physically unable to farm himself, Corbett at first hired four men to work the land for him, but that didn't last long. When his efforts to grow crops failed, he turned to raising cattle and sheep, with which he had more success, but not enough to sustain himself. Still, he kept a sense of humor, naming one of his "unruly sheep" Mrs. Harper after a neighbor he didn't care for. He also kept several dogs and a few chickens, but his prime farm animal was a small horse named Billy, his steady companion and, pulling along a small buckboard, his sole means of transportation.

Corbett made no secret of his identity. Though he spent most of his time alone, he was not a recluse. He became acquainted with his neighbors and fulfilled civic obligations, paying his taxes on time and serving as a juror in a coroner's inquest on July 25, 1880. The dead man was a neighbor named Nathan Wilson; Corbett's role was limited to identifying Wilson's body and testifying that the dead man was about eighty years old, had been in poor health, and talked of sensing that his death was near. The coroner ruled that Wilson had died of natural causes.[4]

Local merchant and one-time post office worker George Henry Palm wrote of Corbett years later, "He was a man of strong peculiarities: very eccentric, and set in his convictions" who "would do all he could for those he esteemed, and nothing for those he disliked; only desired that they should keep away from him and not cross his pathway."[5]

Corbett was an unmistakable figure, with his long hair beneath a Union soldier's hat, his ever-present guns, and Billy. Reid, then a young boy, was fascinated by his first encounter with the living legend.

> [I] was just crossing the street when a man in a buckboard came whirling down the street and flew past me in a cloud of dust. In a moment he drew up his horse, leaped quickly from the buckboard, and then tied his horse to one of the hitch-racks which ran like a line of sentries around the courthouse. He was a small, insignificant-looking little man, with a thin scraggly beard. . . . Around his waist was an old army belt and from the belt dangled two pistols, but in these early days of Kansas little attention was paid to a man just because he felt more at ease in a pistol-belt than out of one. From his pocket he took a small crumpled bag of sugar, poured some of it in the palm of his hand, and gave it to the horse.

Corbett broke his solitude to preach and to gather with fellow Christians. "He always rode Billy all over the country on his preaching work," a Kansan named Clara Myers Brown recalled years later. "He held services in old Enterprise schoolhouse and stayed many nights at our house. We youngsters were a little afraid of him as he always had a gun under his pillow." He was a regular at prayer meetings, where he sermonized about an unforgiving God, occasionally too vociferously for some of the congregants. In one session, he caused such an uproar that fellow churchgoers interrupted the service to demand Corbett be thrown out, but after some discussion he was allowed to stay. "He was a firm believer in a 'hell and eternal burning' for the wicked, and in his discourse he would bring the flames quite vividly before the mind's eye," the merchant Palm said. "He was very fearless in denunciation of evil and crime of all kinds, and he was not afraid of hurting anyone's feelings by plain truth."

Corbett also maintained a lively correspondence, his letters well phrased and polite in a clean and easy-to-read script. Most of the communication was with his friends back east, primarily in and around Camden and Manhattan. But a few were with friends scattered in other places, such as John R. Chesbro, a minister who floated around churches in western New York. Some reached out to Corbett, seeking to reestablish connections severed with Corbett's departure from Camden. The Reverend Richard Pope, who had baptized Corbett in Boston twenty years earlier, was surprised by what he felt was Corbett's abrupt and unannounced exodus.

"I came off the cars from Philadelphia to Camden and look[ed] at the old place where the sunflower stood and saw the foundation of a new brick building before sunrise, I said, where is Brother Corbett?" Pope wrote in a letter to Corbett in April, seven months after Corbett took off for Kansas. "And you know the good old woman who lives close to the ground where we last stood up in that lot and preached Christ together, she told me your pilgrimage." Pope decided that Kansas might be a good spot for him as well. "By the grace of God I will be out with you but I do not know how soon, but I wish to enter an 80 for me close to you and I think we will have a happy home together, and a more extended mission for our Blessed Lord Savior, Jesus Christ." There's no indication, though, that Pope ever made it to Kansas.[6]

In fact, there wasn't much unclaimed homesteading land left. Joseph Wrigley wrote to "Brother Corbett" in May 1879, part of a correspondence in which he earlier asked Corbett about whether any more homesteads might be available; Corbett had told him that the "land is took up" near his own homestead but that he had heard of another piece of land that was still open. "I would like to know how far the plase [*sic*] is from you you mentioned in your letter," Wrigley replied, "how the climate is there and if there is any timber on the land." Wrigley also wondered about the price of coal and other living costs, and mentioned he had given twenty-five cents to a mutual friend to send along to Corbett to help him through the first winter. And echoing the sentiments of Pope and other letter writers, Wrigley said that he wanted to move his family to be closer to Corbett.[7]

Coursing through the letters is a clear stream of affection and support among Corbett's fellow faithful, many of whom apparently were in no better financial shape than he was. That warm embrace contrasts sharply with the portrait history has painted of Corbett as an unstable zealot. It's clear that beyond his religious eccentricities and physical frailties, Corbett established deep friendships in New York City, in Camden, and in his new home, where he engaged in the religious lives of fellow Methodists, to whom he occasionally preached in special services at local schoolhouses and other public buildings.

He also received queries from elsewhere in Kansas about whether he could come preach at meetings. In December 1879, D. C. Fordner, president of the North Kansas District of the Methodist Church, wrote to ask if Corbett was available as a minister in the coming year at struggling congregations in need of a visiting preacher. Corbett did travel about, and much as in his life as a minister in Camden, he seems to have developed a small but devoted band of nearby followers and fellow believers. In one poignant note, a man named John Babb summoned him. "Mr. Boston Corbett: Please come down to our house as soon as you can come. From your friend as ever John Babb . . . Don't stop. Best Come. Nannie is sick." Nannie was Babb's wife, who survived whatever the ailment might have been. That Babb, then twenty-one years old, sought out Corbett in such a time of dire personal stress and need suggests the role the preacher had assumed in the lives of others.[8]

Back at his homestead, however, Corbett was still struggling to get by. Neighbors helped out some, and fellow war veterans took up a collection, but the killer of Booth was reaching a point of desperation. He decided to tap a possible income source of which thousands of others had already taken advantage: a US military pension.

On February 16, 1880, Corbett wrote a letter to the US Bureau of Pensions hoping, as "one of the Andersonville sufferers . . . to see if something can be done on my behalf." He detailed his war history and his time at Andersonville. "I have suffered more or less ever since, not however being entirely disabled, but bearing in my body extreme suffering, caused by my imprisonment mainly." He said that his name had appeared in a recent book about the Andersonville prison and in other publications, which he cited as though it was a supporting affidavit to his request. "I never have applied before for a pension til now, but now I would like to have one if it may be granted. I did write to President Hayes over two years ago, before I left the East for the West, but my letter was disregarded, I never received a reply."[9]

The pension bureau apparently responded with details on how to apply, which included gathering paperwork to prove Corbett was indeed a veteran and that he was physically damaged by his war experience. Corbett had left his discharge papers with the Johnson, Brown and Co. claims agents, but he had been unable to retrieve his papers from Johnson. So he had to amass his personal records from scratch. He wrote to the New York State adjutant general in early March, detailed his history with the state's Twelfth militia and Sixteenth cavalry—though he omitted his role as the killer of Booth— and asked for help with his official records.

"I have put my papers in the hands of claims agents and they were never returned," Corbett wrote. "I desire a certificate of my service for the purpose of procuring a pension, and also to enable me to make proof of my claim." It's interesting that Corbett had to prove a personal history that was such a high-profile part of the end of the war. Still, the adjutant general's office replied that it did not have the company records that would detail Corbett's service, but it did send along a certificate of Corbett's mustering-in and mustering-out dates.

That was sufficient, at least, for Corbett to start the application. On March 23, Corbett, neighbor and fellow Andersonville survivor Joseph Whitehead, and another neighbor, Silas G. Dean, traveled to the Cloud County courthouse in Concordia, where the latter two men witnessed Corbett's affidavit before C. F. Hestetter, the clerk of district court. Even taking into account the possibility of embellishment, Corbett was clearly facing debilitating health problems. Written in the third person, the affidavit offers a detached and brief overview of his military history and his stint in Andersonville, where he "contracted scurvy, chronic diarrhea, intermittent fever, and rheumatism." Corbett also, he reported, "contracted piles while in the service." Corbett then listed the string of hospitals in which he had been treated and his postwar work as a hatter in New York and Camden, though he didn't list his religious work. Prior to the war, he said, "he was a man of good, sound, physical health" and that "now he is partially disabled" and couldn't maintain "his subsistence by manual labor by reason of his injuries."

Corbett submitted the paperwork to the pension bureau in June, but it apparently took months for officials in Washington to make a decision. And it didn't go Corbett's way. On May 19, 1881, the pension bureau sent Corbett a letter asking for a medical report verifying his "chronic diarrhea, scurvy, intermittent fever, rheumatism, and piles." Corbett reacted quickly, submitting to a physical exam on May 31. The physician, L. D. Hall of Concordia, recommended Corbett receive a partial pension for partial disability, but noted that "the disability is likely to grow worse as age advances." The report described a man who was falling apart physically: "Scurvy is affecting ankles and contracting cords under knees, also affects gums and teeth when at worst. Chronic diarrhea has created great emaciation." Corbett complained of "a great deal of pain in pulvis [sic] pain passing up spine to his brain at times, generally worse in hot weather, also causes disentric [sic] condition of lower bowels with bloody muco-purulent evacuation." He had intermittent fever, rheumatism, and piles, and "suffers constantly with pain. His tongue is coated, breath foul, teeth all decaying by effects of scurvy . . . he is a perfect wreck of human suffering."

The records don't show whether that medical report was ever weighed, but a year later US Senator Preston B. Plumb stepped into the process, seeking a prompt update on the status of Corbett's application. Plumb also was a Union army veteran, having served in the Eleventh Kansas Cavalry, and met Corbett at a Grand Army of the Republic reunion in Topeka, where Corbett was one of the featured speakers (along with US Senator James G. Blaine, a failed presidential contender and soon to be secretary of state). Corbett gave a speech recounting his role in the hunt for Booth, and in private conversations complained about what he felt was dismissive treatment by an ungrateful nation. Plumb "was moved by his speech," as were other less influential veterans, and a campaign developed to get Corbett his pension.[10]

Plumb's letter seemed to be the most effective of the efforts; after it was sent, Corbett traveled in June to Junction City for yet another exam, this one by a panel of three doctors. That resulted in a briefer, less detailed report, but a stronger conclusion: "In our opinion the said Boston Corbett is total[ly] incapacitated for obtaining his subsistence by manual labor . . . the disability is permanent."[11]

Corbett also collected a fresh round of affidavits. James H. Brown, the Manhattan hatter for whom Corbett had worked, and in whose stead he had joined the Twelfth Regiment, swore in June that "I have been personally and well acquainted" with Corbett "for the last 25 years." Corbett had been vibrant and in perfect health when he marched off to war. "I see him frequently after the war until I believe 1874, during which time he was in a very feeble condition, was generally used up, was suffering with chronic diarrhea and scurvy and appeared to be used up generally." Similar affidavits came from Allen M. Thompson, a Manhattan tailor; Thomas Brown, who had known Corbett for thirty years and had shared Corbett's Rivington Street address in Manhattan; and Whitehead, the neighbor and former Andersonville survivor, who said Corbett "is now an invalid unable to do anything."

Corbett included his own affidavit, which was more personal than the third-person version he initially submitted. The brief memoir covers the same elements of his life but in more detail. After the war, Corbett said, he worked but "during all this time I was a great sufferer, yet I had to work enough to earn my bread although I was wholly unfit to do so." He mentioned his church work at Camden, and that after moving to Concordia he had done some "preaching at times in this county. I have been very bad for the last six years. I don't think I have been able to earn $20.00 Twenty Dollars [*sic*] during the whole time from 1877 to 1882 by manual labor. I could perhaps do one-fourth of any able-bodied man's work." The cause: his time and maltreatment at Andersonville.

On September 30, 1882, Corbett finally won his pension: six dollars a month beginning on August 18, 1865, the day after he mustered out in Washington, DC, and then eight dollars a month beginning May 31, 1881. The pension was to be paid retroactively, a welcome windfall for a man who had suffered greatly not only from his illnesses and afflictions but also from deep poverty.

Within a month of the pension being entered into the government records, Corbett began receiving letters from claims agents telling him that others had received more for similar afflictions and that they would be pleased to start efforts to gain for Corbett a higher pension—for a cut. There's no indication whether Corbett ever acted on them.

What he did do was pay off debts, including fifteen dollars he still owed his landlord, a Mr. Metz, back in Camden. After Corbett sent the money—four years after he had left town—Metz's agent, James M. Cassady, wrote that "old Mr. Metz was made happy and exclaimed, 'Well, he is an honest man.' What more laudatory could be said of a mortal man—honest with God and man."[12]

While Corbett was pursuing his pension application, rumors and reports swirled anew that Booth was still alive. Newspaper stories that revisited the showdown at Garrett's barn began giving more credit to Doherty, Conger, and Baker. This led James Dalzell, whose published war memoirs and activism in the Grand Army of the Republic made him one of the highest-profile Union veterans, to issue a public defense of Corbett.

"In all printed accounts of the pursuit and capture of Booth, Corbett's name is carefully left out, as if Hamlet were dropped from the play of

'Hamlet,'" Dalzell wrote, then added a detail that seems to have been more legend than fact: that Corbett was robbed of his reward money shortly after receiving it. No contemporaneous reports could be found that he had indeed been robbed, but it eventually became part of the Corbett lore. "Corbett became the target for envy and detraction, settling down into unmeasured contempt among his officers. He was hunted out of the army as if he were the assassin and Booth the hero."

Little of that was true, however. Corbett had received threats, but he had left the military because he was sick, the war had ended, and he was no longer needed. But Dalzell was correct in some aspects.

There is nothing of the egotist, nothing of the fool or of the hypo-crite about him. Yet he is a man of more than ordinary zeal in reli-gion. His place is never vacant in church or Sunday school or prayer meeting. He fills all the conventional requirements of social life and is as pleasant a companion for an evening's chat as you will meet anywhere. Yet he is hated by one-half of the American people and despised by the other half for the only crime ever yet alleged against him—that he shot John Wilkes Booth. . . . This was his supreme offense. He robbed the haughty officers of a pay where they could have all been star actors. He is unmarried, poor, and despised. He bears it meekly and uncomplainingly. . . . It is cruel and unjust, and history will yet rectify the mistake and award Boston Corbett the honor due him.[13]

Corbett had other supporters as well. One John Gillespie of Philadelphia read an article on Corbett in the *Christian Advocate* and sent ten dollars to its author to pass along. And some fellow veterans sought help from Corbett as word circulated that he had won a pension. Abraham Murset of Bucks-town, Pennsylvania, asked Corbett if he remembered enough about their time together in the Sixteenth Cavalry—Murset was the barber—to write an affidavit on his behalf, attesting to a horse-mounting incident in which Murset badly damaged his leg. He also asked for the addresses of other unit members, including Lieutenant Doherty, to gather more testimonials.

Corbett responded:

I am truly sorry that I cannot recollect the fact of your injury. Lincoln Barracks, I remember very well, for I was transferred from there to Lincoln Hospital by order of Surgeon General Barnes. I tried very hard to get Sergeant Gerrard Irvin[e] to help when I was trying to get a pension but could not find out where he was. Your reference to places and names shows conclusively that we were comrades together but when it comes down to positive testimony in regard to your disability, it is impossible for me to testify of an occurrence.[14]

(Sergeant Irvine, under the spelling Gerrard Ervine, had become a naturalized citizen in 1866 in New York City—with Corbett standing witness.)

The mail also brought a reunion, at least in letters, with Richard Thatcher, the young soldier Corbett had befriended at Andersonville, who had visited Corbett briefly in Washington after Lincoln's assassination and the manhunt for Booth. Now the married father of four children, Thatcher moved to Greenwood County, Kansas, east of Wichita, in August 1882, where he was preaching while working as a schoolteacher "to pay expenses." Through a mutual friend, Thatcher obtained Corbett's address and wrote in September seeking to reconnect. He commiserated on the difficulties in obtaining a pension—his own application had gone nowhere.

"I know I have never fully recovered from the effects of my prison life," Thatcher wrote, adding that "I am positive your prison exposure must have ruined your health. I know you had no shelter when I was in prison, and you were not a bit stout." For all the misery and deprivations, though, Thatcher reminded Corbett that there had been uplifting moments. "Above all, I often think of the good times we had serving the Lord, right in that abominable Andersonville. Right there I received impressions that have followed me ever since. I still love the Lord, and am trusting him for salvation, and I realize that he is the same Saviour who did not forsake me in that awful lion's den." That initial letter led to a steady correspondence between the two men for the next five years.[15]

Corbett might have been too sick to work, but he was rarely too sick to preach. In June 1880 George Strickler invited him to Delphos again to preach at a July 3 prayer meeting, for which Corbett received five dollars. Other invitations flowed in, some offering a small honorarium, others silent on the issue.

Some wanted Corbett to preach; some just wanted to hear his war stories. Horace Bushnell invited Corbett to talk to his congregation at the First Presbyterian Church of Concordia about life in Andersonville and the Booth manhunt. Instead, Corbett stepped to the front of Bushnell's church on August 22, 1883, and delivered a haranguing sermon about a wrathful God and the damnation of those who did not follow Christ. "It was a perfect failure as a lecture although a good large audience was out," Bushnell noted in his diary the next day. "We desired to have the simple story of his own exploits. This he omitted entirely and instead gave us a disconnected exhortation. He was very kind . . . in coming—bought himself a new coat and shirt for the occasion, but failed entirely in his lecture because he would not tell us what he knew and what we did not know, and insisted in telling us what we knew as well as he, or better, and giving us exhortations and arguments instead of facts."[16]

Despite his eccentricities, Corbett continued to cultivate a network of friends among the fellow faithful and among his neighbors. William C. Norton, another Union war veteran, lived about one and a half miles from Corbett's homestead, along the route Corbett followed to reach the shops in Concordia. During his frequent trips to town, Corbett usually stopped at Norton's farm for a visit, sometimes spending the night. They would talk late into the evening, reminiscing, one suspects, about their war experiences. But others were less enthused to have the killer of Booth living in their midst. "Some of our neighbors were Confederate sympathizers and they used to tantalize him, but I always took his part," Norton said. "He used to get letters threatening him in different ways."[17]

Corbett also befriended Frank Sorgatz, who was a druggist in Concordia, and his wife, Susan. In 1883, the couple moved their young family to New York City, where Frank worked at a pharmacy during the day and attended classes at night. They moved into an apartment that turned out to be around the corner from where Corbett and his wife had lived before the war. Corbett wrote to Phoebe Palmer, the evangelist, and arranged for

Palmer to visit the Sorgatz family. Susan Sorgatz started attending Palmer's Tuesday afternoon prayer meetings. "Sister Palmer is a most noble woman," she reported in a letter back to Corbett. "I cannot tell you how much I enjoyed her visit or the afternoon meetings. I am not able to go every Tuesday on account of the little boys and household duties, but the heart is always longing to be there when the time comes around."

In another letter, Frank Sorgatz nudged Corbett to move back east. "We . . . often wonder how you are getting along and think about how nice it would be if you could be here and pay us a visit often, for although this is a great city with a great multitude of people, we have so far not found any friends for which we could give up our old friends in Kansas, you among the foremost," Frank Sorgatz wrote nine days before Christmas in 1883. He inquired about Billy the horse, and about how Corbett was faring. "Are you not yet satisfied with stock raising and come to the conclusion to sell out and come east to live? I hope the time will not be to [*sic*] far distant when we shall count you again among our calling friends." Sorgatz noted that while he was learning a lot, his own work wasn't going well and money was tight. Within a few years, the Sorgatzes would return to Concordia.[18]

Corbett didn't express any intention of moving. He seemed happy where he was, selling wool from his small flock of sheep, his income augmented by the war pension. He roamed the countryside on Billy or in the cart pulled by the small horse. Locals shared sightings, some of which were quite odd. Frederick W. Sturges, a lawyer, one-term state legislator, and eventual Cloud County judge, occasionally encountered Corbett on the rural roads. Once Corbett caught sight of the approaching rider, he would slip off Billy "and lie motionless in the grass, his long revolver in one hand, waiting to see what was coming. He never made any attempt to hurt me or, indeed, to hurt any one, but he was always wary."[19]

Albert Reid, the writer whose childhood coincided with Corbett's time in Cloud County, once accompanied his father out into the countryside to assess a farm. As they walked from their wagon to the house they watched a hawk drifting high overhead, wheeling and wafting on the rising thermals. "Suddenly, and, it seemed, almost beside us, there was a terrific boom and there, a few yards away, we saw Boston Corbett lying flat on his back, and twisting down through the air was the hawk we had been watching." The father and son approached Corbett for a brief chat and saw his Bible lying open on the grass beside him. Corbett apparently had been doing some personal Bible study while scanning the sky for targets.[20]

For a young boy like Reid, that Corbett had killed a man—and not just any man, but the man who had assassinated Lincoln—made him a subject of deep curiosity. That Corbett was odd and somewhat reclusive added to the appeal. "The house was a haunt of mystery. He allowed no one to enter it, and it was only when he had dashed away behind Billy that any one could go up and peep into it. . . . It seemed filled with guns and weapons; a rifle stood beside a home-built bunk, and over the head of the bunk was a holster with a brace of pistols in it. Now and then neighbors would come to call, but no one, so far as I know, ever got past that door. When a passer-by rode up, or when Corbett was hallooed to the door, he came and stood in the door with a rifle in his hand."

George Palm, the postmaster and local shop owner, not only counted Corbett among his customers but also once borrowed some of Corbett's pension proceeds. Palm repaid him a short time later, though Corbett declined to accept any interest, an act that Palm said showed "his strong sense of honor and true regard for those he counted as friends."

Yet Corbett was quick to take insult as well. Corbett usually paid cash when he patronized Palm's store, but sometimes when Corbett was short, or unanticipated purchases amounted to more money than he had carried into town, Palm extended credit until Corbett's next trip, a bill that Corbett always paid promptly. "On one occasion he came into the store when I was absent. He bought a few articles of my brother, who had not been with me long and was not much acquainted with him. [Corbett] paid for the articles purchased and remarked, 'I would like to have taken some more things, but haven't any more money.'" Business was tight and Palm was trying to deal mostly in cash, so the brother didn't offer Corbett credit, instead telling Corbett, "It's too bad you haven't any more money." Corbett took the comment as an insult. "He was extremely sensitive and his feelings easily hurt, and he at once went out. Just then I came in, and as soon as I heard it I went out to where he was unhitching his horse and told him to get what he wanted, but he would not return and I could not console him. It was a long time before he felt right about that."[21]

There were other, more public frictions. Somehow Corbett became estranged from Joseph Whitehead, his old friend from Andersonville and now his neighbor. Several Whitehead boys—sons and nephews of Joseph, it seems—made a game of cutting across some of Corbett's property, which drew Corbett from the cabin. (Some versions of the story say the boys were playing baseball on the Sabbath, raising Corbett's ire.) In late November 1885 Corbett opened fire with his rifle in the general direction of the boys. None were hit; given Corbett's considerable marksmanship skills, that he missed suggests he was simply trying to warn the boys off. But even in a time and place where it was not unusual to see people like Corbett riding around armed, it was unusual for the guns to get used. The potshots taken at the boys led to a criminal complaint.

Several variations of what happened next have expanded the legend of Boston Corbett; many of the versions were wildly inflated and seemingly confused with other run-ins with neighbors. What seems certain is that Corbett was summoned to court in Concordia to face trial. As the case unfolded, accusations of lying were exchanged, though it's hard to determine exactly who called whom a liar.

The *Concordia Blade* reported that while Corbett was testifying, Abe Whitehead, Joseph's brother and the father of some of the boys who had been shot at, interrupted Corbett's testimony and said the killer of Booth was spinning lies in the courtroom. The *Republican-Empire*, also of Concordia, reported that the testimony was going against Corbett, who, in his growing paranoia, brandished his revolver and began yelling that he had "fallen among thieves," sending lawyers and the substantial gallery of onlookers ducking and fleeing.

Regardless of the instigation, it was a chaotic scene that ended with Corbett, gun drawn, backing out of the cowed courtroom, mounting Billy, and galloping off to his dugout. The next day, Constable John Linton and a Dr. Dabney went to Corbett's homestead to arrest him; Corbett came to the door with a rifle and in the ensuing discussion made it clear he had no intention of going back to Concordia and the courtroom. Rather than push the conversation into a showdown, the two men retreated, leaving Corbett—heavily armed and well fortressed—right where they found him. No other efforts were made and it appears the case was quietly dropped.[22]

Cloud County officials might have been happy to leave the mercurial Corbett alone, but word of the incident spread around the nation by newswires. This furthered Corbett's notoriety, which in turn led editors of the *Christian Advocate* to issue a scathing denunciation. After a brief overview of the confrontations, the paper wrote that in Cloud County,

> half the people want him arrested, the other half left alone. We have known Corbett for more than twenty years. All churches have members of the crank type. Corbett was of the sort who think that every thing which comes into their heads is inspired by God. They will interrupt meetings, burst out unexpectedly in yells, make interlocutory remarks while another is leading in prayer, and go generally as if they were performers in a circus, instead of being contented with taking their turn and with an occasional old-fashioned Methodist shout, marked by reverence, pathos, and unction, and which does good, and not harm. Corbett used to speak in Fulton Street Prayer Meeting, till he was frozen out, and all who knew him rejoiced when he went West.[23]

There's no way of knowing whether Corbett saw that article, but if he didn't read it himself it seems likely that others would have told him about it. If so, it must have been cutting to be dismissed so categorically by his fellow faithful.

10

CORBETT CRACKS

The financial windfall from Corbett's retroactive pension went fast; it appears that he invested a large portion of it in livestock for his farm. Before the pension, he had at most about forty sheep. In July 1883, nearly five years after he arrived in Kansas and just months after getting the pension, Corbett had four cows and 150 sheep, tended to mostly by James F. Fish, who lived about three miles away. Corbett sold the sheared wool to the Buell Manufacturing Company, which was based in St. Joseph, Missouri, but operated a factory in Blue Rapids, Kansas. Corbett sold 263 pounds of wool for $25.87 in June 1884, though Buell officials advised him at the same time that it was suspending consignment purchases until further notice. It's unknown how long that freeze lasted or whether Corbett was able to sell wool elsewhere.

But he clearly wasn't cut out for farm life, even with the help of hired hands. Cloud County tax forms show Corbett had $32 in personal property in 1882, which jumped to $367 in 1883, the year after the pension was approved. By 1885, his assets had dropped back to $42, and they slipped to $40 in 1886, so he was again facing cash problems.[1] He also continued to suffer from debilitating bouts of illness.

Still, Corbett rejected overtures to trade financially on his fame as the killer of Booth. An offer to go on the lecture circuit apparently went unanswered. Another invitation came from Edward Doherty, his superior officer on that fateful night in 1865, who wrote in September 1886 hoping to draw Corbett into a scheme to travel the country with a "panorama," a popular form of theatrical entertainment in which a machine unrolled a large scroll of painted scenes that told a story, often augmented by a live narrator. The year before, Doherty had filed a copyright for the "Panorama of the assassination of Abraham Lincoln, President of the United States, and the attempted assassination of Secretary William H. Seward."[2]

Doherty saw in the project the chance to make up for some of the riches he felt the Sixteenth Cavalry had been cheated out of by Congress's doling out of the reward money. Doherty wanted to know what Corbett thought of the idea, and "also . . . if you would take a hand in it for a good compensation." Working together, Doherty said, "I think we can make a good deal of money, and now that we are both getting old, we ought to grasp at the opportunity." If Corbett responded, the letter is lost. It's unclear whether Doherty ever launched the project.[3]

Corbett also was having significant trouble making his homestead truly his own. Under federal laws, homesteaders would apply for the public land they desired, upon approval of the application make improvements to the land, then file for the deed to the property. Corbett had filed his application and, with the construction of his dugout home and the plowing of four or five acres of the eighty-acre plot, had sufficiently improved it to submit a claim for the deed.

But his submission coincided with a national suspension of deed grants by lands commissioner William A. J. Sparks, who upon assuming the job in March 1885 had uncovered what he believed to have been massive and persistent fraud and a general lack of diligence by federal officials in ensuring that homesteaders were following the law. There is nothing to suggest Corbett's claim was fraudulent, but the broad suspension meant his deed, or patent, was delayed. And an oddity cropped up. Under the first name Thomas, Corbett was naturalized as a US citizen in Troy in 1855. But he went through the process again in Cloud County, getting his citizenship certificate on June 6, 1885, as he was trying to secure the deed to his homestead. Nothing in the files offers a reason, but it's likely that Corbett wanted to affirm his status under his assumed first name of Boston. Or perhaps he no longer had his naturalization certificate. Notably, when he filed papers in 1878 to apply for the homestead, he listed himself as a US citizen. Yet, eight years later—and three decades after he first became a citizen—Corbett went through the process anew.[4]

Corbett wrote of his frustrations with the deeding process to friends back east, and some of the details found their way to the *Boston Herald*, which reported in April 1886 that Corbett "cannot understand why he should not get his patent. Corbett does not owe a cent." The paper said Corbett was not seeking to borrow against the land, apparently a popular form of fraud at the time, "but he is intensely religious, and, as the assessor made him swear the land was his, he wants his patent so nobody can call him a liar. He says in a letter to a friend here that the republic is ungrateful to him in not giving him his patent, and if he is to be made out a liar, he wishes he had been struck by lightning before he ever settled in Kansas. But for religious tracts sent him by eastern friends, he thinks life would hardly be worth living."

The *Troy Daily Times* reported, apparently based on a different letter to a different friend, that despite his eight-dollar monthly pension, Corbett felt that he had been shorted by the government and that he deserved to be continued in the army at half-pay. Whether the Troy newspaper article is accurate is impossible to measure, but taken together the articles suggest Corbett was becoming increasingly frustrated and isolated. And for someone prone to paranoia, the delay in awarding the deed likely made him quite restive. He finally received the deed on March 20, 1886, though it was some time later before the title was fully cleared.[5]

War-linked friendships run deep, and Corbett still had his supporters among fellow veterans, some of whom sought to find Corbett a stable living that would not tax his ailing body. George W. Knapp, a veteran of Company G, Eleventh Kansas Cavalry, had arrived in Cloud County around the same time as Corbett and opened a livery business in Clyde, about fifteen miles east of Concordia and nearly twenty miles north of Corbett's homestead. Knapp considered himself "a true and tried friend" of Corbett's, and after he took his seat as a freshman member of the Kansas House of Representatives in January 1887, one of the first things he did was to gin up sympathy for Corbett among the other members.

Knapp's wrangling won Corbett an appointment to what was largely a ceremonial post: assistant doorkeeper of the House of Representatives. Corbett would only work when the part-time legislature was in session, but the pay was three dollars a day. Knapp wrote Corbett on January 13 with the good news that Corbett had "been unanimously elected" to the post "and I wish you to come right away. Sell your sheep if you have not done so and get rid of your pony some way and come on at once." Knapp added that Corbett should write him what train he would arrive on "and I will meet you at the depot. Do not fail me as it will injure me very much if you do not come."[6]

For a man getting by on the occasional sale of sheep's wool and an eight-dollar monthly pension, it was too good a job to turn down. Corbett didn't sell the sheep or his beloved Billy; he left the flock in the care of Fish, his regular farmhand, and turned Billy over to a neighbor, John Myers, then headed for Topeka. He rented a room at the home of L. W. Moore, a shoemaker who lived on Jefferson Street, and began his work as the guardian of the hallway in the Kansas State Capitol.[7]

Corbett immediately became something of a tourist attraction for those with business in the capital. People wanted to shake the hand of the man who had avenged Lincoln, and Corbett was happy to accommodate. He also took his duties seriously and, somewhat surprisingly, made friendly overtures to fellow workers in the building, including janitor and messenger Ben Williams.

Not one to let his faith go unexpressed, Corbett also involved himself with the Topeka Salvation Army during his evenings, and each morning he updated Williams on what had transpired the night before. "Whenever anyone was converted, he would tell me about it." Corbett also pitched in to help Williams and the other African American janitors sweep out the hallways in the morning before the building opened for business, an unusual crossing of an unspoken racial line.

But in mid-February Corbett became more withdrawn and "suspicious that someone was following him to do him bodily harm."[8] Skipping his morning chats with Williams and the other workers, he instead went off by himself to brood. He perceived slights in conversations and believed some of the men around the building had been mocking him over his hairstyle, calling him a woman.

Corbett initially had been placed in charge of the gentlemen's gallery, a spectator zone in a balcony reserved for men in the gender-segregated building. But unspecified frictions led to his transfer to the much less used ladies' gallery, which presumably would reduce his contact with the public and potential flashpoints. Long leery of secret societies—Corbett believed that Booth had belonged to one and that its members were the ones sending him threatening letters—Corbett spotted a Masonic Lodge pin on Knapp's lapel. "I believe that your oath to that secret society is stronger than your friendship for me," Corbett told him.

On Tuesday morning, February 15, Williams, a fellow worker named Wilcox, and a few other men were sweeping the hallways and joking with each other. Corbett heard the laughter, thought the men had made a joke at his expense, and went unglued. "I was laughing at one of the other boys," Williams said, "when Corbett came up from behind with a pistol pointed towards me." Williams didn't know Corbett was coming until the other workers began to run, but when he turned and saw Corbett, he began running too.

The legislature was not yet in session for the day, but the capitol building was already full of people holding early meetings and appointments or preparing for the session. Word swept through the building that Corbett had pulled a gun and was in a rage. But Corbett had already tucked away the revolver; he had picked up one of the brooms and was sweeping the hallway as though nothing had happened.

The sergeant-at-arms, Charley Norton, approached and asked Corbett what had led to the confrontation. Corbett dropped the broom and pulled the gun back out and threatened to shoot Norton, who backed away. Corbett then moved to the doorkeeper's station at the entrance to the building's west gallery, an ornately decorated vestibule connecting the balcony stairway to the session room, where he stood guard as though on duty. After a while, Corbett moved into the ladies' gallery, where he sat in one of the empty rows. A local newspaper reporter slowly entered the gallery, walked to Corbett, carefully sat down next to him, and began asking questions. Corbett again pulled out the gun, rose silently, and walked away.

M. V. B. Sheafor of Concordia had known Corbett for several years and was in the capital that morning in his role as clerk for a Cloud County township to discuss some local bonds. Knapp, too, was in the building, and Knapp asked Sheafor to join him in trying to talk Corbett into giving up his gun.

As the two men approached Corbett, Sheafor stretched out his hand in greeting and said, "Hello, Corbett."

"I don't want to have anything to do with you," Corbett replied. "I saw you walking across the floor with Dan Brown, and you are conspiring with him to do me all the harm you can."

Sheafor told Corbett there was no conspiracy with Brown, a Concordia lawyer, Cloud County probate judge, and real estate investor; he was just walking and talking with the man. Corbett drew his gun: "You get out of here." The men backed away, leaving Corbett alone again.

While the drama was playing out inside, police were summoned, and, led by deputy marshal John W. Gardiner, they devised a plan to corral Corbett and, at an unguarded moment when his gun was tucked away, jump him. It took several hours, but they finally had their chance and made quick work of it, grabbing Corbett and pinning him to the floor before he could reach either his gun or a knife he also had tucked into his belt. "Well, you're a pretty gang," Corbett said calmly as they trussed him up and took him away to the city jail.

The next day, Corbett faced a brief sanity trial in probate court before Judge Alfred Bixby Quinton. The key witnesses from the day before, including Williams and the police officers who had subdued Corbett, testified about Corbett's growing eccentricities and the gun-drawn showdowns. Corbett cross-examined some of the witnesses himself, asking about supposed incidents in which he was laughed at or mocked for his hairstyle and other perceived slights.

Then Corbett took the stand and delivered a strange monologue about the forces arrayed against him. They began with a certain unidentified man in Concordia who Corbett was convinced was "seeking to destroy me, and he had told Williams about this," that Williams had insulted him and so "deserved violence," though Corbett noted that he had not hurt Williams. Corbett went on about being "hunted and hounded" and that "people at home have been following me, killing my cattle, and setting fire to my pasture." John Wilkes Booth, he noted, had belonged to a secret society, as had Booth's brother, Edwin, and "some members of that order have been following me ever since I killed Booth."

The judge's verdict was quick and expected. Boston Corbett, the avenger of Lincoln, was insane and a danger to others. Corbett was delivered to the Kansas State Insane Asylum at the Topeka State Hospital, the regional repository for the mentally ill, where, upon admission, he told the doctors that there was something wrong in his head.

Corbett was neither the best nor the worst of the mental patients at the Topeka State Hospital, a sprawling complex on the south bank of the Kansas River less than three miles northwest of the capitol building. The center had been open less than a decade and was already at capacity, with more than five hundred patients and a long waiting list of people housed by their families or being held in county jails.[9]

Corbett now denied that he was insane and argued that his incarceration was the endgame of a conspiracy. Yet partial reports from the hospital say he was admitted with "great mental excitement" after a series of violent or near-violent encounters going back several years. "Corbett is a very civil and comfortable patient, as far as his actions go, but full of cranky notions; and makes frequent demands for liberty; and the possession of his various fighting paraphernalia. He, however, shows his delirium by that he is here by persecution, conspiracy, and fraud. He charges Cloud County officials, his friend Knapp, the legislature, the probate court, and the officers of the asylum with a deep laid plot to get him in here and secure his little property."[10]

The hospital assigned a "special attendant" to keep an eye on Corbett as he moved about and interacted with fellow patients, ever watchful that the man who had been so quick to draw his gun could do no harm to others. At one mealtime, though, the attendant, "neglecting his duty," left his charge untended in the dining hall. "Corbett seized the opportunity on some frivolous pretext to make an assault on the [dining hall] attendant with a knife. He was fortunately disarmed without doing any injury."

By the end of April 1887, Corbett was "in much the same way: in general rather quiet and comfortable; at the same time malicious, fault finding, and disposed to instigate mutiny. He calls down imprecations upon all the Asylum officers, and charges all his misfortunes to them." Corbett viewed any incident as part of the conspiracy. But he was also getting physically healthier, gaining weight, and "is much less annoyed by the maladies that have so long afflicted him." Still, "he is not at all improved mentally" and "clings to the delusions." Among them: "That everything is being done by the officers and attendants of this institution that is possible to undermine his health, and even to take his life by poison, which is placed in his food and drink." And the members of the secret society were still after him. "Believing as he does, and falling back on the vain pride which besets him, he makes numerous threats and seems to continuously long for blood." In short, Corbett wasn't getting out any time soon.

Richard Thatcher, Corbett's Andersonville friend, had moved on to a new job as the superintendent of schools in Neodesha, about 120 miles south of Topeka. Corbett and Thatcher had exchanged a number of letters since Thatcher arrived in Kansas in 1882, but they had not seen each other. Thatcher refused to believe that his old friend and, in some ways, prison and religious mentor had gone insane.

After the school year let out, Thatcher traveled to Topeka and visited Corbett at the hospital, spending thirty to forty-five minutes with him. As a friend, Thatcher was ready to suspend disbelief and join Corbett's view of the world. "He told me just what I already believed, that a deep plot had been laid in his opinion, by one or two men of Cloud County." The aim was Corbett's property, but the conspiracy was also political. Corbett "knew some of their crooked proceedings, which if fully ventilated and exposed, were destined to send them to the 'pen.' And knowing his excitable nature and peculiar eccentricities they had, as he believed, laid a trap for him." It was those conspirators who had "picked a quarrel out of him."[11]

Thatcher went to the probate court in Topeka and requested an audience with Judge Quinton. Thatcher wasn't just some crank; he was a well-regarded educator (two years later he would become the founding president of the Territorial Normal School of Oklahoma, predecessor to the University of Central Oklahoma). Thatcher persuaded Quinton that whatever had been ailing Corbett before had dissipated and he had regained his sanity. Thatcher asked the judge to let Corbett leave the asylum. Quinton found Thatcher persuasive and issued the order; a short time later, though, he spoke with asylum officials and learned that no one at the hospital thought that Corbett was either healthy or safe to be released. Quinton rescinded his order, and Corbett's brief chance at freedom disappeared.

Thatcher, though, did apparently succeed in one other way. On July 14, 1887, Corbett deposited fifteen dollars in an account under his own name at the First National Bank of Concordia, a transaction that was done by mail. It seems highly unlikely that Corbett would have had the opportunity to make such a transaction from inside the asylum; Thatcher was the most likely candidate to have acted on Corbett's behalf. It wasn't much money, but it was a stash that would come in handy.[12]

That Thatcher, an old friend, would give Corbett the benefit of the doubt about his sanity and the forces that landed him in the asylum seems reasonable. But to buy into Corbett's clearly paranoid view of the world says more about Thatcher than it does about Corbett. Still, Thatcher and George A. Huron, the Topeka lawyer who had first met Corbett in Washington at the close of the war, would wind up being Boston Corbett's last and best defenders.

In September, seven months after Corbett was first sent to the insane asylum, Quinton ruled that Corbett was permanently insane and not likely to ever emerge from the asylum. After struggling to find someone to handle guardianship of Corbett and his property, Quinton persuaded Huron to take the assignment. Among Huron's first steps was asking the Bureau of Pensions to send Corbett's pension checks to his care, which he deposited in a bank and began a ledger of Corbett's assets and incomes. Huron also turned his attention to Cloud County and the homestead, where he discovered there was a lot to catch up with.

When Corbett left home for the job in Topeka, he had expected to return by late spring, after the legislative session ended. Fish, Corbett's farmhand, similarly expected to watch over Corbett's flock of sheep only until May. Here it was September heading into October, with winter looming, and Fish still had responsibility for the sheep. Fish saw an item in the local newspaper that Corbett had been judged insane and that a guardian had been appointed, so he wrote to the probate court about the sheep.

"I would be very much obliged if you would see that the guardian disposes of them as soon as possible. It will be impossible for me to keep them much longer, and I am now entitled to pay for the extra time I have kept them." Fish also seemed ready to be rid of Corbett, and the sheep, for good. "I would not take them to keep same another summer for any price, as I had to keep them up and feed them, and I ask to be allowed at least ten dollars per month for keeping them from the first of May until they are disposed of."[13]

Huron sent out letters to other people in and around Concordia to get a sense of Corbett's possessions; he apparently was aided by Corbett himself, with whom he met occasionally at the asylum. It's unclear, though, whether Corbett gave Huron permission to start selling off his possessions—or, for that matter, whether Huron, as the court-appointed guardian, needed Corbett's permission. Regardless, Huron began liquidating Corbett's assets. He wrote to Knapp, Corbett's benefactor at the House of Representatives, who replied that Corbett's pony was still with Corbett's neighbor John Myers. Huron asked Myers to try to sell Billy the horse as well as the guns that had been retrieved from Corbett's dugout; he also instructed Fish to try to find a buyer for the sheep.[14]

Myers had better luck than Fish. He reported to Huron in late October that he had sold two guns—a musket went to Sheafor, the township clerk and Corbett acquaintance who had tried to intercede during the legislature showdown, for $5—and other unspecified property for a total of $15.75. But Myers still had Billy, the horse's harness, and Corbett's buckboard. Myers mentioned to Huron that locals were eyeing Corbett's land and wondered whether that, too, would go up for sale. Others circled as well. The president of the Kansas Historical Society wrote to Huron that he "would be very glad to get for our society the Boston Corbett bootjack and any other relics and papers which you may be able to obtain."

Corbett was penned up, but he still captured the public's attention. In January 1888, nearly a year after the showdown in the capitol building, the *Chicago Herald* reported that among the items Huron had sold was "the identical Enfield rifle with which Corbett shot the slayer of Lincoln," which went to the Concordia post of the Grand Army of the Republic. The article was half true. A rifle was sold, but it had nothing to do with Booth's death. Corbett had shot Booth with a handgun, which disappeared within days of the shooting and remains lost to history.[15]

Despite Corbett's intransigence at the asylum, he was not considered a flight risk, and he—like most of the patients—had the run of the grounds, though always under a watchful eye. Around eight o'clock in the morning on May 26, 1888, Corbett was part of what can best be described as a fitness parade, a daily escorted march of patients around the grounds to get fresh air. The inmates—for that is what they were—were distinctive. Corbett, for instance, wore a gray jeans suit with his name embroidered on the chest, and a dark soft hat to protect from the late spring sun.[16]

As the inmates walked, a boy named Clarence Dennis, about twelve years old, rode up to the main building on a pony, dismounted, tied the animal to a fence, and trotted up the steps and on inside. The custom of the era was for the hospital administrator and family to live on the grounds, and Dennis had arrived to visit the son of hospital chief Dr. Barnard Douglass Eastman.[17]

Corbett noticed the boy's arrival and the tethered pony and saw an opportunity that was too enticing to ignore. As the inmates moved along, Corbett slowed his pace to let the parade go ahead, then broke suddenly for Dennis's pony, quickly untied the reins, and hopped on the animal's back.

Within seconds, Corbett was galloping off down the road, a gray-suited blur leaving the patients, the orderlies, and his incarceration behind.

An alert was sent out immediately that Corbett, the killer of Booth and the madman of Cloud County, was on the loose. Word circulated that Corbett had become more agitated in recent weeks, threatening the lives of the governor, John A. Martin, unspecified officials in Cloud County, and others. Deputies rushed to the statehouse on the presumption that a blood-thirsty Corbett would make that his first stop. But Corbett wasn't there. Telegrams were sent across the state about the escape, and the newspapers were filled with accounts of the vengeance Corbett intended to reap. Officials in Cloud County were on the alert.

Corbett, though, neither hung around Topeka to assassinate his perceived tormentors nor headed home to make some sort of final stand at his fortressed dugout's door. Rather, he directed Clarence Dennis's pony due south, toward Neodesha, where he knew he at least had one friend, Richard Thatcher. Corbett took a few days to cover the 120 miles, likely hiding by day and moving quietly by night. He arrived at Thatcher's home on the evening of May 31, about five days after he fled the asylum. Thatcher was happy to see him and more than willing to help him. Corbett, though, declined Thatcher's offer of a bed, and slept outside on a pile of cobs.

The next day Corbett ate breakfast and dinner with Thatcher and his family, but he wasn't planning on hanging around to get captured and returned to the asylum. Thatcher's brother-in-law, Irvin S. De Ford, took Corbett to a train depot just outside Neodesha. Corbett gave De Ford a draft for the fifteen dollars on his Concordia bank account—the stash Thatcher likely had helped him squirrel away—and De Ford gave Corbett fifteen dollars in cash to fund the journey ahead. Corbett asked that the asylum be alerted that the pony was in Neodesha so it could be returned to the Dennis boy.[18]

Corbett's plan, he had told Thatcher, was to head for Mexico, a place where he presumed the Kansas probate court was unlikely to pursue him and seek his return to the insane asylum. After a flurry of good-byes, Corbett boarded the train and, with the belching of smoke and the crescendo of an engine gaining speed, disappeared.

11

THE RETURN
OF BOSTON CORBETT

T here were rumors, all sorts of rumors, about where the killer
of Booth had wound up. In the first few years after he rode off
on the stolen pony, reports occasionally surfaced, then zipped
around the country by news wire, that Boston Corbett had died in Idaho,
or Montana, or New Mexico, or "Old" Mexico. George Huron picked up
on each rumor and dispatched letters of inquiry to see if there was any truth
behind them, sometimes tapping into networks of his own contacts and
friends of friends. T. B. Mills, a real estate manager and former newspaper
publisher in Las Vegas, New Mexico, knew Simeon B. Bradford, Huron's
former law partner (and Kansas attorney general when Corbett was in the
asylum). Mills responded to a letter from Huron in May 1895 with details
of a search he had undertaken after Huron spotted yet another news item
about Corbett's supposed death.

"I looked over the Territorial papers which I have files of, and made
inquiry of the editors of all the city papers, and they could give me no
information regarding Mr. Corbett. They have no recollection of seeing the
article you refer to in regard to his death. I infer if it took place in Arizona
or New Mexico, it must have been in the former place." Mills reported

that he had forwarded Huron's letter to the New Mexico newspapers for publication, which he expected them to share with the Arizona papers, as was the custom. "No doubt if his death took place in that territory, through this medium you will receive the information you ask for, which I regret I cannot give myself." Huron filed away similar responses from other sources in other states. Despite the sporadic news reports, Huron could run none of them back to the original source. No newspaper editors or law enforcement officers or government officials reported any contact with Corbett. He had disappeared.[1]

Huron continued managing his ward's property, though there wasn't much managing to be done. The sheep were gone, sold off at a price that about squared the debt owed to Fish for feeding and tending them. Corbett's

George A. Huron.

Kansas Historical Society, Topeka (item number 306661, call number B Huron, Judge G. A. *1.; KSHS identifier DaRT ID: 306661)

pony, Billy, and the buckboard were gone, too, sold to cover the cost of their keep at a livery where Myers had sent them for holding.

The farm remained a frustration. Fewer than twenty of Corbett's eighty acres were arable, the rest of it "very broken and very stony" and hard to till and to harvest. Huron had leased out the tillable land but the renters had no more luck farming it than had Corbett. Farmers preferred rental contracts based on a share of the crop, and for a few seasons Huron entered into agreements for one-third of the harvest, deals that were negotiated through Concordia realtor and insurance man John M. Brumbaugh until 1892. Thereafter, Huron paid Concordia lawyer E. L. Ackley five dollars a year to act as his local agent. Some seasons brought no crops and earned the estate nothing.

Eventually Huron managed to rent it out for cash, at first $36 for the season then raised to $40, most often to Corbett's near neighbors A. S. Harrington and Lorenzo Acton, who lived across the road. One unidentified renter reneged when his crop failed and he had no cash reserves to pay the debt. "There have been so many crop failures since I have had charge of the land that some years it produced almost nothing, and one or two years I got nothing at all from it," Huron reported. "The expenses of looking after a piece of land so far away are large enough to keep the accumulations down to a very low point. Consequently, there has been no accumulation of consequence from the rentals, after paying the court expenses, and other expenses of looking after it."[2]

Huron kept detailed records and submitted reports to the probate court. He wrote to old friends of Corbett, names apparently culled from the papers Corbett had left behind in the dugout, to see if they might know a relative to whom Huron could turn over the property and the responsibility. But all anyone knew about Corbett's life were the scant details. Corbett had had a wife who died childless. Corbett's self-castration precluded any further chance of an heir. There was a sister, but she had fallen out with the rest of the family and faded away. The brother, John, couldn't be found either. Huron contemplated selling the farm and sticking the proceeds in the account he was managing for Corbett; he had been offered $400 for it. But he decided to pass that up in case Corbett someday reappeared and wanted to return to the homestead.

So the estate sat.

As a lawyer, Huron had other clients and business to tend to from his office in room 6 of the Office Block, a three-story building on East Fifth Street adjacent to the post office and federal courtrooms in Topeka. He eventually became a police judge, a high-profile position handling infractions of city ordinances. As a war veteran, Huron received regular invitations to speak at Memorial Day gatherings, and he played an active role in Lincoln Post No. 1 of the Grand Army of the Republic. He stumped for political candidates, always Republican, and belonged to an array of social organizations: the International Order of the Odd Fellows, the Ancient Order of United Workmen, and the Knights and Ladies of Security, an insurance collective. He and his wife, Mary, were longstanding members of the Methodist Episcopal Church, which gave Huron a bond of common faith with Corbett.[3]

Some of Corbett's friends, too, sought information on his disappearance; others who had missed the news wrote to Corbett directly, including Edward Doherty, Corbett's former cavalry commander. After giving up his panorama scheme and other business ventures, he had decamped New Orleans for New York City, where he was working as a city street-paving inspector.[4] Apparently unaware of Corbett's meltdown and eventual escape from the asylum, Doherty wrote Corbett that a friend had mentioned reading an article purportedly by Corbett about the night Booth died, and Doherty wanted a copy of it. Doherty used stationery from the Grand Army of the Republic's Veteran Post No. 436, headquartered at 54 Union Square, and the tone sounds like a man trying to reconnect with an old service buddy who may not have been as keen to renew the relationship.[5]

"I have been very anxious to hear from you, have written you several times without receiving a reply," Doherty wrote. "I hope this epistle will not meet the same fate of the others. Write me a long letter about yourself and what you are doing, and how you are getting along. If I can be of any service, you must command me. Tho we are getting old, we are brothers in our holy savior who wields all things to suit himself." The religious reference was unusual: none of Doherty's earlier letters to Corbett included such phrasing, suggesting he either had found religion or sought to ingratiate himself. Doherty added "the kindest regards" from a "Miss

Thompson," a hint that Doherty had managed to overlap Corbett's old life in New York.

But no word surfaced from Corbett himself. For all his peculiarities, street preaching, and noisy public proclamations of faith, he proved to be very effective at staying quiet, or at least not drawing enough attention to himself to raise suspicions among local authorities, wherever he might have landed.

Among the richest men in Topeka at the time was William W. Gavitt, who owned a loan and investment firm and a printing company as well as real estate around the city, including the Office Block, where Huron maintained his law office. Gavitt made his fortune, though, by marketing a top-selling laxative, Gavitt's System Regulator, sold primarily through mail orders and a wide system of regional traveling representatives to whom he would ship cases of the product, leaving it up to salesmen to either vend it themselves or establish their own local networks of dealers.

Gavitt maintained close communications with his sales force, always exhorting them to do better, steering them to possible regional markets, and pressing them for more sales. As part of those communications, he wrote regularly to his regional salesman covering Texas and the Indian and Oklahoma territories. The salesman went by the name of John Corbett, and something about the exchanges stirred Gavitt's memory. Eventually he asked Corbett if he had ever spent any time in Topeka and whether he might be the very same Boston Corbett with whom Gavitt had crossed paths. "We are under the impression that we met you here six or eight years ago, when you were Assistant Sergeant or door keeper in the State Legislature," Gavitt wrote in June 1900.

Yes, the salesman replied, he was Boston Corbett. After more than a decade, the killer of Booth had apparently resurfaced.[6]

Corbett's letters to Gavitt didn't survive, but from Gavitt's responses it's clear they discussed Corbett's legal standing and the possibility that he remained a wanted man a dozen years after he had fled Topeka. Gavitt offered to help get "a pretty good statement of some party here in Topeka that you could use in connection with the statements that you already have, so that you can travel without molested [*sic*] in Texas or almost any other place."

A few days after getting Corbett's response, Gavitt popped into Huron's office and told the lawyer that he had found Corbett. Huron wrote to the salesman, then in Enid, Oklahoma, telling him that if Gavitt was correct and he was indeed Boston Corbett, Huron had "good news." Huron wrote that Corbett had left his pension unclaimed after his disappearance, and that it could be resumed with back payments for the uncollected years. He also updated Corbett on the steps he had taken to preserve and administer the small estate that held the proceeds from the sale of Corbett's personal property, the sheep, and Billy; and on the status of the eighty acres and dugout home Corbett owned outside Concordia. Gavitt sent his own letters advising Corbett how to go about reclaiming his life and offering to gather whatever documents Corbett would need from Dr. Barnard Eastman, the former director of the asylum.[7]

Corbett replied to Huron on July 18 in a letter scrawled in pencil on thin and narrow notepaper, words misspelled and grammar broken, and following peculiar rules of punctuation. Corbett told the lawyer he "was glad to hear from you. Someone at the asylum told me that they had a pointed me a guardian but I never thought any more a Bout it as i was so glad to make my escape and gane my liberty in the world onse more I never expected to ever claim my pension any more I would rather die at onse than to Ever have to go back to that Hauling hole of Satan, as I use to call it. And i want to say rite now that if i thought that i wood hav to go back to the sylum i wood rather looze my pension intirely than to ever hav any more to Do with it."

Corbett told Huron he believed Kansas officials had sent him to the asylum as part of a conspiracy to steal his pension, but that he would welcome Huron's help as his guardian to get the pension reinstated, so long as Corbett would remain free of the mental hospital. He reminisced a bit about the day he was arrested when he "was faithfully discharging my duties" as "assistant sergeant or doorkeeper in the State Legislature." He said he would do whatever he needed to "get my pension and citizenship back . . . except going Back to Kansas. That I will not do." Yet he also described Dr. Eastman as "a perfect gentle man and he will cheerfully recommend me to you. i know that he was a good man and he was good to all of his patients" and not part of the conspiracy that Corbett believed led to his incarceration. It was that conspiracy, he added, that had propelled him to flee and start calling himself John or James Corbett; "i was afraid that i wood Be taking Back to the Sylum at Topeka and left there to die." (For the sake of easier reading, the misspellings in the rest of Corbett's letters will be corrected.)[8]

The guardian and his ward exchanged letters sporadically over the ensuing months as Huron began figuring out what he needed to do to have Corbett's pension resumed. Part of the slowness was Corbett's travel—he moved often throughout the Southwest. Part of it was Corbett's legendarily odd behavior and his inconsistent correspondence; part of it was the steps that were required to get the pension resumed, which included a positive identification of the recipient. Huron advised Corbett that he would likely be required to undergo another medical examination. Corbett demurred. A lot of years had passed, he said. He had been insane for a while, and sick, and his memory wasn't that clear. The original examination should still hold, he argued. "It seems but it would be a small matter to have my pension started again and further my pension should be increased to the very best dollar that it could be raised." Corbett also asked Huron about selling the farm, and about transferring his "business"—the guardianship—to Pecos County, Texas, where Corbett then lived. "Please write to me and tell me what is best for me to do as you know what is best and I don't, me being feeble both physically and mentally and I certainly need some help to know what is best for me to do."[9]

Huron continued to manage the farm. He began forwarding letters that came to him as Corbett's guardian, including one from Edward Kirk, Corbett's cavalry buddy, now a director of Kirk's Cornice Works Co. in Chicago. Kirk wrote Huron to thank him for getting him in touch with his "old comrade," and that Corbett had responded. "He was, as you have been informed, a peculiar man," Kirk wrote. "Very set and determined, and made no promises on engagement but he kept both in letter and spirit." Kirk added that he hoped Corbett could regain his pension so "that he might be made comfortable in his old age," suggesting that Corbett had enlisted Kirk to lobby on his behalf.[10]

Huron finally determined that the best tactic would be to file a request with the federal government to reopen Corbett's pension and let the government sort out the specifics of how to proceed. In January 1902, he wrote to the pension bureau that he was Corbett's guardian, that Corbett had been found, and that he wanted to restore the pension. But the pension bureau apparently moved too slowly for Huron; he wrote Congressman William A. Calderhead, whose subsequent letter to the bureau apparently sped up the process. In late April, pension commissioner H. Clay Evans wrote Huron that the bureau would need "medical testimony showing whether the soldier has been disabled by chronic diarrhea, scurvy, and rheumatism continuously since December 4, 1889," when Corbett's last pension check had been issued. The bureau would also have an inspector meet with Corbett to verify his identity.[11]

Huron passed the word to Corbett and urged him to travel to Topeka for the medical exam and to deal with the legal issues surrounding his assignment to the insane asylum. Huron was convinced that whatever mental problems Corbett might have had that led to the episode at the state capitol, he had recovered and was fit to resume control of his own life and assets. Corbett wanted Huron to sell the land for $500, but under the terms of the guardianship, Huron would not be able to pass along the proceeds in a lump sum but could only dole it out in small amounts as needed, subject to court overview. Corbett asked Huron to arrange for the land sale but hold any agreement in abeyance. Once the probate court released Corbett from oversight, he would sign the deed transfer. Corbett was already counting his cash. He told Huron to keep $25 for his handling fee and set aside some cash to cover court costs, leaving him with $455. He'd use that sum, he said, to buy a small home somewhere else for himself and his wife—apparently he'd remarried since his disappearance.

Corbett agreed to make the trip, though with a murky timetable. He and his wife had been planning to visit his mother-in-law in Oklahoma City in the summer and would include a side trip to Topeka, about three hundred miles to the northeast. Corbett wrote on May 2 that his "wife and I shall start at once for the north," which stretched out until around May 21.

Huron passed along word to Washington that the pension bureau could assign an inspector to meet with Corbett in Topeka. "He is possessed of a wagon and team of horses and has been in the habit of traveling over the country following the avocation of selling medicines prepared by the W. W. Gavitt Co. of Topeka," Huron wrote. "If he comes in this way it will take him weeks to reach Topeka; otherwise if he comes by train he is liable to be here at any time." The Bureau of Pensions had a special examiner based in Topeka, a man named Hiram Kingsley, and he set an August 18 start date for taking depositions in the request to reopen Corbett's pension case.[12]

The sporadic communications with Corbett frustrated Huron. He wrote to Corbett at different stops along the route, but if Corbett received the letters he didn't respond. Because Corbett communicated more frequently with Gavitt, his boss, Huron enlisted the wealthy laxative maker to urge Corbett to get to Topeka soon. Corbett, though, decided at the last minute to skip Kansas. He told Gavitt, who passed the details along to Huron, that he had fallen ill in Oklahoma. The weather was bad for his rheumatism, and for the sake of his health he and his wife were returning immediately to west Texas and the dry heat of the semi-desert.

So Corbett and his wife loaded up their wagon and headed back home.

It's remarkable, in hindsight, that it took Huron so long to become suspicious of the elusive Boston Corbett, traveling salesman. The first clues were in the original letter from the man, when he told Huron that "someone at the asylum told me that they had appointed me a guardian but I never thought any more about it as I was so glad to make my escape." Huron had met Corbett in Washington, had seen him in the Topeka capitol building before the meltdown and again several times at the asylum after he had been appointed guardian. Yet the letter suggested Corbett had not met with Huron as part of the court oversight. It could be that Huron suspended natural skepticism because he wanted to believe that Corbett had finally been found.

But by fall of 1902, after Corbett skipped the Topeka trip and following a brief exchange of letters, Huron's doubts blossomed, fed by "the tenor" of what Corbett was writing. While Corbett told Gavitt he had returned to Texas for health reasons, he wrote to Huron that in addition "my best friends told me that I had better stay away from Topeka if I wanted to keep out of the asylum." But Corbett also told Huron he no longer needed him to serve as his guardian and suggested Huron turn that job over to Corbett's wife.

Huron began making inquiries. He hired T. T. Harding, a cousin in Oklahoma City, to go talk to Corbett's mother-in-law, Paralee Williams, and supplied him with the address. When Harding knocked on the door, though, he found someone else living in the house. Williams had moved three or four miles out into the country, and the current resident knew nothing about Corbett. Harding began asking around the neighborhood and found people who said that yes, Corbett had been there, but he had left, telling people he was heading for Enid, or back to Texas, but not to Topeka because he "still has his queer ways that you speak of" and feared being sent back to the asylum.[13]

"The neighbors seem to think that his wife and the mother-in-law are not strictly decent," Harding reported. "When he was away they would have a gang of men out at nights, and when he was at home he would put a stop to it so he and the old lady had a falling out and she called the police and gave him notice to quit the place, and at once, or they would have to take him into custody. So he took his wife and lit out."

A few days later Harding asked around further about Corbett; apparently Huron wanted him to double-check and make sure that it had indeed been Corbett. He reported back that some neighbors believed Corbett might have stopped in Lawton, about ninety miles southwest of Oklahoma City, and Harding offered to go find him and bring him to Topeka. He included descriptions from others in Oklahoma City of what Corbett looked like, details that must have confirmed Huron's suspicions. "Corbit," as police officer H. S. Baker knew him, was about six feet tall and around fifty-five years old. Boston Corbett was at least half a foot shorter and would have been seventy years old. A Mrs. MacGruder was even more detailed, though Harding had to pay her a dollar to assuage her fears that Corbett might return and "do her some harm." She, too, said Corbett was about six feet tall and added that he had "slender form with broad shoulders, long legs and arms" with black hair that he combed over the top of his head to cover up a large bald spot.

Huron had his own memories of what his ward looked like—short, compact, no evidence of emerging baldness—but he wanted something more definitive. He asked the pension bureau for the description of Corbett in their records. The response from deputy commissioner E. F. Ware noted the discrepancy in height: the new Corbett was a half-foot taller than the original. The commissioner sent along a sample of Corbett's signature for Huron to compare, but also said that Kingsley, the special examiner in Topeka, had yet to turn up sufficient evidence to determine whether Corbett was Corbett.[14]

Huron became convinced that the man with whom he had been corresponding was a fake and that he was trying to defraud the government of Corbett's pension and the court of Corbett's estate. Huron knew that the salesman was living somewhere near the post office in Truscott, Texas, in Knox County about 180 miles northwest of Fort Worth, because that was where he was collecting his mail from Gavitt. Huron went to the probate judge, W. E. Fagan, with his suspicions, and he suggested the court order him to travel to Texas and track the man down. He also suggested that he take with him John W. Gardiner, the former Topeka cop and private railway detective, one of the men who subdued Corbett during the capitol incident and had spent most of two days with him until Corbett was signed into the asylum. Both men would be able to identify the real Corbett on sight.

Judge Fagan agreed. He issued the order on January 9 and set a daily rate of $2.50 for Gardiner and $15 a day for Huron, reflecting the income the lawyer would lose being away from his practice. And, oddly, the expenses were to come from Corbett's estate, which meant that Corbett, wherever he was, would be paying for the investigation into the man who was trying to steal his property and pension.[15]

Huron and Gardiner left on February 12, a Thursday, traveling by train. They worked methodically, tracing the salesman through some of the places Huron knew he had been—a trail of post offices at which he had collected and sent letters. They stopped in Enid, Oklahoma, then traveled on to Texas, first by train to Wichita Falls, where they likely rented a horse team and wagon for the rest of the trip. They went on to Seymour, where they linked up with Robert T. Dickson, most likely hiring him as a local guide to help them get around. They carried on to Benjamin and finally Truscott. The travel was difficult, covering more than seventy-five miles after leaving the train "over very bad roads, through heavy snow drifts, in very inclement weather, immediately following a Texas blizzard." Through inquiries in Truscott they learned that their man was living on a nearby ranch owned by Louis Chesser, a successful cattle dealer who also ran the town's biggest general store.

Huron, Gardiner, and Dickson rode four miles west out of town and found the salesman living in a dugout, a more rustic version of the stone-walled, wood-floored shelter Corbett had built back in Cloud County. The Texas version was built into the south side of a low hill, fronted by a stone wall and with a chimney that emerged from the bluff itself. As they arrived, a tall man of about fifty with one hand heavily bandaged and a younger man emerged from the hovel. Huron said they were looking for Boston Corbett, and the tall man said that he was Boston Corbett, which Huron and Gardiner knew instantly was a lie.

Huron didn't identify himself by name but told the man that he had been sent by the pension bureau to identify him as Boston Corbett so that they could resume his government pension. (It wasn't a lie; Huron had gained permission for the ruse from the pension bureau.) Inside they met Corbett's wife of four years, who was then nineteen years old, who told Huron that when she married him he went by the name John Corbett but that he recently had told her his true identity.[16]

Huron took the lead and began questioning the man about his life. It was quite a tale, but it wasn't the life history of Boston Corbett. This Corbett told the inquisitors he had been born in Maine along the Delaware River (there is no such river in the state). He ran away around age sixteen and wound up in New York City working as a common laborer (no mention of hat making), then enlisted in the Sixteenth Cavalry, his only service (Corbett served three stints in the Twelfth New York State Militia before joining the Sixteenth), and had never been taken prisoner, though he had contracted during his army service the debilitating "diarrhea, rheumatism, and scurvy" that initially led to the pension. He listed the wrong names for his commanding officers. He said that after mustering out he immediately headed west, stopping for a brief time in Indianapolis, then working in a quarry at Terre Haute before moving on to Kansas. After escaping from the asylum, he traveled west on foot to Colorado, then stayed in a long list of towns and villages before working his way back to Kansas, stopping for a time in Wichita, then moving on to Texas and starting work selling Gavitt's remedies. He brought out a packet of letters from Gavitt—and also from Huron, not knowing that it was Huron who was peppering him with questions.

The specificity of the towns and people with whom the man said he lived makes it seem as though he meshed true details of his own life with concocted details from what he thought Corbett's life was, particularly in the years after Corbett disappeared. He also said he had been sick continually since leaving the asylum but had not sought a doctor's help, relying instead on Gavitt's laxative concoctions, an odd bit of self-medicating for what was supposed to be chronic diarrhea. The investigator asked him how tall he was. Just under six feet, the man said, though he was taller before rheumatism bent his knees. Huron must have mentioned the enlistment measurement supplied by the pension bureau, because the man said he had been five feet, eight inches when he enlisted, but had grown two inches while in the army.

Huron asked to measure him. Their host agreed but immediately took off his boots, saying the pension bureau had his height listed too short. When Huron arrived the man was upright and limber; now he hobbled to the doorway against which Huron planned to measure him. "He stood at the door with his knees bent, his feet forward from the door, threw his head back and to one side and drew his neck down," trying to game the measurement. Gardiner and Huron stepped forward, each taking an arm, and straightened him out. Gardiner pushed the man's feet back against the doorjamb and held him as straight as he could while Huron marked the level of the top of his head on the doorway, then measured it. Even with the contortions, the man was five feet, nine inches tall, some four or five inches taller than Corbett.

Huron noted that he also appeared to be younger now than the real Corbett had been when he knew him at the asylum.

The man was "voluble" through most of the interview, but when "asked questions that he had not seemed to have previously considered," such as his whereabouts after leaving Topeka and the details of his health problems, he "did not answer readily and some questions he declined to answer at all, saying he would have to look those matters up." Notably missing from his answers and, for that matter, from his letters with Huron was any sign of religious faith, the driving power of the real Boston Corbett's life.

John Corbett clearly was not Boston Corbett. Huron told him they would need to have his statement written up and notarized. The man said he had spent the winter trapping wolves, and two weeks earlier one had bitten him on the hand. The weather was cold, and the combination of the healing hand and cold air precluded him from traveling to the nearest good-sized town, Benjamin, where they could have the statement typed up and witnessed. So Huron wrote the statement out in longhand, covering four pages, then read it aloud and had the man sign it, witnessed by Gardiner, Dickson, and himself.

For Huron, it was the evidence he needed to establish the attempted fraud. And even if the statement became problematic, the investigators would soon turn up another damning detail: this Boston Corbett and his young bride were about to start a family.

Huron and Gardiner arrived back in Topeka around February 22, where Huron had some unfinished Corbett business to complete: the sale of the eighty-acre homestead in Cloud County. What should have been a simple transaction was complicated by two competing bids and a bit of overstepping by Huron's agent in Concordia, Alvin Wilmoth, one of the remaining two partners after Ackley left the law firm of Caldwell, Ackley & Wilmoth. Wilmoth leased the farm for the 1902 growing season to F. W. Clawson, one of Corbett's neighbors, for $40, a lease that was to expire in March 1903. But in April 1902 Wilmoth had written to Huron that he had sold the land to Clawson for $550 and that Huron would need to process it through probate court. Once the deed was clear, Clawson would pay.

But with Corbett supposedly found, Huron had been uncertain of what he should do. To sell it through probate meant adding the proceeds to Corbett's estate, which could only be doled out as Corbett needed it, through Huron and with the court's permission. During the summer, when Huron thought Corbett had been found, he delayed acting until Corbett's status was clarified. In early September, Huron received a second offer for the property—$550 from Lorenzo Acton, whose farm adjoined Corbett's land and who wanted it for pasture land.

Huron told Acton that, given the unsettled situation, the land was no longer for sale. And he told Clawson the same thing. But Clawson had a contract signed by the lawyer Wilmoth, and he threatened to sue to enforce the sale agreement. Acton upped his bid to $625. It was around that time that Huron began to suspect that the Boston Corbett in Texas was a fake. There was a flurry of letters between Clawson and Wilmoth and Huron, and between Acton and Gavitt and the probate court and Huron, a legal land-sale dustup that was complicated in late November when it was discovered that Corbett's deed to the land was never entered, so it technically still belonged to the US government. Another wrinkle: if the Texas Corbett was indeed a fake and the real Corbett was dead, then the land technically would belong to his heirs—whoever they might be—which raised questions of whether Huron, as the guardian of a presumably dead man, had the authority to sell the land.

Huron ultimately unscrambled the mess, the deed was recorded correctly in Corbett's name, and in the end Acton got the farm for $650 in January 1903. But Clawson, armed with his contract, refused to move his farm equipment and other possessions, and in February he began cutting down some of the few trees. Clawson was half right; his lease was valid until the start of March. The squabble continued on through the summer, but Acton—who at one point demanded a refund and the voiding of the sale—eventually got his land.

The dispute over the land now ended, Huron still had the fake Boston Corbett issue dangling before him.

Why Huron continued to press the issue isn't clear. His role was to protect Corbett's estate; it was up to law enforcement to go after John Corbett if he had broken the law, or to pension officials if they felt the salesman had committed a crime trying to claim a pension to which he was not entitled. Yet Huron continued to pursue the man as though he had been personally wronged. He likely felt culpable, and a bit foolish, for writing that first letter to the fake Corbett, giving the con man enough information about the real Corbett to try to press the fraud.

On March 6, 1903, Huron was in Washington on business and gave affidavits and a request to the pension bureau to withdraw his appeal to restore Corbett's pension, a request the bureau honored, given the evidence he supplied. He took a side trip to Camden and spent a day interviewing people who knew Corbett.

In May 1903 the pension bureau sent Huron's affidavits back to Topeka to the special examiner with an eye toward trying to bring charges against John Corbett. Commissioner Ware wrote to Huron thanking him for "the interest you have displayed in determining whether or not the man claiming to be Boston Corbett is an impostor or is, in fact, the pensioner." He also told him to expect a visit from the examiner, who was going to try to interview the fake Corbett himself.[17]

Huron continued amassing evidence, which supplemented the formal investigation underway by the pension bureau. They worked slowly until, by the summer of 1905, there was enough material to turn over to federal prosecutors, who convened a grand jury in San Angelo, Texas, and in early September 1905 indicted John Corbett on charges of attempted fraud and perjury. A month later, the accused was convicted after a brief trial in San Angelo in which Huron, Thatcher, and others from Boston Corbett's past testified. The sentence was three years in federal prison.

So what happened to the real Boston Corbett? He simply vanished from documented history.

Conjecture arose decades after Corbett disappeared that he might have been among the more than four hundred people who perished in the disastrous 1894 Hinckley wildfire in Minnesota. But the conjecture was based on speculation about the appearance of the name Thomas Corbett on the list of the dead, and a secondhand account by someone who said the fire victim had claimed to be Boston Corbett. It is too tenuous a connection to credit.[18]

Over the years, journalists and local historians occasionally returned to Boston Corbett's story, drawn by the oddities and eccentricities of the man himself but also by the bit part he played in one of the critical junctures of American history. The major players in that coda to the Civil War were, obviously, Abraham Lincoln and John Wilkes Booth. Though contemporaries held mixed opinions about Lincoln in his time, he is now a revered American figure, among the most popular of presidents and a martyr in both the fight against slavery and the fight to keep the nation united.

Booth, on the other hand, remains a scorned creature, an actor defined by his final role and stage appearance, as it were, as a craven assassin. History would not have treated Booth kindly no matter how he killed Lincoln, but creeping up behind the unsuspecting president as he watched a play and blasting a bullet into the back of his head added a layer of cowardice to the deed.

Though history has largely forgotten Boston Corbett, of the three men connected by those long-ago killings, he was the closest to an average, everyday person. Lincoln was the elected leader of the entire nation, a man recognized on sight, whose political beliefs helped propel the country to war against itself. Booth didn't have Lincoln's fame, but as a successful stage actor, one of the best of his generation, he, too, was a celebrity several steps removed from the daily lives of his fellow countrymen—the farmers and liverymen, the shopkeepers and hotel men, the rail workers and steelworkers and others eking out a living through the heavy industries propelling the nation's economic rise.

Yet those are the ranks from which sprang Corbett, a regular, run-of-the-mill American—albeit a strange one—who did his job as a hatter, and then as a soldier, and in the process inextricably linked himself with an unforgettable event in American history. His was a fleeting fame, fifteen minutes in the spotlight more than a century before Andy Warhol's famous observation about the duration of celebrity in America. But it was fame nonetheless, and it stemmed from an action that riveted the nation. Had he not shot Booth on that April morning, someone else in the Sixteenth New York Cavalry may well have—if, indeed, Corbett was right and the assassin was preparing to shoot his way out, or to shoot as a prompt to his own end. Had Booth survived the showdown and been captured with Herold, he too would have dangled from the end of a rope on the Washington gallows.

But then, if Booth had been killed by another or hanged with his gang of murderers, Boston Corbett would never have risen from the background of daily life. Such is the nature of fleeting fame, and of small lives brushing up against large moments in history.

ACKNOWLEDGMENTS

Historians, military buffs, and conspiracy theorists began obsessing over the Civil War while gunpowder smoke still wafted over the battlefields, and so much of what happened during those riveting and pivotal years has long been settled history. Yet Boston Corbett remains something of an enigma. I didn't know about him until my editor at Chicago Review Press, Jerome Pohlen, mentioned Corbett as I was scouting around for a fresh book project. The broad contours of Corbett's life—a self-castrating religious zealot who killed Lincoln assassin John Wilkes Booth, escaped from an insane asylum, and then disappeared from history—were hard to resist for a journalist drawn to interesting stories about unusual people caught up in historic events.

So I dove in. Rather than reinvent the wheel, I relied on the work of others for such well-documented events as the onset of the Civil War, the assassination of Abraham Lincoln, and the pursuit of Booth. And there has been some standout work done, including but not limited to Shelby Foote's *Civil War* trilogy, James H. McPherson's *Battle Cry of Freedom: The Civil War Era*, Michael W. Kauffman's *American Brutus: John Wilkes Booth and the Lincoln Conspiracies*, and James L. Swanson's *Manhunt: The 12-Day Chase for Lincoln's Killer*. Many of the details contained in this account are from widely cited and available sources, so I opted to go light on the footnotes on those events.

Corbett's life is another matter, and it posed some significant challenges. It was difficult to sift through records establishing his early years as Thomas Corbett. I was aided by newspaper stories published in 1866 about an elderly hoarder in London who had been found in his overstuffed apartment suffering from a debilitating, and ultimately fatal, medical condition. It identified the ailing Bartholomew Corbett as a naturalist and the father of Boston Corbett, the avenger of Lincoln. That was sufficient to pick up the trail of Corbett's early life, uneventful as those years were. But there are dead ends—the fate of his mother eluded me, as did the last name of Corbett's wife and the date they were married. And there are confusions. Thomas H. Corbett became a US citizen in 1855 in Troy, New York; Boston Corbett became a US citizen in 1885 in Concordia, Kansas. Yet in 1878 Corbett claimed in the homestead application for the Cloud County property that he was an American citizen. Despite the dueling naturalization records, I'm confident that Thomas H. Corbett is Boston Corbett, though I also acknowledge the proof is circumstantial.

For details of Corbett's life and travels, I sought out primary sources in a wide range of depositories and archives with the help of librarians and archivists, some of whom deserve singling out. I was aided greatly by the warm and welcoming staff, particularly Lin Frederickson, of the Kansas State Archives in Topeka, as well as their roster of volunteers, including Jan Johnson, who was kind enough to share some of her own research on Corbett. There I also had a serendipitous encounter with Peter Vanderwarker, a lawyer working on his own Corbett project and with whom I explored (unsuccessfully) options for getting the archives to open Corbett's medical records from the Kansas State Hospital for the Insane, which are sealed under state law despite their historical significance. Marilyn Johnston, a volunteer at the Cloud County Historical Museum, provided knowledge and, as needed, legwork to run down elusive facts about Corbett's life in Concordia. In New Jersey, Chris Anderson, head of special collections and Methodist librarian at the Drew University Library, Madison, was generous with his time and knowledge in tracking down details of Corbett's ministerial life. In Massachusetts, similar aid was provided by Kara Jackman, archivist and research collections librarian at the Boston University School of Theology Library. My son Andrew joined me at the National Archives in Washington and shared some of the drudgery of sifting through old military and pension files, and I am grateful for his help (not to mention having the pleasure of his company). And longtime friend and occasional research assistant Ivan Roman did me the favor of retrieving records I missed during my visits to the Archives.

Thanks, too, are owed Jerry Pohlen for directing me to Corbett in the first place; to his colleagues—Mary Kravenas and Meaghan Miller, among others—at Chicago Review Press and the Independent Publishers Group for their help in the book's birthing chamber, as it were; to Jane Dystel and her literary partner, Miriam Goderich, at Dystel & Goderich Literary Management for their good sense, deep patience, and stalwart support; and most of all to the Lovely Margaret, for more reasons than a simple thank you can express.

NOTES

PROLOGUE

1. Details of the events at the Garretts' barn are drawn primarily from statements and testimony by Everton J. Conger (April 27, 1865, and May 22, 1865), Luther B. Baker (April 27, 1865, and May 22, 1865), and Willie Jett (May 6, 1865, and May 17, 1865), compiled in James O. Hall, *On the Way to Garrett's Barn: John Wilkes Booth and David E. Herold in the Northern Neck of Virginia* (Clinton, MD: The Surratt Society, 2001). For a good overview of that night, see James L. Swanson, *Manhunt: The 12-Day Chase for Lincoln's Killer* (New York: HarperCollins, 2006), chap. 9.

2. Statement by David E. Herold, April 27, 1865, collected in Hall, *On the Way to Garrett's Barn*, 19. Much of Herold's statement is pure fabrication as he sought to hide his involvement in the conspiracy, but the details from the night of his capture ring true.

3. The witnesses disagree on some of the particulars of the confrontation, including what weapon Booth was holding. I put the most weight on the account of the man who shot Booth.

1. LOSS AND REDEMPTION

1. "Shipping News," *Liverpool Mercury*, July 31, 1840, and August 14, 1840.

2. Quote from *Knickerbocker Magazine* 32 (1848), reprinted in Edward K. Spann, *The New Metropolis* (New York: Columbia University Press, 1981), 1–2.

3. Details drawn from the passenger list for the *Zenobia*, accessed via Ancestry. com.

4. For details see Tyler Anbinder, *Five Points: The 19th-Century New York City Neighborhood That Invented Tap Dancing, Stole Elections, and Became the World's Most Notorious Slum* (New York: Penguin, 2001).

5. There are many good histories of this era in New York. Spann, *New Metropolis,* particularly chaps. 1, 4, and 5, is succinct yet broad on the economic and population growth.

6. Spann, *New Metropolis*, 71–72.

7. Thomas Bender, *New York Intellect: A History of the Intellectual Life in New York City, from 1750 to the Beginnings of Our Own Time* (New York: Alfred A. Knopf, 1987), 125.

8. Addresses culled from city directories; for details of New York City life in that era, see Robert Ernst, *Immigrant Life in New York City 1825–1863* (Syracuse, NY: Syracuse University Press, 1994).

9. David Bensman, *The Practice of Solidarity: American Hat Finishers in the Nineteenth Century* (Urbana: University of Illinois Press, 1985), 5–7.

10. Ibid., 9.

11. See Alice Hamilton, "The Hatters' Trade," chap. 18 in *Industrial Poisons in the United States* (New York: The Macmillan Co., 1929); and Bensman, *Practice of Solidarity*, 3–4.

12. E. A. Bruner to Huron, December 17, 1905, in Boston Corbett–George A. Huron Collection, Kansas State Archives, Kansas Historical Society, Topeka.

13. The naturalization certificate is in the Corbett-Huron Collection. A caveat: this and a later medical record have "H." as the middle initial, but other sources give him a middle initial of "P." Despite the inconsistency, I believe this is very likely Boston Corbett, given how the few known details of his life mesh with the timing of this naturalization certificate. But I acknowledge there is room for doubt as well as need of better proof.

14. There have been several accounts of Corbett's early life and marriage, all thin on grounded details. This is pieced together from the best and most verifiable sources I could find, including contemporary city directories, affidavits by friends in the Boston Corbett file, Legal Records, Bureau of Pensions, RG 15.2.2, National Archives, Washington, DC, and in the Corbett-Huron Collection. Part of the legend has it that Corbett's wife died in childbirth, but those mentions show up in newspaper articles and other later accounts;

tellingly, affidavits by those who knew Corbett well do not mention the child-birth story.

15. Alex Beam, *American Crucifixion: The Murder of Joseph Smith and the Fate of the Mormon Church* (New York: Public Affairs, 2014), 15.

16. Kathryn Teresa Long, *The Revival of 1857–58: Interpreting an American Religious Awakening* (New York: Oxford University Press, 1998), 13, 26–33.

17. Affidavit of William C. Norton, December 12, 1904, in Boston Corbett file, Bureau of Pensions. Biblical passages are from the King James version.

18. Efforts to get original medical records from Massachusetts General Hospital were unsuccessful under the hospital's policies. This is drawn from notes and reports gathered in Dr. John B. Scofield, "The Assassination of Abraham Lincoln," maintained by the Lincoln Financial Foundation in Indianapolis and available online at www.lincolncollection.org/search/results/item/?q=corbett&item=44474. The medical records seem to be a later copy, since they identify Corbett as the killer of Booth, which hadn't yet occurred, and use the first name Boston, which Corbett had yet to adopt.

19. "Boston Corbett," undated private recollection of fellow Twelfth New York Cavalry member Edward Kirk, likely sent to George Huron in the early 1900s, in Corbett-Huron Collection.

20. Newspaper accounts refer to his annoying tendencies, but the peculiar speaking style is included in John J. Redjinski's overview of Corbett's life in Scofield, "Assassination of Abraham Lincoln." Unfortunately, Redjinski does not cite his source.

21. Corbett's relationship with Gardner is mentioned in the unsigned "Anecdotes of Corbett, The Executioner of Booth," *Rochester Democrat*, reprinted in *New York Times*, May 7, 1865.

22. Long, *Revival of 1857–58*, 40.

23. "Serious Disturbance at Fulton Ferry," *New York Herald Tribune*, February 18, 1851; "Awful Gardner Sentenced for Six Months," *New York Daily Times*, October 3, 1855; "Arrest of 'Awful' Gardner," *New York Daily Times*, December 10, 1856.

24. "Religious Experience of 'Awful' Gardner," *Evening Star* (Washington, DC), April 7, 1858.

25. Brown to Huron, August 12, 1895, in Corbett-Huron Collection.

26. There are numerous mentions of his habits in contemporary newspaper articles on Corbett in the weeks after Booth's death, including "Boston Corbett,"

Philadelphia Inquirer, May 4, 1865; the quote is from "The Daily Prayer Meeting," *New York Observer and Chronicle*, May 11, 1865.

27. For a succinct discussion of Palmer's theology and life, see Elaine A. Heath, *Naked Faith: The Mystical Theology of Phoebe Palmer* (Eugene, OR: Pickwick Publications, 2009), part of the Princeton Theological Monograph Series.

28. Heath, *Naked Faith*, 7–9.

29. Fulton Street details from "The Daily Prayer Meeting," *New York Observer and Chronicle*, May 11, 1865; see also Richard Thatcher's handwritten and unpublished "Boston Corbett's Prison Life," in Corbett-Huron Collection.

2. BOSTON CORBETT GOES TO WAR

1. William Howard Russell, *My Diary North and South* (Boston: T.O.H.P. Burnham, 1863), 33.

2. Horace Greeley, *Recollections of a Busy Life* (New York: J. B. Ford & Co., 1868), 404.

3. "The New Administration," *New York Times*, March 5, 1861.

4. Bureau of Military Statistics of the State of New York, *Third Annual Report* (Albany: Wendell Printers, 1866), 31.

5. *The Union Army: A History of Military Affairs in the Loyal States 1861–65*, vol. 2 (Madison, WI: Federal Publishing Company, 1908), 25.

6. Adam Goodheart, *1861: The Civil War Awakening* (New York: Alfred A. Knopf, 2011), 187–88.

7. After the war, President Ulysses S. Grant appointed Butterfield treasury secretary, where Butterfield became embroiled in a bribery scandal as Jay Gould and James Fisk sought to corner the gold market by getting advance word from Butterfield on when the federal government would sell gold. Grant got wind of the insider deal and sold gold without telling Butterfield, and the resulting panic led to the Black Friday economic crisis of September 24, 1869. Butterfield was not charged but he resigned his position and returned to American Express. For details on Butterfield's relationship with Grant and involvement in the Gold Bug scandal, see William S. Feely, *Grant: A Biography* (New York: W. W. Norton, 1981), 253, 324, 328, 414.

8. M. Francis Dowley, *History and Honorary Roll of the Twelfth Regiment Infantry* (New York: T. Farrell and Son, 1869), 55.

9. Brown to George Huron, August 12, 1895, in Corbett-Huron Collection.

10. Details are drawn primarily from Corbett's war records obtained from the National Archives, Washington, DC, also contained in Scofield, "Assassination of Abraham Lincoln"; and from contemporary news accounts, including "Twelfth Regiment," *New York Tribune*, April 19, 1861; "Departure of the Twelfth, Seventy-First and Sixth Regiments," *New York Sun*, April 21, 1861; and "Departure of the Twelfth Regiment," *New York Herald*, April 22, 1861.

11. Kirk to Huron, undated, in Corbett-Huron Collection.

12. "News from the Twelfth Regiment," *New York Herald*, April 27, 1861.

13. Dates and deployments of the Twelfth Regiment are contained in many sources. A succinct version can be found in Bureau of Military Statistics of the State of New York, *Third Annual Report*, 293–97.

14. Kirk to Huron, undated, in Corbett-Huron Collection.

15. "The New York Regiments," *New York Herald*, May 2, 1861.

16. See US War Department, "Riot in Baltimore," chap. 9 in *The War of the Rebellion*, series 1, vol. 2 (Washington, DC: Government Printing Office, 1880), 9–23; and James M. McPherson, *Battle Cry of Freedom: The Civil War Era* (New York: Oxford University Press, 1988), 285.

17. Kirk to Huron, undated, in Corbett-Huron Collection.

18. Julia Lorrilard Butterfield, *A Biographical Memorial of General Daniel Butterfield* (New York: The Grafton Press, 1904), 31.

19. Ibid., 34.

20. Unless otherwise noted, troop movements and battle descriptions are drawn from the *War of the Rebellion* series.

21. Details from a letter by William Raynor, who had been a captain in Corbett's I Company, to the *Evening Post* newspaper, reprinted in the *New Orleans Times*, May 17, 1865. The later reminiscence by Edward Kirk attributed Butterfield's outburst to frustration over the men's care of their equipment.

22. Butterfield, *Biographical Memorial*, 25.

23. McPherson, *Battle Cry of Freedom*, 279.

24. Butterfield, *Biographical Memorial*, 27–28.

25. Ibid., 19.

26. The general details are recounted in a wide range of postwar articles on Corbett; the court-martial and fine are in his military records, copies of which are included in Scofield, "Assassination of Abraham Lincoln." Unfortunately,

the National Archives has no records of the Twelfth New York State Militia, Corbett's first foray into military life, nor of his first court-martial while a member of that regiment; the New York State Archives also has no records on the Twelfth. Legend has it that Corbett was ordered shot and that an appeal to Lincoln brought a reprieve, but no evidence of that has surfaced.

27. JWB, "Reminiscences of a Schoolmaster in Another Field," *American Educational Monthly*, April 1875. It's unlikely the quotes are verbatim, given the time between the incident and the publication of the article. The quotes may in fact be embellished to match JWB's perceptions of Corbett as violent.

28. "Corbett, the Executioner of Booth," *Philadelphia Inquirer*, May 5, 1865.

29. "The Late Riot," *New York Tribune*, July 20, 1863.

30. War Department, *War of the Rebellion*, series 1, vol. 33, pt. 1 (New Berne), 159–60.

31. Ibid., 315–16.

32. The details of Corbett's capture are drawn primarily from three sources: his own account; War Department, *War of the Rebellion*, series 1, vol. 37, pt. 1, 168–69; and James J. Williamson, *Mosby's Rangers: A Record of the Operations of the Forty-Third Battalion of Virginia Cavalry from Its Organization to Surrender*, rev. ed. (New York: Ralph B. Kenyon, 1895), 463–66.

3. ANDERSONVILLE: A JOURNEY TO HELL

1. Details drawn from reports contained in War Department, *War of the Rebellion*, series 1, vol. 37, 166–69.

2. James J. Williamson, *Mosby's Rangers*, 2nd ed. (New York: Sturgis and Walters and Company, 1909), 464–66.

3. Casualty figures from Frederick Phisterer, *New York in the War of the Rebellion, 1861–1865*, 2nd ed. (Albany: J. B. Lyon Company, 1890), 316.

4. William Marvel, *Andersonville: The Last Depot* (Chapel Hill: University of North Carolina Press, 1994), x.

5. War Department, *War of the Rebellion*, series 2, vol. 7, 117–19.

6. McPherson, *Battle Cry of Freedom*, 796.

7. Corbett's descriptions of his time in Andersonville are from his testimony in the trial of camp superintendent Henry Wirz, as transcribed in "Trial of Henry Wirz," in US House of Representatives, *Executive Documents Printed by Order of the House of Representatives During the Second Session of the Fortieth*

Congress, vol. 8 (Washington, DC: Government Printing Office, 1868), exec. doc. no. 23, p. 73.

8. John L. Ransom, *Andersonville Diary, Escape, and List of the Dead* (Auburn, NY: John L. Ransom, 1881), entry for July 12, 1864.

9. "Trial of Henry Wirz," 71.

10. Thatcher, "Boston Corbett's Prison Life."

11. Letter to unidentified nurse reprinted in "Boston Corbett," *Crutch* (weekly hospital newspaper, Annapolis, MD), May 6, 1865.

12. John McElroy, *Andersonville: A Story of Rebel Military Prisons* (Toledo: D. R. Locke, 1879), 214–15.

13. Robert Knox Sneden, *Eye of the Storm: A Civil War Odyssey* (New York: The Free Press, 2000), 253.

14. John L. Maile, *Prison Life in Andersonville: With Special Reference to the Opening of Providence Spring* (Los Angeles: Grafton Publishing Co., 1912), 65–66.

15. Ovid L. Futch, *History of Andersonville Prison* (Hialeah: University of Florida Press, 1968), 95.

16. Isaac N. Sutton, "The Glorious Second Corps," *National Tribune* (Washington, DC), November 8, 1906.

17. Joseph H. Whitehead affidavit, July 26, 1882, in Boston Corbett file, Bureau of Pensions.

18. Details of Thatcher's experience with Corbett are drawn from Thatcher, "Boston Corbett's Prison Life."

19. Robert Scott Davis, *Ghosts and Shadows of Andersonville: Essays on the Secret Social Histories of America's Deadliest Prison* (Macon, GA: Mercer University Press, 2006), 73–76; "Trial of Henry Wirz," 147.

20. Boston Corbett affidavit, undated, filed August 26, 1882, in Boston Corbett file, Bureau of Pensions.

21. "Our Prisoners," *New York Times*, November 26, 1864.

22. "The Prisoners," *Crutch*, December 3, 1864. While the *Crutch* doesn't include Corbett as among the new patients in a list published a week later, his military record puts him there at the dates noted.

23. Corbett testimony in "Trial of Henry Wirz," 74; Corbett letter to US Pension Bureau, February 16, 1880, in Boston Corbett file, Bureau of Pensions.

24. "Boston Corbett," *Crutch*, May 6, 1865.

25. "The Man Who Shot Booth," *Cleveland Leader*, May 3, 1865; "The Daily Prayer Meeting," *New York Observer and Chronicle*, May 11, 1865.

26. James H. Brown affidavit, June 12, 1882, in Corbett-Huron Collection. Brown was referring to the postwar years but the description is likely apt for this period as well, since it's unlikely that Corbett recovered his health then lost it again.

27. Byron B. Johnson, *Abraham Lincoln and Boston Corbett, with Personal Recollections of Each* (Waltham, MA: Byron Berkeley Johnson, 1914), 27, 37; William Thomas Davis, *Bench and Bar of the Commonwealth of Massachusetts*, vol. 1 (Boston: The Boston History Company, 1895), 171.

28. Corbett to Brown, February 1, 1865, reprinted in the *New York Times*, April 29, 1865.

4. THE ASSASSIN

1. For a detailed list of Booth's stage appearances, see Gordon Samples, *Lust for Fame: The Stage Career of John Wilkes Booth* (Jefferson, NC: McFarland & Co., 1982), 196–234.

2. Asia Booth Clarke, *The Elder and the Younger Booth* (Boston: James R. Osgood and Company, 1882), 53–54; "U.S., Atlantic Ports Passenger Lists, 1820–1873," National Archives, accessed via Ancestry.com.

3. "Obituary," *New York Evening Post*, December 2, 1852.

4. Gene Smith, *American Gothic: The Story of America's Legendary Theatrical Family—Junius, Edwin, and John Wilkes Booth* (New York: Simon and Schuster, 1992), 24.

5. Michael W. Kauffman, *American Brutus: John Wilkes Booth and the Lincoln Conspiracies* (New York: Random House, 2004), 81–82.

6. Ibid., 85–89.

7. Numerous contemporary newspaper accounts. Detail about June Booth is from "Theatricals in California," *Boston Herald*, September 15, 1852.

8. Details of his transit are pieced together from numerous newspaper accounts; Nora Titone, *My Thoughts Be Bloody: The Bitter Rivalry Between Edwin and John Wilkes Booth That Led to an American Tragedy* (New York: Free Press, 2010), 118.

9. Several sources put the debut at Wheatley's Arch Street Theatre in Philadelphia, but the Baltimore debut seems more likely, given the proximity to the Farm.

10. Kauffman, *American Brutus*, 105–6.

11. McPherson, *Battle Cry of Freedom*, 198, 212. For background on the political and cultural reverberations of Brown's raid, see also Brenda Wineapple,

Ecstatic Nation: Confidence, Crisis, and Compromise, 1848–1877 (New York: HarperCollins, 2013), chap. 6.

12. Asia Booth Clarke, *John Wilkes Booth: A Sister's Memoir*, ed. Terry Alford (Jackson: University Press of Mississippi, 1996), 88.

13. Kauffman, *American Brutus*, 124–25.

14. Ibid., 107.

15. Swanson, *Manhunt*, 126.

16. The letters are reprinted in John Rhodehamel and Louise Taper, eds., *"Right or Wrong, God Judge Me": The Writings of John Wilkes Booth* (Urbana: University of Illinois Press, 1997), 124–31. The details of Booth's forays into Charles County have been recounted too many times to cite individual sources, but again, Swanson's *Manhunt* offers a solid overview.

17. There's disagreement over whether Booth had asked Mudd to Washington to introduce him to Surratt, but Mudd reported in his statement that he had traveled to the city with a neighbor and cousin, Jeremiah Mudd, to do some shopping and chanced across Booth. There's no overwhelming reason to disbelieve him on that detail. See Nettie Mudd, *The Life of Dr. Samuel A. Mudd* (New York: Neale Publishing Co., 1906), 42–43.

5. A President Is Murdered

1. Many of these details are drawn from Kauffmann, *American Brutus*, 183–85.

2. Clarke, *John Wilkes Booth*, 88–89.

3. "Bulletin," *Evening Star*, April 14, 1865.

4. Kauffman, *American Brutus*, 218.

5. See testimonies of William H. Bell, Sergeant George F. Robinson, and Major A. H. Seward in Benjamin Perley Poore, *The Conspiracy Trial for the Murder of the President* (Boston: J. E. Tilton and Company, 1865), vol. 1, 471–80, and vol. 2, 1–9. The details of that night are contained primarily in Poore's volumes; rather than bog down this chapter with a flood of footnotes, I invite those interested in specific details to consult each person's individual testimony therein.

6. See the conspiracy trial testimony of John Lee and Leonard Farwell, in Poore, *Conspiracy Trial*, vol. 1, 62–69, and vol. 3, 174–76. See also Swanson, *Manhunt*, 88–90; and Kauffman, *American Brutus*, 30–32.

6. The Hunt for Booth and Herold

1. See the conspiracy trial testimony of John M. Lloyd, in Poore, *Conspiracy Trial*, vol. 1, 125.

2. See Swanson, *Manhunt*, chap. 5.

3. Thomas A. Jones, *J. Wilkes Booth: An Account of His Sojourn in Southern Maryland After the Assassination of Abraham Lincoln, His Passage Across the Potomac, and His Death in Virginia* (Chicago: Laird and Lee, 1893), 78.

4. Telegram to Eastman, April 22, 1865, in Navy Department Records, RG 45, M599, p. 376, National Archives, Washington, DC.

5. See the conspiracy trial testimony of Willie Jett, in Poore, *Conspiracy Trial*, vol. 1, 308–12.

6. Statement of Willie Jett, May 6, 1865, in Letters Received and Statements of Evidence Collected by the Military Commission, Investigation and Trial Papers Relating to the Assassination of President Lincoln, National Archives, accessed via www.fold3.com/image/7341020/, pp. 54–69; "Pursuit and Death of John Wilkes Booth," *Century* (New York) 39 (November 1889–April 1890), 443–44.

7. Welles to Montgomery, April 15, 1865, in Navy Department Records, RG 45, M599, p. 333.

8. Details drawn from, among other sources, "Annals of the War," *Philadelphia Weekly Times*, April 14, 1877, reprinted in Hall, *On the Way to Garrett's Barn*. The article was written twelve years after the assassination, when Corbett was living in Camden, NJ. The language differs from that used in Corbett's letters and other statements, so it's likely the article was ghostwritten by a journalist. But nothing suggests that the details aren't true.

9. "The Assassination," *New York Times*, April 19, 1875.

10. Swanson, *Manhunt*, 281–85.

11. Statement of Edward P. Doherty, in War Department, *War of the Rebellion*, series 1, vol. 46, pt. 1 (Appomattox Campaign), 1317–22.

7. Celebrity, and Infamy

1. Hall, *On the Way to Garrett's Barn*, 156. If a statement was taken from the soldier witness Corbett mentioned, it doesn't seem to have made it into the files. Also, conspiracy theorists over the years have posited many different scenarios

of what happened at Garrett's barn and the identity of the dead man, but the statements given by participants at the time of the capture make it certain that Corbett fired the shot, and that Booth was the man killed.

2. The scene at Garrett's barn and the immediate aftermath is drawn from witness statements gathered aboard the *Montauk* in the days after the capture and from testimony in later trials and hearings. I've drawn mostly from the first statements of the participants, seeing those as the freshest and not as self-serving as in the later testimony, when the participants were jockeying for credit and cash.

3. Baker's testimony at the Johnson impeachment trial, reprinted in Hall, *On the Way to Garrett's Barn*, 91; Benjamin P. Thomas and Harold M. Hyman, *Stanton: The Life and Times of Lincoln's Secretary of War* (New York: Alfred A. Knopf, 1962), 420.

4. "Booth's End: The Shooting of the Assassin of the President," *New York Herald*, April 28, 1865.

5. "The Assassination," *New York Tribune*, April 28, 1865.

6. Johnson, *Abraham Lincoln and Boston Corbett*, 37–38.

7. Corbett to Stanton, May 6, 1865, in Records of the Office of the Secretary of War, RG 107.2.1, National Archives, Washington, DC.

8. Poore, *Conspiracy Trial*, vol. 1, 8; and illustration accompanying "Military Court Trial of the Lincoln Conspirators: President Lincoln's Assassination," *Harper's Weekly*, June 3, 1865; telegram from Fox to Montgomery, April 24, 1864, Navy Department Records, RG 45, M599, p. 385, National Archives, Washington, DC.

9. Compiled from reports by *Philadelphia Daily Inquirer* staff writers, *The Trial of the Alleged Assassins at Washington* (Philadelphia: T. B. Peterson and Brothers, 1865), 20.

10. Poore, *Conspiracy Trial*, vol. 1, 11–13. Contemporary news accounts offered similar takes, each seeming to cast the defendants in an unfavorable light.

11. Entry for May 22, 1865, in *The Diary of Horatio Nelson Taft, 1861–1865*, vol. 3 (January 1, 1864–May 30, 1865), Manuscript Division, Library of Congress, accessed at www.loc.gov/item/mtaft000003.

12. Poore, *Conspiracy Trial*, vol. 1, 325. For the sake of brevity much of the testimony was edited into narrative form. I've chosen to quote Corbett verbatim here, but recognize the words were likely not exactly his.

13. No one has put forward a convincing case that Booth was not shot dead by Corbett in Garrett's tobacco barn, though the conspiracy theories enjoy a

robust life. See William Hanchett, *The Lincoln Murder Conspiracies* (Urbana: University of Illinois Press, 1986).

14. Details drawn from testimony and Corbett's statement contained in the court-martial file, RG 94, Records of the Adjutant General's Office Book Records of Volunteer Union Organizations, Sixteenth New York Cavalry, National Archives, Washington, DC.

15. Thatcher to George A. Huron, undated, but provided as research for a report Huron made on Corbett to the Kansas Historical Society in December 1907, in Corbett-Huron Collection.

16. "The Review," *Evening Star*, May 23, 1865.

17. Entry for May 24, 1865, in *Diary of Horatio Nelson Taft*.

18. The surgeon's note is included in the court-martial papers.

19. See Huron's testimony before the special pension examiner, undated, in Corbett-Huron Collection; Weston Arthur Goodspeed, *The Province and the States*, vol. 7 (Madison, WI: The Western Historical Association, 1904), 536–37.

20. Charles Smart, *The Medical and Surgical History of the War of the Rebellion*, vol. 3, pt. 1 (Washington, DC: Government Printing Office, 1888), 942.

21. The Corbett quote is from his February 16, 1880, pension application, in Boston Corbett file, Bureau of Pensions.

22. Boston Corbett affidavit, 1882 (date not listed), as part of his application for a war pension submitted to the US Commissioner of Pensions, and subpoena letter, July 29, 1865, both in Corbett-Huron Collection.

23. Glenna R. Schroeder-Lein and Richard Zuczek, *Andrew Johnson: A Biographical Companion* (Santa Barbara, CA: ABC-CLIO, 2001), 315–16.

24. "Trial of Henry Wirz," 75.

8. CITIZEN CORBETT, PREACHER

1. "The Daily Prayer Meeting," *New York Observer and Chronicle*, September 21, 1865.

2. Copies of the autograph requests are in the Corbett-Huron Collection. While the records contain no specific threats, later letters and affidavits by Corbett's friends established the threats as part of his postwar life.

3. Undated affidavits by Boston Corbett as part of his application for a war pension, and by Thomas Brown, folder 5, in Boston Corbett file, Bureau of Pensions.

4. "Fleet Street Young Men's Christian Union," *Brooklyn Eagle*, November 28, 1865.

5. Edward Kirk pension inquiry testimony, and a letter from Kirk to George Huron, included in Corbett-Huron Collection.

6. See US House of Representatives, "Awards for the Capture of Booth and Others: Letter from the Secretary of War," April 19, 1866, 39th Cong., 1st sess., exec. doc. no. 90.

7. The affidavit is included in Lafayette C. Baker's self-serving memoir, *History of the United States Secret Service* (Philadelphia: L. C. Baker, 1867), 532–38.

8. For a good and detailed discussion of the rewards, see Robert G. Wick, "Battle for the War Department Rewards for the Capture of John Wilkes Booth," *Journal of the Abraham Lincoln Association* 32, no. 2 (2011).

9. Johnson to Corbett, October 3, 1866, in Scofield, "Assassination of Abraham Lincoln."

10. Details drawn from contemporary newspaper accounts, including the *London Morning Post*, October 26, 1865, and the *Reading (England) Mercury*, December 2, 1865; and Bartholomew Corbett's death certificate, obtained from the General Register Office, London.

11. "In the Grove," *Brooklyn Eagle*, July 24, 1868.

12. Reference letter for Corbett, signed by T. Taylor Heiss, president of the New Jersey District, Methodist Church, May 8, 1869, in Corbett-Huron Collection; *Minutes of the New Jersey Annual Conference of the Methodist Church* (Philadephia: J. Grand and Son, 1870), 3.

13. Clergy pocket diary details contained in Scofield, "Assassination of Abraham Lincoln."

14. "The Tool of a Conspiracy in the Church," *Pomeroy's Democrat* (Chicago), May 10, 1871.

15. "The Midland Railroad," *New York Times*, May 26, 1873.

16. Richard White, *Railroaded: The Transcontinentals and the Making of Modern America* (New York: Norton, 2011), 81–83; H. M. Hyndman, "The Crisis of 1873," chap. 7 in *Commercial Crises of the Nineteenth Century* (New York: Charles Scribner's Sons, 1902).

17. Details drawn from Cleveland city directories; "Personal," *Cleveland Plain Dealer*, April 19, 1875; soldiers' regiments at www.nps.gov/civilwar/soldiers-and-sailors-database.htm.

18. "Boston Corbett in the Pulpit," *Cleveland Plain Dealer*, May 17, 1875.

19. "Boston Corbett: Further Facts About His Persecution," *Cleveland Leader*, July 22, 1881; James M. Dalzell, *Private Dalzell: His Autobiography, Poems*

and Comic War Papers (Cincinnati: Robert Clarke and Co., 1888), 43; R. B. Hoover, "Slayer of J. Wilkes Booth," *North American Review* 149, no. 394 (September 1889), 382–84.

20. Untitled article, *New York Tribune*, September 29, 1876.

21. Corbett to postmaster general, January 12, 1878, in Corbett-Huron Collection. Original edited to correct distracting misuse of parentheses.

22. [Illegible] to Corbett, February 9, 1878, and Kirby to Corbett, February 17, 1878, in Corbett-Huron Collection.

23. Strickler to Corbett, June 16, 1878, in Corbett-Huron Collection.

24. Corbett's departure date is included in a letter from his former landlord's agent, James M. Cassady, November 18, 1882, in Corbett-Huron Collection.

9. CORBETT GOES WEST

1. "Lincoln's Avenger in the City," *Pittsburgh Commercial-Gazette*, September 24, 1878.

2. Rail pass letter in Corbett-Huron Collection; untitled item from *Chicago Journal*, reprinted in *San Francisco Bulletin*, October 5, 1878.

3. Albert T. Reid, "Boston Corbett: The Man of Mystery of the Lincoln Drama," *Scribner's Magazine*, July 1929.

4. Reminiscence of Clara Myers Brown from 1958, and *Coroner's Journal*, vol. A, 43, according to notes contained in Boston Corbett files, Cloud County Historical Museum, Concordia, KS. The name of the note taker is not listed.

5. George Henry Palm recollection, undated, Boston Corbett files, folder 1, Cloud County Historical Museum.

6. Pope to Corbett, April 9, 1879, in Corbett-Huron Collection.

7. Wrigley to Corbett, May 14, 1879, in Corbett-Huron Collection.

8. Fordner to Corbett, December 12, 1879, and Babb to Corbett, August 7, 1879, in Corbett-Huron Collection. Nannie Babb shows up in the next year's decennial US Census.

9. Unless otherwise noted, all the affidavits quoted here are from the Boston Corbett file, Bureau of Pensions.

10. E. A. Bruner to Huron, December 17, 1905, in Corbett-Huron Collection.

11. "Boston Corbett," *National Tribune*, November 16, 1882; undated medical affidavit by Kennedy, Hunter, and Hays, in Corbett-Huron Collection.

12. The exchange is included in the Corbett-Huron Collection; "Boston Corbett Pays His Old Debts," *Bridgeton Chronicle*, New Jersey, reprinted in the *New York Times*, November 26, 1882.

13. "Boston Corbett's Fate," *Cleveland Leader*, July 20, 1881.

14. Murset's letter is in the Corbett-Huron Collection. Corbett's response is in the Murset pension files, National Archives, Washington, DC.

15. Thatcher to Corbett, September 17, 1882, in Corbett-Huron Collection.

16. Bushnell affidavit, November 14, 1904, in Boston Corbett file, Bureau of Pensions.

17. Norton affidavit, November 25, 1904, Boston Corbett file, Bureau of Pensions.

18. Frank Sorgatz to Corbett, December 16, 1883, in Corbett-Huron Collection.

19. Quoted in "Boston Corbett, Lost Slayer of Booth," *San Francisco Call*, June 29, 1913.

20. Reid, "Boston Corbett."

21. Palm reminiscence in Boston Corbett files, Cloud County Historical Museum.

22. Like many tales of Boston Corbett, this anecdote has several conflicting versions. This one is cobbled from the closest contemporary accounts that could be found, augmented by personal memoirs written years later. Unfortunately, the court file could not be found. "Boston Corbett Crazy," *Concordia (KS) Blade*, reprinted in the *Kansas City Star*, December 11, 1885; "Boston Corbett, the Slayer of Booth: How He Adjourned Court," *Concordia (KS) Republican-Empire*, November 26, 1885; affidavit of M. V. B. Sheafor, October 1, 1904, in Boston Corbett file, Bureau of Pensions.

23. *Christian Advocate*, December 17, 1885.

10. CORBETT CRACKS

1. Corbett's livestock holdings are detailed in notes culled from Horace Bushnell's diary, in Boston Corbett files, Cloud County Historical Museum; Buell Manufacturing to Corbett, June 26, 1884, in Corbett-Huron Collection; tax forms and asset details also in Corbett-Huron Collection.

2. Library of Congress Copyright Office, *Dramatic Compositions Copyrighted in the United States* (Washington, DC: Government Printing Office, 1918), 1761.

3. Doherty to Corbett, September 10, 1886, in Corbett-Huron Collection.

4. Details on Corbett's homestead claim are included in Bureau of Land Management, Records of the Concordia land office (1870–89), RG 49.9.12, National Archives, Washington, DC.

5. "Boston Corbett Dreadfully Afraid Somebody Will Call Him a Liar," *Boston Herald*, April 22, 1886; "Rushing Reports in Pension Cases," *Troy (NY) Times*, April 22, 1886; a copy of the deed is held by the Cloud County Historical Museum, Concordia, KS.

6. Knapp to Corbett, January 13, 1887, and a second undated letter apparently written several weeks later, both in Corbett-Huron Collection.

7. Unless otherwise noted, details are drawn from "Crazy Corbett," *Topeka Daily Capital*, February 16, 1887; "Corbett Corralled," *Topeka Daily Capital*, February 17, 1887; "Freaks of a Crank," *Wichita (KS) Daily Eagle*, February 16, 1887; M. V. B. Sheafor affidavit, October 1, 1904, in Corbett-Huron Collection.

8. Huron affidavit, August 18, 1902, in Boston Corbett file, Bureau of Pensions.

9. See State Board of Charities, *Combined Kansas Reports* (Topeka: Kansas Publishing House, 1888).

10. Corbett's medical file, like all those of former patients at the asylum, is sealed under a modern state law tied to the transfer of records from the closed facility to the state archives. However, this partial report was obtained before the records were sealed and is included in Scofield, "Assassination of Abraham Lincoln."

11. "Boston Corbett," *Topeka Daily Capital*, May 10, 1888.

12. Affidavit of W. W. Bowman, December 3, 1904, in Boston Corbett file, Bureau of Pensions.

13. Fish to probate court, September 29, 1887, in Corbett-Huron Collection.

14. The letters are included in the Corbett-Huron Collection. For the sake of simplicity, I opt not to cite each individual letter; sources outside the letters are cited.

15. "Boston Corbett's Gun," *Chicago Herald*, reprinted January 11, 1888, in the *Canton (OH) Repository*.

16. Unless otherwise noted, details are drawn from accounts over the next several days in the *Topeka Daily Capital* and the *Topeka State Journal* newspapers.

17. B. D. Eastman affidavit, December 7, 1904, in Corbett-Huron Collection.

18. Details of that final scene in Neodesha are hard to nail down. These are drawn from Thatcher family stories retold by others, so chances are good that Corbett's boarding of the train didn't occur exactly as the family lore depicted it. See the undated memoir of Richard Harrington, in Boston Corbett files, Cloud County Historical Museum. Also from George A. Huron testimony in Corbett-Huron Collection.

11. THE RETURN OF BOSTON CORBETT

1. George Huron affidavit, August 18, 1902, in Boston Corbett file, Bureau of Pensions; Mills to Huron, May 23, 1895, in Corbett-Huron Collection.

2. Huron to John Corbett, January 29, 1902, in Boston Corbett file, Bureau of Pensions; rental agreement for each year are in the Corbett-Huron Collection.

3. James L. King, *History of Shawnee County, Kansas, and Representative Citizens* (Chicago: Richmond and Arnold, 1905), 334–35; J. H. Hubbell, *Hubbell's Legal Directory for Lawyers and Business Men* (New York: The Hubbell Legal Directory Company, 1892), 65.

4. "E.P. Doherty Passes Away," *New York Times*, April 4, 1897.

5. Doherty to Corbett, October 9, 1889, in Corbett-Huron Collection.

6. Gavitt to Corbett, June 21, 1900, in Corbett-Huron Collection. The correspondence is maddeningly incomplete; Corbett's letters to Gavitt are not included.

7. Huron affidavit, March 1903, in Corbett-Huron Collection.

8. Corbett to Huron, July 18, 1900, in Corbett-Huron Collection.

9. Corbett to Huron, August 18, 1900, in Corbett-Huron Collection.

10. Kirk to Huron, January 9, 1901, in Corbett-Huron Collection.

11. Evans to Huron, April 23, 1902, in Corbett-Huron Collection.

12. Huron to Calderhead, May 8, 1902, in Corbett-Huron Collection.

13. Two letters from Harding to Huron, October 1902, in Corbett-Huron Collection.

14. Ware to Huron, October 18, 1902, in Corbett-Huron Collection.

15. The details of Huron's time in Texas are drawn from a series of affidavits by him and by Gardiner, all in Corbett-Huron Collection.

16. Some of the details drawn from Huron's testimony in the John Corbett trial in 1905, part of the Corbett-Huron Collection.

17. Ware to Huron, May 19, 1903, in Corbett-Huron Collection.

18. Grace Stageberg Swenson raised the possibility, unconvincingly, in her *From the Ashes: The Story of the Hinckley Fire of 1894* (Stillwater, MN: Croixside Press, 1979).

Sources

Archives

Cloud County Historical Museum, Concordia, KS
Kansas State Archives, Kansas Historical Society, Topeka
Library of Congress, Washington, DC
National Archives, Washington, DC

Periodicals

American Educational Monthly
Boston Herald
Brooklyn Eagle
Canton (OH) Repository
Century (New York)
Christian Advocate
Cleveland Leader
Cleveland Plain Dealer
Concordia (KS) Republican-Empire
Concordia (KS) Blade
Crutch (weekly hospital newspaper, Annapolis, MD)
Evening Star (Washington, DC)
Harper's Weekly
Journal of the Abraham Lincoln Association
Liverpool Mercury
London Morning Post

National Tribune (Washington, DC)

New Orleans Times

New York Daily Times

New York Evening Post

New York Herald

New York Herald Tribune

New York Observer and Chronicle

New York Sun

New York Times

New York Tribune

North American Review

Philadelphia Inquirer

Philadelphia Weekly Times

Pittsburgh Commercial-Gazette

Pomeroy's Democrat (Chicago)

Reading (England) Mercury

San Francisco Bulletin

San Francisco Call

Scribner's Magazine

Topeka Daily Capital

Topeka State Journal

Troy (NY) Times

Wichita (KS) Daily Eagle

SELECTED BIBLIOGRAPHY

Anbinder, Tyler. *Five Points: The 19th-Century New York City Neighborhood That Invented Tap Dancing, Stole Elections, and Became the World's Most Notorious Slum*. New York: Penguin, 2001.

Baker, Lafayette C. *History of the United States Secret Service*. Philadelphia: L. C. Baker, 1867.

Beam, Alex. *American Crucifixion: The Murder of Joseph Smith and the Fate of the Mormon Church*. New York: Public Affairs, 2014.

Bender, Thomas. *New York Intellect: A History of the Intellectual Life in New York City, from 1750 to the Beginnings of Our Own Time*. New York: Alfred A. Knopf, 1987.

Bensman, David. *The Practice of Solidarity: American Hat Finishers in the Nineteenth Century.* Urbana: University of Illinois Press, 1985.

Bureau of Military Statistics of the State of New York. *Third Annual Report.* Albany: Wendell Printers, 1866.

Butterfield, Julia Lorrilard. *A Biographical Memorial of General Daniel Butterfield.* New York: The Grafton Press, 1904.

Clarke, Asia Booth. *The Elder and the Younger Booth.* Boston: James R. Osgood and Company, 1882.

———. *John Wilkes Booth: A Sister's Memoir.* Edited by Terry Alford. Jackson: University Press of Mississippi, 1996.

Dalzell, James M. *Private Dalzell: His Autobiography, Poems and Comic War Papers.* Cincinnati: Robert Clarke and Co., 1888.

Davis, Robert Scott. *Ghosts and Shadows of Andersonville: Essays on the Secret Social Histories of America's Deadliest Prison.* Macon, GA: Mercer University Press, 2006.

Davis, William Thomas. *Bench and Bar of the Commonwealth of Massachusetts.* Vol. 1. Boston: The Boston History Company, 1895.

Dowley, M. Francis. *History and Honorary Roll of the Twelfth Regiment Infantry.* New York: T. Farrell and Son, 1869.

Ernst, Robert. *Immigrant Life in New York City 1825–1863.* Syracuse, NY: Syracuse University Press, 1994.

Feely, William S. *Grant: A Biography.* New York: W. W. Norton, 1981.

Futch, Ovid L. *History of Andersonville Prison.* Hialeah: University of Florida Press, 1968.

Goodheart, Adam. *1861: The Civil War Awakening.* New York: Alfred A. Knopf, 2011.

Goodspeed, Weston Arthur. *The Province and the States.* Vol. 7. Madison, WI: The Western Historical Association, 1904.

Greeley, Horace. *Recollections of a Busy Life.* New York: J. B. Ford & Co., 1868.

Hall, James O. *On the Way to Garrett's Barn: John Wilkes Booth and David E. Herold in the Northern Neck of Virginia.* Clinton, MD: The Surratt Society, 2001.

Hamilton, Alice. *Industrial Poisons in the United States.* New York: The Macmillan Co., 1929.

Heath, Elaine A. *Naked Faith: The Mystical Theology of Phoebe Palmer.* Eugene, OR: Pickwick Publications, 2009. Part of the Princeton Theological Monograph Series.

Hubbell, J. H. *Hubbell's Legal Directory for Lawyers and Business Men*. New York: The Hubbell Legal Directory Company, 1892.

Hyndman, H. M. *Commercial Crises of the Nineteenth Century*. New York: Charles Scribner's Sons, 1902.

Johnson, Byron B. *Abraham Lincoln and Boston Corbett, with Personal Recollections of Each*. Waltham, MA: Byron Berkeley Johnson, 1914.

Jones, Thomas A. *J. Wilkes Booth: An Account of His Sojourn in Southern Maryland After the Assassination of Abraham Lincoln, His Passage Across the Potomac, and His Death in Virginia*. Chicago: Laird and Lee, 1893.

Kauffman, Michael W. *American Brutus: John Wilkes Booth and the Lincoln Conspiracies*. New York: Random House, 2004.

King, James L. *History of Shawnee County, Kansas, and Representative Citizens*. Chicago: Richmond and Arnold, 1905.

Library of Congress Copyright Office. *Dramatic Compositions Copyrighted in the United States*. Washington, DC: Government Printing Office, 1918.

Long, Kathryn Teresa. *The Revival of 1857–58: Interpreting an American Religious Awakening*. New York: Oxford University Press, 1998.

Maile, John L. *Prison Life in Andersonville: With Special Reference to the Opening of Providence Spring*. Los Angeles: Grafton Publishing Co., 1912.

Marvel, William. *Andersonville: The Last Depot*. Chapel Hill: University of North Carolina Press, 1994.

McElroy, John. *Andersonville: A Story of Rebel Military Prisons*. Toledo: D. R. Locke, 1879.

McPherson, James M. *Battle Cry of Freedom: The Civil War Era*. New York: Oxford University Press, 1988.

Minutes of the New Jersey Annual Conference of the Methodist Church. Philadephia: J. Grand and Son, 1870.

Mudd, Nettie. *The Life of Dr. Samuel A. Mudd*. New York: Neale Publishing Co., 1906.

Philadelphia Daily Inquirer staff writers. *The Trial of the Alleged Assassins at Washington*. Philadelphia: T. B. Peterson and Brothers, 1865.

Phisterer, Frederick. *New York in the War of the Rebellion, 1861–1865*. 2nd ed. Albany: J. B. Lyon Company, 1890.

Poore, Benjamin Perley. *The Conspiracy Trial for the Murder of the President*. Vols. 1 & 3. Boston: J. E. Tilton and Company, 1865.

Ransom, John L. *Andersonville Diary, Escape, and List of the Dead.* Auburn, NY: John L. Ransom, 1881.

Rhodehamel, John, and Louise Taper, eds. *"Right or Wrong, God Judge Me": The Writings of John Wilkes Booth.* Urbana: University of Illinois Press, 1997.

Russell, William Howard. *My Diary North and South.* Boston: T.O.H.P. Burnham, 1863.

Samples, Gordon. *Lust for Fame: The Stage Career of John Wilkes Booth.* Jefferson, NC: McFarland & Co., 1982.

Schroeder-Lein, Glenna R., and Richard Zuczek. *Andrew Johnson: A Biographical Companion.* Santa Barbara, CA: ABC-CLIO, 2001.

Smart, Charles. *The Medical and Surgical History of the War of the Rebellion.* Vol. 3, pt. 1. Washington, DC: Government Printing Office, 1888.

Smith, Gene. *American Gothic: The Story of America's Legendary Theatrical Family—Junius, Edwin, and John Wilkes Booth.* New York: Simon and Schuster, 1992.

Sneden, Robert Knox. *Eye of the Storm: A Civil War Odyssey.* New York: The Free Press, 2000.

Spann, Edward K. *The New Metropolis.* New York: Columbia University Press, 1981.

State Board of Charities. *Combined Kansas Reports.* Topeka: Kansas Publishing House, 1888.

Swanson, James L. *Manhunt: The 12-Day Chase for Lincoln's Killer.* New York: HarperCollins, 2006.

The Union Army: A History of Military Affairs in the Loyal States 1861–65. Vol. 2. Madison, WI: Federal Publishing Company, 1908.

Thomas, Benjamin P., and Harold M. Hyman. *Stanton: The Life and Times of Lincoln's Secretary of War.* New York: Alfred A. Knopf, 1962.

Titone, Nora. *My Thoughts Be Bloody: The Bitter Rivalry Between Edwin and John Wilkes Booth That Led to an American Tragedy.* New York: Free Press, 2010.

US House of Representatives. *Executive Documents Printed by Order of the House of Representatives During the Second Session of the Fortieth Congress.* Washington, DC: Government Printing Office, 1868.

US War Department. *The War of the Rebellion: A Compilation of the Official Records of the Union and Confederate Armies.* Washington, DC: Government Printing Office, 1880.

White, Richard. *Railroaded: The Transcontinentals and the Making of Modern America*. New York: Norton, 2011.

Williamson, James J. *Mosby's Rangers: A Record of the Operations of the Forty-Third Battalion of Virginia Cavalry from Its Organization to Surrender*. Rev. ed. New York: Ralph B. Kenyon, 1895.

———. *Mosby's Rangers*. 2nd ed. New York: Sturgis and Walters and Company, 1909.

Wineapple, Brenda. *Ecstatic Nation: Confidence, Crisis, and Compromise, 1848–1877*. New York: HarperCollins, 2013.

INDEX